THE
WORST PRESIDENT--
The Story of James Buchanan

THE
WORST PRESIDENT--

The Story of James Buchanan

Garry Boulard

THE WORST PRESIDENT--THE STORY OF JAMES BUCHANAN

iUniverse books may be ordered through booksellers or by contacting:

iUniverse
1663 Liberty Drive
Bloomington, IN 47403
www.iuniverse.com
844-349-9409

ISBN: 978-1-4917-5961-5 (sc)
ISBN: 978-1-4917-5962-2 (e)

Print information available on the last page.

iUniverse rev. date:12/16/2021

For Rochelle Williams
and Sid Hamilton

Contents

Acknowledgments

This book would have been impossible without the assistance of a large number of librarians and archivists, beginning with the staffs of the University of Florida George A. Smathers Libraries.

During the writing of this book, I was also helped by the fact that UF's Library West, through the generous support of the UF Student Senate, has a 24-hour schedule. To be researching and writing late into the night in a library filled with people who are doing the same is a good thing.

I am additionally indebted to Andrea Anesi, research assistant, Susquehanna County Historical Society; Lee Arnold, director of library and collections, the Historical Society of Pennsylvania; Sylvia Ashwell, library specialist, Alachua County Library District; Marjorie Bardeen, director of library services, Lancaster Historical Society; Christine Beauregard, senior librarian, New York State Library; Kimberly Brownlee, manuscripts librarian, Ward M. Canady Center for Special Collections, University of Toledo; Christine Colburn, readers services manager, Special Collections Research Center, University of Chicago Library; Kate Collins, research services librarian, David M. Rubenstein Rare Books and Manuscript Library, Duke University; Keli Conroy, adult services librarian, Alachua County Library Distrct; Robert Coomer, director, Illinois Historic Preservation Agency; Uwe Michael Dietz, microfiche/microfilm reference librarian, George A. Smathers Library West, University of Florida; Will Griebal, student technical specialist, Zimmerman Library, University of New Mexico; Suzanne Hahn, director, reference services, Indiana Historical Society; Paige Harper, program assistant, Marston Science Library, University of Florida; Molly Kodner, associate archivist,

Missouri Historical Society; David Haugaard, director of media services, Historical Society of Pennsylvania; Lisa Long, reference archivist, Ohio Historical Society; Curtis Mann, director, Sangamon Valley Collections, Springfield Public Library; Meg McDonald, interlibrary loan specialist, Albuquerque Public Library; Dana Miller, processing archivist, Hargett Library, University of Georgia Libraries; and Cheryl Schnirring, curator of manuscripts, Abraham Lincoln Presidential Library; Ed Shipley, researcher, Historical Society of Pennsylvania; Robert Ticknor, reference assistant, Historic New Orleans Collection.

A special word of thanks also goes to Cody Francis Hall, Dallas Khamiss, Bao Qiang Li, Cong Luo, Chris Philip and Andres Vergara

Cover concept by Katy Jordan.

A Recurring Historical Mistake

On December 20, 1860, as the country teetered on the edge of secession and civil war, President James Buchanan and his 30 year-old niece Harriet Lane climbed into a carriage that would take them from the White House grounds to the corner of 4th and C streets, a journey of less than 2 miles.

There the carriage pulled to the front of a three-story brownstone mansion described by the ebullient Virginia Clay, wife of Alabama Senator Clement Clay, as a "palatial residence known for its fine conservatories, its spacious parlors and glistening dance floors." [1]

The mansion was the home of George Parker, a wealthy man who made his fortune in the grocery business. Well-connected politically, Parker this afternoon was engaged in a ritual certain to give any father pause: the wedding of his daughter. Mary Elizabeth Parker was marrying the fiercely independent John Bouligny, a young New Orleans Congressman who, unlike the vast majority of his Southern colleagues, was opposed to secession.

Entering the mansion the 69 year-old bachelor Buchanan was greeted by the people he had always been the most comfortable with during his many decades in Washington: wealthy white pro-slavery Southerners, members of Congress and his own administration, who told witty stories, knew all the latest gossip, and hosted the best parties in the city.

What a welcome relief all of this was from the recent stress and non-stop crisis atmosphere of his job as president. Ever since the November election of Abraham Lincoln it was as though the whole country had gone crazy. Southern leaders, convinced that Lincoln's pledge to stop the expansion of slavery meant that he in reality had a secret agenda to end it altogether, began meeting in the immediate aftermath of the election to plot their response, which in almost every instance meant one thing: organizing state conventions that would officially vote for secession, starting, it was hoped, with South Carolina, ground zero in the movement.

Northerners, meanwhile, decried the Southern talk of disunion, calling out instead for a firm federal response the moment the first Southern state seceded, and demanding that Buchanan declare his determination to stop any movement in that direction, using military force if need be.

The problem was that Buchanan, tired and hoping that somehow the crisis would simply fade away, or at the very least not reach a point of explosion until Lincoln took office in March, was stumped.

He had, in mid-November, asked Attorney General Jeremiah Black to research the constitutionality of secession. On December 3, drawing heavily on Black's opinion, Buchanan declared in his annual message to Congress that while it was certainly unconstitutional for any state to leave the union, if one did, there really wasn't much he could do about it.

"The fact is that our Union rests upon public opinion and can never be cemented by the blood of its citizens shed in civil war," Buchanan said. "If it cannot live in the affections of the people, it must one day perish. Congress possesses many means of preserving its conciliation, but the sword was not placed in their hand to preserve it by force." [2]

Buchanan's argument bombed. The *New York Times* condemned what it characterized as an "incendiary document" that "promises the seceding states that the power of the federal government shall not be used for their coercion."

"The country has to struggle through three more months of this disgraceful imbecility and disloyalty to the Constitution," the paper added. [3]

New York Senator William Seward, soon to be Lincoln's Secretary of State, said Buchanan's message gave evidence of two strands of thinking: "That no state has the right to secede unless it wishes to," and that "It is the president's duty to enforce the law, unless somebody opposes him." [4]

Responding to his argument that secession was unconstitutional, Southerners were unhappy with Buchanan's message, too. On December 8 Treasury Secretary Howell Cobb, one of those Southerners who gave some of the most glittering parties in Washington, handed in his resignation to Buchanan. To add to the president's mortification, Cobb shortly headed out for South Carolina where he threw in with the secessionist cause. In another nine days, Secretary of War John Floyd, a Virginian, would claim policy differences with the president and also quit. Mississippi Senator Jefferson Davis and former Georgia Congressman Alexander Stephens, soon to be the top officers in the new Confederacy, also registered their disgust.

How nice, as Buchanan settled into a parlor chair in the Parker mansion, to be away from all this madness   if only for a few hours. The always amusing Sara Pryor, wife of Virginia Congressman Roger Pryor, found a spot standing directly behind the President.

Suddenly someone started to yell outside the Parker home. Buchanan nodded his head in the direction of the noise and asked Mrs. Pryor whether or not the mansion was on fire.

Mrs. Pryor promised a speedy investigation. Opening the doors to the home's entrance hall she saw the tall, muscular black-bearded 36 year-old Lawrence Keitt, until recently a Congressman from South Carolina, leaping in the air and waving a paper over his head,

"Thank God! Oh, thank God!" Keitt exclaimed.

"Mr. Keitt, are you crazy?" The President hears you and wants to know what's the matter," Mrs. Pryor said.

"Oh!" Keitt cried. "South Carolina has seceded. Here's the telegram. I feel like a boy let out from school."

Mrs. Pryor returned to the mansion where she bent over the back of the chair Buchanan was sitting in and whispered "It appears South Carolina has seceded from the Union. Mr. Keitt has a telegram."

Buchanan appeared stunned. He fell back, grasping the arms of the chair. The moment he had long dreaded, and never really believed would come, had arrived. South Carolina had seceded. And with it would undoubtedly follow most, if not all, of the other Deep South states. The country was indeed falling apart—and while the exhausted Buchanan was still president.

"Madam," Buchanan finally said to Mrs. Pryor, desperate to return to the White House as soon as possible, "Might I beg you to have my carriage called?" [5]

The story of how Buchanan first heard the news of South Carolina's secession is one of the great stories of the immediate pre-Civil War months; an exhausted, clueless, elderly chief executive, Caligula-like, partying away the pleasant hours with his wealthy friends at the very moment that the country was coming apart.

Almost every prominent historian of the period for more than a century has gleefully repeated this story, including Doris Kearns Goodwin in her epic 2005 biography of Lincoln, *Team of Rivals;* Ernest Ferguson in his 2004 book on life in Washington in the Civil War, *Freedom Rising;* Bruce Catton in his seminal early 1960s *The Coming War;* Margaret Leech in her award winning 1941 *Reveille in Washington;* and two prominent Buchanan biographers, Philip Shriver Klein in his 1962 *President Buchanan* and Elbert Smith in his 1975 study *The Presidency of James Buchanan.* [6]

Indeed the story has been repeated so much and in so many places, including a 2010 column in the *New York Times* by author Jamie Malanowski, that it has become one of the things most remembered, at least by historians, about Buchanan, next to the fact that he preceded Lincoln in office, may have been a homosexual, and probably hastened the dismantling of the Union through his own inertia. [7]

The only problem with the story is that it isn't true. It never happened. Or at least it certainly did not happen the way everyone thinks.

The first clue that something is wrong comes with Lawrence Keitt. "Life, in the very texture of the word, means struggle, motion, purpose, object," Keitt had once declared to the woman who would become his wife. Energy, action, movement—*doing something*, these were the young Keitt's bywords, glimpses into the soul of a man who admitted that his own nervous energy made it difficult for him to even pause long enough to have his daguerreotype taken. [8]

In the weeks following Lincoln's election, Keitt was characteristically in full motion. He resigned his seat in Congress and returned to his native South Carolina where he loudly beat the drum for secession. By mid-December Keitt was a proud member of the special convention organized to decide whether or not South Carolina should secede, and on the pivotal day, December 20, Keitt enthusiastically voted in favor of the secession ordinance dissolving South Carolina's ties with the United States.

It's a fact easily verified through a survey of the South Carolina secession convention's *Journal of the Convention of the People,* which records Keitt in Charleston, 536 miles away from Washington, where he was supposed to have been yelling outside the Parker mansion. [9]

But the second clue that something is wrong comes with a scan of the Washington newspapers. Surely some mention would be made of what undoubtedly must have been the wedding of the season. But none of the city's papers, including the *Washington Evening Star, Daily National Intelligencer* and *Washington Constitution,* covered it. Not one story, not one graph, not one sentence. Nor do any of the New York papers, in particular, the *New York Times* and *New York Herald,* both of which had busy Washington bureaus with reporters who emphasized society news, say anything at all about the nuptials.

At least not on December 20.

But they did mention the wedding when it *really* happened, more than seven months earlier, on May 1, 1860.

That ceremony was described in detail by the *Washington Evening Star* in its May 2nd edition in a story headlined "A Brilliant Wedding." The story goes on to describe a bride dressed in a white satin dress with a lace veil, flowers in her hair, and "rich sparkling diamonds in the ornaments she wore." [10]

The article additionally notes that the wedding guests included a "number of gentlemen in distinguished public positions here and their families," including Buchanan. [11]

This wedding, the real wedding, was additionally covered in the *Daily National Intelligencer, Harper's Weekly,* (calling it "perhaps the most brilliant wedding that has ever taken place in the Federal metropolis"), and the *New York Times,* which said the Bouligny-Parker nuptuals were "celebrated with much splendor." The *New York Herald* called the wedding "the social event in the fashionable world." [12]

A final, conclusive piece of evidence comes in a document housed in the Historic New Orleans Collection's Bouligny-Ganin Family Papers. On October 16, 1860 a letter was written to Amanda Bouligny, the sister of Congressman Bouligny. It is a pleasant, elegantly written letter touching on Washington society, family illnesses, and a recent storm that had swept through New Orleans. The letter is signed: "Mary E. P. Bouligny," otherwise known as Mary Elizabeth Parker Bouligny, who only naturally signed off using the last name of the man she had married five and a half months before, but obviously could not use that name two months before the mythical wedding of lore. [13]

How to explain such a widespread discrepancy between the many erroneous historic accounts of a particular event and what really happened?

The problem is rooted in the memoirs of Sara Pryor, memoirs that are full of inviting, colorful descriptions of social life in pre-war Washington. Mrs. Pryor was 30 years old in 1860, and, as recalled by Virginia Clay, was the "beautiful wife" of Virginia Congressman Roger Pryor, a woman with "soft brown hair and eyes," who wore a "distinctive coiffure, and carried her head charmingly." [14]

Writing in 1905 of Sara Pryor in the months leading up to the Civil War, Mrs. Clay added: "Even at that time Mrs. Pryor was notable for the intellectuality which has since uttered itself in several charming books." [15]

But nearly half a century had passed between the Bouligny-Parker wedding and Mrs. Pryor's memoirs recalling the event. During the intervening years she had accompanied her husband on his duties as a commissioned officer during the Civil War, eventually returning by herself to Petersburg, Virginia where she raised the couple's six children.

After the war, the Pryors moved to New York. Roger Pryor started a law practice while Mrs. Pryor took care of their growing family (a seventh child was born in 1868). She would remember the late 1860s as financially challenging years for their family. Even so, she and several friends eventually established a home for impoverished mothers and their children. In the decades to follow, Mrs. Pryor was a whirlwind of activity, involved in a large number of philanthropic, historical and preservation groups, before seeing the publication of her first book in 1904, *Reminiscences of Peace and War*. [16]

She was in her early seventies when that book came out, and would be dead a short eight years later from chronic pernicious anemia, a disease that, among other things, causes memory loss. [17]

But to not remember the specific date of a particular event more than four decades after it happened is one thing, to invent out of whole cloth dialogue, and both Keitt and Buchanan's responses to a particular historic moment, is quite another.

How to explain Mrs. Pryor's vivid memory of Keitt jumping and yelling outside the Parker mansion, and Buchanan's slumping in his chair before asking Mrs. Pryor to fetch his carriage for him?

One explanation would be that Mrs. Pryor was a liar. Simple enough. She told a good story, and generations of historians have since fallen for it. But nothing else in her two memoirs, *Reminiscences of Peace and War* and *My Day: Reminiscences of a Long Life,* rings false.

Why then did she remember Keitt and Buchanan behaving as they did? Where does this memory come from?

It is entirely possible that, having confused the dates of the Bouligny-Parker wedding, Mrs. Pryor also confused the events surrounding the actual and imagined weddings. The mistaken wedding date, December 20, was indeed the day that South Carolina seceded from the United States. But the real wedding day, May 1, was the day that the Washington papers carried the sensational news that the South Carolina delegation had walked out of the Democratic National Convention, meeting in Charleston, on the previous afternoon. That state's delegation decided that the party platform did not go far enough to protect slavery. The South Carolinians would be accompanied by similar walk-outs, also reported on May 1, from the Alabama, Florida, Mississippi and Texas delegations. The South Carolina delegation's decision to leave the Democratic Convention was widely referred to in the contemporary press as a "secession."

The announcement of this secession was big news, especially to Keitt, who wanted his native state to not only abandon the national Democrats, but the Union as well. A guest at the May 1 wedding, Keitt could well have been outside the Parker mansion when he learned of South Carolina's exit from the convention, and may well have jumped in the air, as Mrs. Pryor remembered, instantly appreciating that the secession of the five individual Southern state delegations, during a time when a two-thirds convention vote was required for a presidential nomination, most likely meant that no one would now be nominated. Chaos, to Keitt's satisfaction, reigned. [18]

But Buchanan, too, may have well responded the way Mrs. Pryor remembered. A Democratic Convention incapable of naming a nominee meant that Buchanan's beloved party was coming apart at the seams. The young Republican Party, just weeks away from selecting Lincoln as its nominee, seemed, by contrast, confident, unified and headed for victory.

"Madam, might I beg you to have my carriage called?" Buchanan, who was often theatrical, may well have asked after learning of the implosion of the Democratic Party in Charleston.

The irrefutable fact that Mrs. Pryor got her dates wrong, and that generations of historians, using her memoirs as their only source, have retold the incorrect story, is interesting in and of itself, the sort of dusty discovery that scholars enjoy finding and making much of.

But in Buchanan's case, Mrs. Pryor's mistaken tale takes on a much more important meaning. The episode, as remembered by Mrs. Pryor and unquestioned by historians, serves as a metaphor for James Buchanan's entire presidency: a four-year period of executive inertia that is regularly served up as one of the worst in American history, as, indeed, Buchanan is generally regarded as the worst president in history.

The persistence of this story, and the unwillingness of any historian during the past century to question it, shows how powerfully etched Buchanan's reputation has become as the country's worst president. Surveys of presidential scholars consistently rate Buchanan at the bottom of every list regarding performance and effectiveness. That he immediately precedes Lincoln, who is roundly regarded as America's greatest president, only seems to further doom Buchanan, linking him forever with an iconic figure who came to office to supposedly right all of Buchanan's wrongs. To put it another way, the mistaken story of what happened on December 20, 1860, and what Buchanan did on that day, persists because it re-enforces all notions of an out of touch, clueless Chief Executive. And there can be no doubt about it, the fictional imagining of what James Buchanan did on December 20, 1860 does indeed make for a good story.

But what James Buchanan actually did on that same important date is just as interesting.

Chapter One

What Really Happened
on December 20, 1860

Everyone had had it with James Buchanan, his endless equivocations, his bureaucratic mind, his melodrama, his lack of vision, the way he let things get so out of control, the way in which it seemed impossible for him to, in fact, regain control, his plodding, doddering, aimless oldness in a nation obsessed with direction and youth.

The country had never before known such an aged chief executive. The "Old Public Functionary," as he was often called, was just short of 70 years of age. The last president, Franklin Pierce, left office when he was only 52. The soon-to-be next president, Abraham Lincoln, would enter at 52.

There would, in the future, be presidents equal in age to Buchanan. Dwight Eisenhower would leave office at 70. Ronald Reagan would be nearly 70 as he came in. But Eisenhower and Reagan, as they entered their seventh decades, were still intellectually vibrant men, inspired with purpose and ideas.

Buchanan really was old, shuffling around the White House in a worn robe and patent leather pumps, regaling listeners with tales of days long since passed, wondering, as many do when they age, why the world could not have at a certain point stopped, when everything seemed so perfect, remembering random and sometimes trivial events of long ago that were important to himself only.

His life was populated with ghosts: friends, foes, and family members who had long since died but remained very much alive for him, populating his conversations with stories of who did what when, decades in the past.

He smoked cigars throughout the day, read late into the night, and affected an air of icy indifference when anyone asked him how he was holding up in a time of national crisis, telling his remaining friends that history would vindicate him, that he had done right by his country and that he was really quite unconcerned about what people were saying about him. Theatrically, he declared, he was ready to meet his God.

Cartoonists liked him. His wispy white hair came to a point on a pale white head that sometimes appeared concave. He was drawn to look like a rodent or a sheep or a pig. Because he was fussy and prim, because he had always been fussy and prim, he was most often portrayed as a dowdy old maid.

In truth, Buchanan was entirely odd: He had, the biographer of financier August Belmont would memorably write, "The look of a man watching a street riot from behind a curtain in an upstairs window." Just over 6 feet tall, he cocked his head forward to one side in conversation, squinting to compensate for an unusual vision problem: he was near-sighed in one eye and far-sighted in the other. For no apparent reason he had taken recently to shaking the hands of visitors by offering two fingers, a gesture which, one reporter noted, "has been the occasion of considerable private speculation." When he caught the eye of a woman, or several, at a distance, he would kiss his fingertips to them three times in a roll. [1]

Those leather pumps could be slippery on the floor. One day Attorney General Jeremiah Black and Treasury Secretary Howell Cobb, men who were many years Buchanan's junior and had come to enjoy his quirks, were talking at the bottom of a White House stairwell. Suddenly they heard a large thump and looked up to see that Buchanan, at the top of the stairwell, had fallen royally on his rear. The comic scene was made all the more absurd when Buchanan stared blankly at the two men (a quick wit was never his calling card) before silently righting himself and walking away. [2]

The charge that Buchanan was fussy had little to do with his attire. Also known as "Old Buck," Buchanan wore boots that were invariably dusty and a broadcloth coat habitually flecked in cigar ash. When he was the minister to Britain and the novelist Nathaniel Hawthorne was serving as the U.S. consul there, Buchanan one evening tied a silk handkerchief in a knot by way of a reminder after Hawthorne's wife asked him to get a pass for her to visit Parliament. Hawthorne observed that the cloth "ought to have gone into this week's wash." [3]

Some even regarded Buchanan as being somewhat feminine, or at least lacking in masculine virtue. The crusty publisher Frank Blair told former president Martin Van Buren that the country was cursed with "Hermaphrodites, and of all, Old Buck has proved the worst." [4]

But women were attracted to him, or at least to his power.

"Tradition whispers legends wild and mystical as to why and wherefore the venerable President has failed to take onto himself a wife," the family-oriented *Boston Saturday Evening Gazette* pondered, adding that "His good humored smile and benignant manner are adapted to win hearts." [5]

Any number of women in Washington would have married him. Why he decided to remain single was never fully explained. Many speculated. Some thought he had just never found the right woman. Others thought he liked men. Everyone missed the point.

Buchanan liked women. He also liked men, or at least one man in particular. But he despised being put out by anyone, man or woman, and only had to think about a single searing, painful incident in his life to be reminded of how incredibly inconvenient romance could be.

Her name was Anne Coleman. She was tall, dark-haired, and 23 years old. She was also a member of one of the wealthiest families in Lancaster, Pennsylvania. Buchanan, a rising young attorney, also in Lancaster, declared his love for her and one day asked her to marry him. The young woman gave her ascent but soon discovered, as eventually everyone did in his orbit, that Buchanan could be cold and remote.

Distraught, Anne Coleman was vulnerable to manipulation. When a woman friend whose intentions were never explained suggested that the ambitious 28 year-old Buchanan might be most interested in the Coleman family's treasure and social connections, the young girl committed suicide.

"I have lost the only earthly object of my affection without whom life now presents to me a dreary blank," Buchanan wrote upon learning of Anne's death. "My prospects are all cut off and I feel that my happiness will be buried with her in the grave."

My prospects are all cut off: Buchanan often had a clumsy and mechanical way of expressing himself. Whatever he really meant was further clouded when he begged Anne's father, Robert Coleman, to be allowed to attend her funeral, adding, in a sentence that made his plea seem like a contrivance: "I would like to convince the world, and I hope convince you, that she was infinitely dearer to me than life." [6]

Anne's father sent Buchanan's letter back to him unopened.

Buchanan was never serious, if indeed, he had been even that with Anne Coleman, with another woman again. He flirted with them, winked at them, kissed his fingertips in their direction, listened to their stories and told better stories in return. He was particularly suggestive around married women, most likely because he knew they would be unlikely to respond. Through a friend, New York Congressman and former aide Dan Sickles, who was known to cavort with prostitutes, Buchanan may have even found unsaid ways to satisfy his occasional need for feminine physical companionship.

But his romantic life was over.

For the Navy Lieutenant David Porter, it was all so damn pedestrian. "What could one expect at a court presided over by an old bachelor whose heart was dead to poetry and love; who sat at dinner with no flowers to grace the festive board, and never even wore a *boutonniere* on his coat-lapel; who eschewed everything like official state, and was content to live out his term of office in plain republican simplicity?" [7]

But Buchanan in fact did think about romance, if only from a pecuniary perspective. "You ought never to marry any man to whom you are not attached," he advised his niece Harriet Lane, who patiently endured her uncle's lectures. "But you ought to never marry any person who is not able to afford you a decent & immediate support."

Revealing more sympathy than usual, Buchanan warned Harriet of the life that would await her should she marry unwisely. "I have witnessed the long years of patient misery & dependence which fine women have endured from rushing precipitately into matrimonial connection without sufficient reflection," he said, urging Harriet to marry for love *and* money. [8]

There were those who could never get over the fact that Buchanan had never married, fellow politicians and reporters brought it up repeatedly in their speeches and stories. But his bachelorhood in a country that revered family never really hurt him as he rose in the ranks, mostly out of public view, serving as Andrew Jackson's Minister to Russia in the early 1830s, James Polk's Secretary of State in the mid-1840s and Franklin Pierce's Minister to Great Britain in the mid-1850s. Nor did the subject come up in any particularly damaging way during his long service in the House of Representatives and Senate, or in the most important election of his life, the one that made him president in 1856.

What really made a difference in that latter election was the Democrats' superior vote-getting ability and the solid support of the South, where state leaders looked at Buchanan's career-long support of slavery and decided he was as good as they were likely to get (Buchanan's total national vote in 1856, in fact, would be off by more than 5 percent from what Democrat Pierce had won four years before, but his Southern vote was up 6 percent).

Despite the fact that Buchanan was not a particularly exciting, or for that matter, even popular candidate, he lucked out, more than he would ever admit, in 1856. He had an opponent, the explorer John Fremont, who was the first-ever Republican presidential nominee and not an effective politician. The young Republicans were feeling their way, almost running the 1856 campaign as a dry run for 1860 when they were certain to be better organized and funded and led by a more politically astute nominee.

By 1858, Republicans, capitalizing on a series of Buchanan missteps that had permanently alienated large numbers of Northern voters, most notably his support for a pro-slavery constitution in the still-to-be-formed state of Kansas, made sweeping gains in the mid-term elections. As 1860 dawned it was clear that any of the most known Republican leaders, in particular New York Senator William Henry Seward, could very well be elected president.

When Republicans, meeting in Chicago in the late spring of that year, instead chose Abraham Lincoln, they landed on a candidate who built on the 1856 Fremont vote and was substantially helped by an angry split in the Democratic Party. On the day of the election, November 6, 1860, Lincoln carried almost every state of the more populous North to become president-elect.

Within hours, leaders in the South, many of whom were Buchanan's personal friends, openly announced plans to secede, with the fever for secession reaching a particularly high point in South Carolina. Throughout the rest of November Buchanan holed up almost daily with his cabinet exploring options: Should he be more conciliatory towards the South? Should he adopt a harder line? Should he do nothing at all?

By early December matters had reached a crisis point. Southern secession passion had only grown more intense since Lincoln's election. The nation waited for a response from Buchanan. That response would come with his annual message to Congress, delivered on December 3; a document that attempted to strike a balance between sympathy for the South while also opposing any move to secede. In the end, Buchanan only further enraged Southerners when he said there was no provision in the Constitution allowing a state to secede. But at the same time he disgusted Northerners when he strangely added that if a Southern state actually did secede, there was nothing the federal government could do to stop it.

Treasury Secretary Howell Cobb resigned on December 8, taking a train to South Carolina where he joined the secessionist cause. Four days later Secretary of State Lewis Cass of Michigan also called it quits, blaming Buchanan for what he thought was a policy that encouraged secession.

By the third week of December, Southern federal office holders by the hundreds were leaving Washington to join the secessionists, Congress was paralyzed in sectional recrimination, the stock market was drastically off as investor confidence plummeted, and Buchanan, everyday looking older and less resolute, was getting the blame.

Pennsylvania Congressman Thaddeus Stevens, who had loathed Buchanan for decades, once describing him as a "bloated mass of political putridity," was making hasty plans to return home. He had no particular desire to be back in the Keystone State for the holidays, wanting instead to just be far away from the disaster in Washington, which he regarded as entirely of Buchanan's making.

"I do not care to be present while the process of humiliation is going on," wrote Stevens, whose principle vice after swearing off the more pleasant past-times of smoking and drinking was wearing a strange-looking crimson-colored wig. [9]

Iowa Senator James Grimes passed along a rumor to a friend: "Mr. Buchanan, it is said, about equally divides his time between praying and crying."

"Such a perfect imbecile," added Grimes, "never held office before." [10]

Associate Supreme Court Justice Robert Grier, an old Buchanan friend, dropped by the White House and walked away shaken. "He is getting *old*—very *faint*—poor fellow, he has fallen on hard times." Noting how Southerners in general had influenced Buchanan throughout his presidency, Grier continued, "He put his confidence and gave his power to his enemies and not to his friends and now he is enjoying the fruits of his mistakes." [11]

The abolition leader in the Senate, Massachusetts Senator Charles Sumner, who despite his opposition to everything the President stood for somehow managed to remain on social terms with him, penned a long letter to the Duchess of Argyll predicting that South Carolina would soon take the steps needed for secession—"That is the mild phrase for treason!" he exclaimed. Sumner continued: "She will be followed, in all probability, by the 'Cotton States,' being the ultra slave states on the Gulf of Mexico. All this will be done before the 4th of March, when the new Administration comes into power."

"It could not take place," Sumner added, "if Mr. Buchanan were not playing into their hands. His irresolution, timidity & positive sympathy have encouraged them in their treason."

Two days later Sumner again picked up his pen to report on the possibility of both Maryland and Virginia also joining the secession cause. "The imbecility of Mr. Buchanan is more apparent every day," Sumner said. "A vigorous will on his part would have arrested this movement." [12]

Others, at the same time, were suspicious that Buchanan was somehow involved in some kind of dark plot to keep himself in office beyond his term, shutting out Lincoln entirely. On December 18, Major David Hunter, who had become lately deranged on the topic of coups, claimed to know of a plot hatched by Southern radicals in 1856 that, should Fremont have won the presidential election, would have seen some 20,000 Southern men marching on Washington in order to prevent him from taking office. The coup, claimed Hunter, would have had the support of President Pierce, and was a movement whose single purpose was to "keep possession of the government."

"Now Sir," Hunter told Lincoln, "from Mr. Buchanan's Message, and from a careful study of the signs of the times, I am very much inclined to believe that they intend to attempt the same game with you—to have the Old Public Functionary hold over, and thus demoralize your Administration and bring about the same anarchy and confusion at the North as they will have plunged into at the South." The only hope of frustrating the evil designs of both the Southerners and Buchanan, thought Hunter, was to recruit 100,000 men to protect the federal government. "By a coup-de-main we could arm them in Washington." [13]

Two days later, on the morning of December 20, the *Chicago Tribune* made a front-page declaration: "Timidity, imbecility and treason rule in the White House." The *Daily Constitutionalist* of Augusta, Georgia, weighed in on this same day from the other side. "The Chief Magistrate is left almost alone," the paper said, alluding to the Southern defections from his cabinet, and adding that Buchanan had "sinned against his party and his country." [14]

Also this same morning the *New York Times* ran a bizarre piece: a letter purported to have been written by Buchanan to a Philadelphia friend justifying his failure to organize a militia in response to events in South Carolina. Had he done so, a fabricated Buchanan said, "A warlike spirit would have been aroused in every state in the Union," Southerners would "fall in their spirited defense," leaving slaves to mass in a "black wave of terror, rolling with its strength against the North." Northerners, in response, would be "compelled by necessity to mow them down." [15]

Why the paper felt a need to publish what it subsequently admitted was a forged document went unsaid, unless the goal was to embarrass Buchanan by putting words in his mouth that made him seem both unduly alarmist and even hysterical.

Buchanan was angered by such distractions, but on this overcast morning he was preoccupied with other matters, aware as he was that secession leaders had called for a convention in South Carolina. His close friend, Lawrence Keitt, who had just days before announced he was resigning his seat in Congress to join the Southern cause, was a secession leader, and had met several times with Buchanan, impressing upon him the seriousness of the situation. Keitt's take on things was supported by the amiable 36 year-old Assistant Secretary of State William Henry Trescot, a pleasant-looking Harvard-educated South Carolinian who kept in touch with leaders in his native state and knew secession was coming.

But Buchanan couldn't wrap his mind around it: secession meant disunion—*states actually leaving the Union of their own accord.* Why, he wondered, would they want to do that? Particularly with a generation whose fathers and grandfathers had sacrificed much in forming the United States in the first place. Buchanan had grown up listening to tales of the American Revolution handed down to him from his elders. America, he knew, was the greatest nation in the world, and he assumed all other Americans, but in particular Southerners who revered tradition, shared his sentiments.

Besides, why would these Southerners want to leave now when they had the protection of perhaps the most South-loving, slavery-supporting president in history? To leave after Lincoln took office and his presumed anti-Southern, anti-slavery policies became a reality was one thing, but to leave under a president who always genuinely saw the Southern point of view and endlessly catered to Southern interests was quite another. It was a curious thing, observed the *Economist,* trying to fathom the coming divorce in the American family, this cry for secession that "is the loudest in those quarters which to all appearances would suffer most from it and have the greatest reason to dread it." [16]

On this day Buchanan formally accepted the resignation of Trescot, who had earlier made the rounds in the State Department saying goodbye to all of the clerks who had worked for him. Like Cobb, Trescot told Buchanan he could no longer divide his loyalties between his state and his country. But Trescot was at heart a diplomat, telling Buchanan that he planned to stay on in Washington, hopefully serving as a messenger of sorts between Charleston and Washington.

By mid-morning, in Trescot's presence, Daniel Hamilton, the U.S. Marshal for the District of South Carolina, arrived at the White House to deliver by hand to Buchanan a message from the newly elected Governor of South Carolina, Francis Pickens. Pickens, described by a biographer as a man of "aloofness and overbearing personality," was now suddenly threatening to throw out of whack what was left of the delicate relations between the federal government and South Carolina: He demanded that all federal forts along the South Carolina coast be turned over to the state government. [17]

Astonished, but trying to keep his cool, Buchanan told Hamilton he could not give the Governor an official response until the next day. Alarmed, Trescot ran from the White House to seek out South Carolina Congressmen Milledge Bonham and John McQueen and tell them of Pickens' demand.

While this was going on, Buchanan had time to write a short note to James Gordon Bennett, the unpredictable publisher of the powerful *New York Herald*. In the last four years, Buchanan had worked assiduously to keep Bennett happy, letting him in on major administration decisions before they were publicly announced, sending him speeches and documents by carrier, and opening up the White House to *Herald* reporters.

Now Buchanan griped to Bennett about the way he was being portrayed in smaller rural papers which were publishing stories suggesting that he was coming to pieces under the weight of his job. Such stories, said Buchanan, were "short and spicy, and can be easily inserted in the country newspapers. In the city journals they can be contradicted the next day; but the case is different throughout the country. Many of them are sheer falsehoods, and especially those concerning myself."

Buchanan went on to assure Bennett that despite the pressures of the moment, he "never enjoyed better health or a more tranquil spirit. All of our troubles have not cost me an hour's sleep or a meal's victuals, though I trust I have a just sense of my high responsibility."

Self-righteously, Buchanan added: "I weigh well and prayerfully what course I ought to adopt and adhere to it steadily, leaving the results to Providence. That is my nature, and I deserve neither praise nor blame for it." [18]

It was raining by early afternoon as dispatches arrived at the Washington office of the American Telegraph Company on West 6th Street reporting the startling news: within the last half hour South Carolina secession leaders, meeting at the St. Andrew's Hall in Charleston, had enthusiastically voted to pull their state out of the Union.

Virginia Representative Muscoe Garnett, who had warned his colleagues that this moment was coming, was on the floor of the House of Representatives when he was handed the news in a note by an aide. Crisply, he announced: "One of the sovereign states of this confederacy has, by the glorious act of her people, withdrawn from the Union, as the telegraph announced to us at half past one." [19]

An audible gasp was followed by shouts of joy. Southern members of the House, in an ecstatic defiance of decorum, bounded over to what was left of the South Carolina delegation to offer congratulations. Republican members, in response, moved to deprive the South Carolinians of the drama of walking out of the House *en masse* by voting to adjourn for the day. [20]

Buchanan was handed a dispatch in the White House at roughly the same time, although the information it contained was confusing, incorrectly reporting that the South Carolinians had agreed not to leave the Union until Lincoln actually came into office. Either way, Buchanan knew this was serious. A Washington correspondent for *New York Times*, tipped off by an insider studying Buchanan's reaction, reported "I learn that he exhibited much agitation on hearing the news." [21]

By early evening the endless rain had transformed Washington's streets into sloughs of mud. Lieutenant Porter stopped by the residence of Jefferson Davis on I Street N.W, some 5 blocks from the White House. There he encountered Davis' darkly attractive wife Varina who asked him to give her a ride to see Buchanan. Convinced that Buchanan had secretly been a secessionist all along, Mrs. Davis said she wanted to congratulate him in person regarding the news from South Carolina.

The visit with the President would prove brief, but when Porter and Mrs. Davis returned to the Davis residence they encountered other secession enthusiasts who said they, too, wanted to visit Buchanan and celebrate with him. It was all evidence, thought the skeptical Porter, that Buchanan had long ago thrown in with the secessionists, and that the secessionists had accepted him as one of their own. [22]

How Buchanan, who was always gracious in the extreme to any woman, but in particular a member of the Southern ruling elite, responded to Mrs. Davis was not known (five days later, on Christmas Day, Mrs. Davis sent him a pair of slippers, which he hopefully wore in lieu of his dangerous patent leather pumps). But after Mrs. Davis left, he finally found enough time to sit down and write out a response to Pickens. He began his message by telling Pickens that he had done all that he could to "prevent a collision between the army and navy of the United States and citizens of South Carolina in defence of the forts within the harbor of Charleston." [23]

At the same time, Buchanan continued, he had done nothing to re-enforce the forts, even though the federal troops there could be at risk, because he relied "upon the honor of South Carolinians that they [the forts] will not be assaulted whilst they remain in their present condition."

Buchanan then noted that he had no power to turn over the forts anyway, only Congress could do that. Civics lecture over, Buchanan sternly warned Pickens: "If South Carolina should attack any of these forts, she will then become an assailant in a war against the United States."

Reiterating the same point in different words, just in case Pickens missed his meaning, Buchanan wrote: "Between independent governments, if one possesses a fortress within the limits of another, and the latter should seize it without calling upon the appropriate authorities of the power in possession to surrender it, this would not only be a just cause of war, but the actual commencement of hostilities."

Because he had formerly appointed Pickens as Minister to Russia and thought the Governor was his friend, Buchanan added: "I have, therefore, never been more astonished in my life, than to learn from you that unless Fort Sumter be delivered into your hands, you cannot be answerable for the consequences." [24]

It was after 9 p.m. when an excited Trescot returned to the White House. He reported to Buchanan that earlier in the evening he had sent a telegraph to Pickens, urging the Governor to officially withdraw his insulting demand to Buchanan. Trescot's message had been co-signed by Congressmen Bonham and McQueen who, with South Carolina's secession, were now out of jobs (Republican Speaker of the House William Pennington would graciously make certain they were paid in full up to the date of their departures). Surprisingly, Pickens responded positively, obviating, in turn, the need for the communication Buchanan had just completed, a copy of which he decided to file away for the official record. [25]

On this anticlimactic, exhausting note, as Southerners throughout the night in parlors and taverns across Washington celebrated South Carolina's secession, and Northerners in other parts of the city drank in despair, did the eventful, historic day of December 20, 1860 finally come to an end for James Buchanan.

Chapter Two

A Roseate and Propitious Morn

More often that he cared to admit, Buchanan looked at the faces of his Cabinet members, aides and visitors to the White House and realized they were too young to know anything about the country and times he had come up in. How absurd, he must have thought, that his vice-president wasn't even yet born when Buchanan had won his first election to Congress.

By the time Edwin Stanton, his Attorney General, was born, Buchanan had already served in the military and had won the first of his two terms to the Pennsylvania Legislature. When his new Secretary of State Jeremiah Black opened his eyes for the first time, Buchanan had already graduated from college and was studying law under the guidance of a prominent Lancaster attorney.

Buchanan realized that only a handful of the current members of Congress had served when he first entered the House in 1821 and legislated with the giants of the day, Daniel Webster and Henry Clay and John Calhoun, all now long since deceased. He had known them all and worked with them and fought with them, so many decades in the past, when the country was just decades old and most of the politicians of 1860 were still in diapers.

When Buchanan was born, George Washington had been president for only 24 months. The U.S. Supreme Court had convened for the very first time the year before. There was no telegraph, no train, no Library of Congress, no Ohio, Michigan, Illinois, Florida, Texas or California. There wasn't even a *New York Times*.

But there was Pennsylvania, celebrating its third year as a state when Buchanan came to life in the tiny, forested Cove Gap, near the Maryland border, on April 23, 1791.

He was the son of James Buchanan, Sr., an Irish immigrant, local merchant and justice of the peace, whose taciturnity kept the young Buchanan at bay. His mother, Elizabeth Speer Buchanan, was easier and more accepting, a thoughtful woman who cherished books and liked in particular the works of Alexander Pope and John Milton.

"She had a great fondness for poetry," Buchanan would later recall of the woman who catered to him throughout his youth, "and could repeat with ease all of the passages in her favorite authors which struck her fancy." [1]

His mother's interest in everything he did, along with the attention he received from his younger sisters, four of whom were born in the decade after Buchanan's birth, made him feel not just loved but adored. For the rest of his life he would believe that he was a cut above most other people and could never find a really good reason to think otherwise.

Enrolling at the age of 16 in Dickinson College, nearly sixty miles to the north, after studying Greek and Latin at the Old Stone Academy in Mercersburg, Buchanan demonstrated to his own and his instructors' satisfaction his prowess in logic and metaphysics. But it wasn't enough. "To be a sober, plodding industrious youth was to incur the ridicule of the mass of the students," he later wrote. [2]

"Without much natural tendency to become dissipated and chiefly from the examples of others, and in order to be considered a clever and spirited youth," Buchanan added, "I engaged in every sort of extravagance and mischief." [3]

This meant smoking cigars and drinking, although he rarely if ever got drunk, and disrespecting his superiors. But soon came a stunning turn of events: the school, when Buchanan was visiting his family, sent him a letter of expulsion. One could only imagine Buchanan's horror. This was the first time in his life he had faced rejection. How could this be explained? How could anyone, including a group of humorless educators, so treat him?

Desperate, Buchanan begged John King, the president of the school's board of trustees, to give him another chance. He vowed to reform. King relented, not necessarily because he liked Buchanan but due to his respect for Buchanan's father. Over the course of the next two years Buchanan proved good to his word, successfully completing all of his course work and staying out of trouble.

But even his graduation was etched in controversy: the school's administrators denied him a scholastic honor that he very much felt he deserved. It was possible that they took the action they did because they thought that while Buchanan had certainly worked and studied hard, he still had a chip on his shoulder and deserved one last comeuppance. Whatever the reason, Buchanan was outraged and threatened to boycott the graduation ceremony. Subsequently Buchanan would claim that his fellow students were also ready to protest with him. But because he didn't want them to be hurt academically, he claimed, he called the boycott off. Whatever really happened, Buchanan would harbor a grudge against the school for decades.

Just two months later Buchanan moved more than 100 miles to the east, from Cove Gap, to Lancaster, to take advantage of an opportunity to study law under prominent attorney James Hopkins. Hopkins would also introduce Buchanan to a number of the city's political leaders. Suddenly Buchanan was in a larger world than he had ever been before, and took it seriously. "I studied law and nothing but law," Buchanan later said of his days working his way through thick legal texts. At night he went for long walks, a habit he maintained throughout his life, trying to commit to memory what he had read. [4]

He was admitted to the bar in 1812 and less than two years later was in uniform after volunteering for service when news of the British sacking of Washington made it to Lancaster.

He marched the nearly 80 miles into Baltimore with a special company of dragoons led by Judge Henry Shippen, slept outdoors in the rain, and stole horses under the order of his commander who feared the animals would be used by the British. The British then abandoned Baltimore and Buchanan's company returned home where he was able to claim in his first and successful campaign for the Pennsylvania House of Representatives that he was a veteran.

Altogether Buchanan would serve two terms in the state legislature before opting to spend more time on his law practice in Lancaster and becoming engulfed in the single romantic tragedy of life: his romance with

Anne Coleman, who killed herself on a cold winter day in late 1819, some six months after she had agreed to marry him.

Lancaster had been good to Buchanan, but now he suddenly felt isolated there. He could hear, or imagined he did, what they were saying about him, that he only wanted to marry Anne Coleman to get access to her family's wealth and power, that the troubled girl died a horrible death because Buchanan was a terrible fiancé, cold, selfish, remote, and unfeeling.

But the following year, to the surprise of his detractors, Buchanan, whose law practice in no way suffered from the Coleman tragedy, jumped back into politics, announcing his candidacy for Congress in Pennsylvania's competitive Fourth District. And while he definitely had his detractors, there were also those who automatically supported him, especially in Lancaster. Local Federalist Party leaders couldn't help but be impressed, noting that Buchanan was always good for a drink in neighborhood pubs, slapped backs like a seasoned politico, and seemed to know what he was talking about when he gave one of his rare public speeches.

Years later Buchanan would paternalistically describe his relationship with the mostly working class voters of Lancaster: "Among these people I had acquired a competence for a man of moderate wishes, and I think I may say without vanity my professional and personal character stood very high." [5]

Buchanan ran as a Federalist-Republican and won easily, moving in 1821 to Washington to begin what would turn out to be a ten-year stay in the House of Representatives. But even in Washington, a city whose bars, hotels and boardinghouses appealed to him, he never stopped thinking about Pennsylvania politics. He accurately predicted that the state, which would possess, behind New York, the second largest number of electoral votes in the 1824 presidential election, would inevitably play a pivotal role in that contest, and he wanted a part of the action.

To that end, Buchanan initially flirted with supporting John Calhoun, President James Monroe's stern Secretary of War. But Calhoun's support beyond his native South Carolina was often overstated in the national press and that certainly was the case in Pennsylvania. The woods instead was on fire for Andrew Jackson. When Buchanan saw how popular the General and hero of the Battle of New Orleans was in the Keystone State, he was converted into a Jackson man, eventually also declaring himself, like Jackson, a Democrat.

Buchanan would be easily re-elected to Congress in 1822 and 1824. Generally regarded by his fellow members in the House as a hard-working, if plodding legislator, he enjoyed the male bonhomie of the House, was good at backroom bargaining, and now and then was willing to give speeches which were usually remembered more for their legalistic content than dramatic flair.

In his private hours Buchanan boarded on F Street with the handsome Senator William King of Alabama, five years his senior and a fellow bachelor. The two men had much in common. They were both known for their hard working habits, possessed with dreams of national office and supported slavery (King, in fact, owned roughly 500 slaves on his family plantation in Alabama). King had more money than Buchanan and, as a Senator, more influence. But there was also something about him that was effete and perhaps even effeminate: when, decades later, King died, the *Mobile Daily Register* diplomatically regaled him for his "amenities of character and polished deportment [which] shed a softness and 'daily beauty' over his political life." [6]

"He was my most intimate friend, for I was more intimate with him than I ever was with any other man in my life," Buchanan would say years later of King. Keeping in mind that the word "intimate" has many meanings, it's hard to imagine that Buchanan in this remark was admitting to what some scholars have since argued seems certain: that he and King had a homosexual relationship. As a man who was always self-absorbed, Buchanan was probably incapable of maintaining a meaningful and lasting romantic and physical relationship with members of either sex because it required the one thing he was unwilling to surrender: himself. But this much is clear: Buchanan's friendship with King would give him an appreciation of and even sympathy for Southern life, culture, and politics as seen from the personal perspective of a slaveholder. And that perspective would very much influence Buchanan's thinking and politics in the decades to come.[7]

By the fall of 1826 life for Buchanan was good. Very good. He had money in the bank from his law practice, owned property in Pennsylvania, and was widely regarded both in the Keystone State and Washington as young man with a future. Then all of a sudden, Buchanan's world threatened to come apart. A letter arrived from Duff Green, who had served as Calhoun's campaign manager in the recent presidential election, asking Buchanan if he could explain his activities in that contest and "advise me of the manner in which you would prefer that subject to be brought before the people." [8]

Specifically Green wanted to know the details of a charge made by Henry Clay, the ex- Speaker of the House and also a candidate in the 1824 election, claiming that Buchanan in the weeks after that election had gone to Jackson and suggested that he had inside word that Clay would throw his support to the General if Jackson would favor Clay with an executive post.

The election of 1824 had turned out to be one of the most controversial in the nation's history. Jackson won a plurality of the popular vote, but not enough electoral votes to become president. John Quincy Adams was the eventual winner after Clay threw his support to him in balloting that ended up in the House of Representatives. When Adams subsequently named Clay as his Secretary of State, Jackson partisans decried what they labelled a "corrupt bargain" and promised revenge at the polls in 1828.

Through it all, Jackson maintained his reputation for honesty. His supporters repeatedly noted that the General himself would never be a part of any such bargaining for political office. But now Green's letter threatened to undo all of that. If Buchanan had indeed gone to Jackson and dangled the possibility that Clay might support him in return for a place in the cabinet, and if Jackson responded with intrigue, the General would seem as morally venal as Clay and Adams.

Buchanan initially fudged a response, telling Green that if any bargaining had been done, it was done by Adams and Clay. But eventually Jackson himself was drawn into the controversy, writing to tell Buchanan that it had become "necessary for the public to be in possession of the facts." [9]

Buchanan was 35 years old when the news of his 1824 election maneuverings became a scandal. The other men in the controversy— Adams, Clay and Jackson—were all in their 50s, big men of national stature. Buchanan, by contrast, suddenly looked like a small man, a young upstart playing very much out of his league. Clay and Daniel Webster, who had also been a candidate in the 1824 race and enjoyed seeing Buchanan put in "an awkward situation," relished his discomfort. [10]

Finally, and because he had no other choice, Buchanan wrote a letter for publication in his hometown *Lancaster Journal* explaining that his motivation in the embarrassing episode had only been to get an office for Clay, unbeknownst to Clay, while at the same time promoting Jackson's election. Two days later a desperate but still amazingly cocky Buchanan told Jackson: "I have ever been your ardent, decided & perhaps without vanity I may say, your efficient friend. Every person in this part of the state of Pennsylvania is well acquainted with the fact." [11]

Jackson never again wholly trusted Buchanan, who would be called by Jackson biographer Robert Remini a "fidgeting little busybody" for his amateurish maneuverings in the 1824 contest. But after at last winning the White House in 1828, and after Buchanan decided not to run for re-election to Congress in 1830, Jackson was willing to at least acknowledge that Buchanan was competent, and, also wanting to keep Pennsylvania Democrats happy, nominated Buchanan as his Minister to Russia. [12]

Buchanan had many reasons not to accept the post. He was worried that being sent to the other side of the world might be a form of political exile, and wondered about the price he would have to pay to leaving behind his friends and family (his mother, who would die while he was abroad, advised him to turn the job down). But he accepted the mission, perhaps out of a fear of yet one more time offending Jackson, although he bluntly told the President that he didn't intend to stay in Russia for the entirety of Jackson's term.

Ultimately Buchanan served Jackson well in Russia. He successfully negotiated a commercial treaty between the U.S. and Russia (but he fell short trying to do the same with a treaty addressing U.S. maritime rights), and kept in regular touch with the President, sending him lengthy dispatches regarding Russian society and politics and at one point candidly observing: "The great objection which an American must feel to a residence in this country does not arise from the climate, though that is bad enough. It is because here there is no freedom of the press, no public opinion, and but little political conversation, and that very much guarded." [13]

At some level Jackson must have been impressed with Buchanan's service, yet Buchanan's uncanny knack for annoying the President was once again displayed after he returned to the U.S. in the summer of 1833 and dropped by the White House. Learning that a distinguished Englishwoman was about to visit the President, Buchanan suggested that Jackson should quickly discard the comfortable, but down-scale clothing he was at the moment wearing for something more elegant. "When I went to school I read about a man who minded his own business and made a fortune at it," Jackson coldly replied. [14]

Buchanan obviously by this time knew that Jackson didn't particularly like him, yet he remained politically devoted to the President (a decision undoubtedly influenced by Jackson's continuing popularity well into the last years of his second term). Winning election in 1834 as U.S. Senator (elected by state legislators in Pennsylvania), Buchanan entered the Upper Chamber days later as a Jackson Democrat, loyally voting for both Jackson's remaining legislative initiatives as well as, eventually, those of his successor, Martin Van Buren.

The Senate that Buchanan sat in for the rest of the 1830s shined in what historians have since called a Golden Age. It was a period, according to Senate scholar Elaine K. Swift, "in which the chamber was unprecedentedly powerful and prominent." Unfortunately for Buchanan, the legends Clay, Calhoun and Webster, all of whom were like so many walking statues, also served during his Senate years, making Buchanan seem insignificant by contrast, with the devilish Clay frequently ridiculing and destroying Buchanan in debate. [15]

On one notable occasion, the Whig Clay accused the Democrats of failing to state in public their stands on the major issues of the day. "Let us hear from you, I call for the leaders of the party."

Taking the bait, Buchanan rose and said that he never shrank from taking a stand on the issues, prompting Clay to remark: "I called for the leaders of the party." [16]

On another day, as Buchanan was regaling the members with stories of his service in the War of 1812, Clay asked: "You marched to Baltimore?"

Buchanan responded in the affirmative.

"Armed and equipped?" asked Clay.

Again, Buchanan said yes.

"But the British had retreated when you arrived," continued Clay.

"Yes," said Buchanan.

"Will the Senator from Pennsylvania be good enough to inform us," Clay proceeded, a cat toying with a mouse, "whether the British retreated in consequence of his valiantly marching to the relief of Baltimore, or whether he marched to the relief of Baltimore in consequence of the British having already retreated?" [17]

The loud laughter of his fellow Senators must have long burned in Buchanan's ears.

Rarely more than a marginal presence during all of his years in the Senate, Buchanan nevertheless continued unbroken from his House service his support for legislation protecting states' rights and slavery and promoting American expansionism. "He never, in all of his legislative career, had his name attached to an important bill or became the focal point of public interest in a debate," said Buchanan biographer Philip Shriver Klein. When Buchanan left the Senate in early 1845 to become President James K. Polk's Secretary of State, it was not a particularly noteworthy event. [18]

But if Buchanan had been an obscure presence in the Senate, he suddenly became a forbidding, critical, and even explosive Secretary of State in the Polk administration, a vital center of controversy working for a president he appeared to have little respect for or appreciation of. His reason for accepting the post was clear: the Secretary of State office was then seen as a traditional stepping stone to the presidency, and by as early as 1844 Buchanan was no longer just idly imagining himself as president. But the State job would prove a bad fit, not just because Buchanan thought he was smarter than Polk, but also because he resented Polk for having won the 1844 Democratic presidential nomination.

By now in his mid-fifties, Buchanan was a permanently grumpy presence in the Polk White House, endlessly complaining about his duties as Secretary of State and arguing over administration policy. Often, Buchanan's approach to Polk was high-handed: When his former roommate William King returned to Alabama to run for the U.S. Senate, after serving as Minister to France, Buchanan read in the *New York Evening Post* that the President preferred incumbent Dixon Lewis in that race. Angered, Buchanan wrote to Polk, telling him that he was certain the report must be wrong. Without bothering to give Polk a chance to respond, Buchanan said he would take it upon himself to inform King that "you have not encouraged & you do not prefer" Lewis. Buchanan added: "I consider myself fully warranted in these operations." Only naturally Polk soon came to resent Buchanan's attitude and arrogance, savoring any victory over a cabinet officer who repeatedly challenged him. One day the President pointed out to Buchanan that the form of a diplomatic letter he was writing was incorrect. Buchanan, naturally, disagreed. Polk then bet Buchanan a "basket of champagne" that he couldn't find a precedent for the letter. Buchanan searched, but finally had to admit that he was wrong. Triumphant, Polk declined the champagne, happy enough for having for once put Buchanan in his place. "The members of the Cabinet laughed heartily at this incident," Polk later wrote, obviously enjoying Buchanan's defeat. In remarks that could have been easily made by Clay, Jackson or Webster, Polk would eventually characterize Buchanan "an able man, but is in small matters without judgment and sometimes acts like an old maid." [19]

Buchanan, of course, failed to see his negatives in the same light. He regarded himself ultimately as a patriot above everything else, and because he loved his country he remained convinced that anything he did or said was right, even if he was sometimes brusque or bumptious in the process. He didn't want Jackson to look like a slob before an English noblewoman because he thought the country Jackson led was better than England. He argued with Polk over the correct form of a diplomatic letter because he studied such things and wanted to show the ambassadors of other countries that even though America might be young and new to diplomacy, it was nevertheless capable of doing things correctly.

Buchanan's love of country and belief in American exceptionalism was due to some degree to the fact that he was a member of the second generation in a country that had institutionalized self-celebration. Newspapers of the day gave passing mention to Christmas and Easter, but lavishly splashed July 4th events, events that inevitably included parades, picnics, and outside concerts, across their pages. But Buchanan's patriotism was additionally informed by his world travels, travels which were unusual for a man of his day. He took in everything he saw during those travels, made notes to himself and observations in letters to others, and was frankly shocked by what he viewed as the oppression, defeatism and class prejudices of other lands.

"How happy ought we to be in America!" Buchanan had written to a friend while he was still Minister to Russia. "Would that we knew our own happiness! Coming abroad can teach an American no other lessons but to love his country, its institutions & its laws better, much better than he did before." [20]

Years later, serving as Minister to England, Buchanan told his niece Harriet Lane: "I have never met an American gentleman or lady who, whatever they may profess, was pleased with London. They all hurry off to Paris as speedily as possible, unless they have business to detain them here. A proud American who feels himself at home to the best does not like to be shut out by an impassable barrier from the best or rather highest society in this country." [21]

If these ruminations represented a particularly 19th century American point of view on the shortcomings of every other place except America, revelations of this xenophobia would have cost Buchanan few votes back home. On the contrary, Democratic bosses thought Buchanan's world travels, buoyant nationalism, and firm stand as an anti-abolitionist, coupled with his years in Congress, might serve him well as a candidate for the presidency, touting him seriously for the first time in 1844, before he lost the nomination to Polk. Buchanan claimed indifference, telling one supporter "I think there never was a man whose name had been mentioned for the Presidency who took the subject less to heart than myself." [22]

Four years later, again approached by supporters to run, Buchanan said he found the whole thing distasteful and insisted he would do nothing personally to advance his cause. This time he placed a distant second to Michigan Senator Lewis Cass, who humiliated him in the convention delegate balloting, 179 to 33. "I bore my defeat," Buchanan later told his friend Robert Tyler, "with perfect resignation." But, as with Polk, Buchanan would forever resent Cass for beating him. [23]

What prevented Buchanan from mounting more focused and professional campaigns for the nomination? He was clearly ambitious, and having known and served both Jackson and Polk, was convinced he could do the job at least as well, or in Polk's case, better. It would have been impossible for him not to have imagined himself as President. Yet he hesitated, letting two promising election years, 1844 and 1848, get by him when he was only in his mid-fifties and at the height of his personal powers.

He may have wondered if the public, and the opposition press, might make too much of his not being married. But that was only a part of it. The truth was that at middle age Buchanan's ego was just as inflamed, and thus, fragile, as it had been when he was a boy. He could not bear the thought of running for such a prominent office and losing. He had hoped in both 1844 and 1848 that somehow or other the White House would come to him, rather than the other way around.

Then, in 1852, Buchanan shifted tactics, launching an energetic effort to win that year's party nomination.

Even though he still continued to claim an "unconquerable repugnance for anything like personal electioneering for the highest office in the world," Buchanan sought delegate support throughout the spring of that year. By the time of the Baltimore convention, he was certain that the Democratic nomination was at last within his grasp. [24]

His surprise must have been palpable then when the delegates, after protracted balloting that showed the young 39 year-old Illinois Senator Stephen Douglas as his strongest opponent, settled late in the game on the likable Franklin Pierce, the former Senator from New Hampshire and one of history's great dark horses. In a letter revealing more bitterness than he intended, Buchanan congratulated Pierce by claiming "my own defeat, I can assure you, did not cost me a single pang." He sourly added that the presidency was a "crown of thorns" and Washington a city of corruption populated with "contractors, speculators, stock jobbers & lobby members which haunt the halls of Congress." Pierce may have wondered, if Buchanan really felt that way, why he had campaigned for the nomination in the first place. [25]

After Pierce won a landslide election in November, Buchanan saw the results as a personal tragedy, believing his career had been cut short before it reached its natural climax. He would now retire to his comfortable two-story brick mansion in Wheatland, a mile from Lancaster, forgotten by an unappreciative public.

"I am rapidly becoming a petrification," he confided melodramatically to a woman friend, Eliza Watterson, adding "I have seen enough of public life to satisfy a wise man." [26]

The petrification would have to wait.

Only months after his victory, Pierce asked Buchanan to serve as his Minister to England. Buchanan, unsure of the political advantage, negotiated for weeks with the President regarding the power and duties of the post (Buchanan was additionally put out that Pierce had not yet appointed any Pennsylvania Democrats to office). Meeting with Pierce in Philadelphia in the summer of 1853, Buchanan painstakingly hashed matters out with him over dinner and continued the negotiations up to the moment that Pierce boarded a train heading back to Washington.

Even then, Buchanan was uncertain about the post, but knowing that his name was being widely circulated in the press, he finally decided to accept the job, after a confusing exchange of letters with Pierce, on the theory that declining it might seem unpatriotic and would offend Pierce Democrats who seemed to represent the party's future.

Ultimately, Buchanan proved a capable and well-connected minister in Britain, although he would find himself tripped up by the enthusiasms of his own secretary, Daniel Sickles, who somehow managed to talk both the President and Pierre Soule, the American Minister to Spain, into a scheme that resulted in the notorious Ostend Manifesto, a document justifying taking Cuba by force if negotiations with Spain failed. "I cannot for myself discover what benefit will result," Buchanan had protested to Pierce when he learned of the meeting that would result in the controversial manifesto. After the manifesto became reality, and Buchanan was attacked in American newspapers for his participation in it, he protested to Secretary of State William Marcy: "Surely, this ought to be corrected. Never did I obey instructions so reluctantly." [27]

The Ostend controversy did Buchanan no lasting harm. What was much more important for a possible future presidential campaign was the fact that he had been out of the country during the angry domestic slavery debates sparked by the passage of the Kansas-Nebraska Act of 1854. As Pierce's political fortunes, by at least the fall of 1855, declined, attention increasingly focused on Buchanan as a likely nominee in 1856. "I am not, nor shall I be, a candidate for any office," Buchanan told Robert Tyler. He was certain, he told Harriet Lane, that "President Pierce is daily growing stronger for a re-nomination." [28]

But in fact, by early 1856 it was clear that Pierce was in trouble. Although the economy was strong, divisions over the settlement of Kansas had sparked a political firestorm as Northern abolitionists and Southern slaveholders (if not those who served in the latter group's interest) poured into the flat, dusty territory to wage what would become a violent struggle to make Kansas free or slave.

Pierce and Douglas were both tainted by their involvement in the Kansas question. Buchanan seemed a safer bet for the Democrats, although in reality his position on Kansas was indistinguishable from Pierce's, due to the fact that voters did not readily associate him with the controversy.

Buchanan had told Pierce he would retire from his post in Britain by the spring of 1856. His subsequent return in late April to the U.S. was only naturally big news. Arriving in New York, he publicly proclaimed his love for America: "I have been abroad in other lands. I have witnessed arbitrary power. I have contemplated the people of other countries," he announced.

"If you could see how despotism looks on," Buchanan continued, "how jealous the despotic powers of the world are of our glorious institutions, you would cherish the Constitution and Union to your hearts, next to your belief in Christian religion—the Bible for heaven and the Constitution of your country for earth." [29]

He spent a tiring day in New York, ushered from one Democratic function to the next. At one point he even provided a moment of unintended comedy: a prankster approached him from behind and gently placed a small wreath of flowers on his head. When Buchanan saw the people in front of him smiling perhaps more than the occasion required, he reached up to his head and removed the flowers without comment. [30]

Meeting in Cincinnati two months later, Democrats re-auditioned their 1852 choices: Pierce, Douglas and Buchanan. Buchanan, perhaps reading the newspaper reports of Pierce and Douglas getting together in the White House before the convention, worried that at some point the two men would unite in opposition to him.

But a Pierce-Douglas combine never materialized, even though Douglas personally liked Pierce more than he did Buchanan. After 15 ballots that saw his vote steadily decreasing, Pierce graciously had his name withdrawn, making no deals with anyone. That left Douglas and Buchanan and the prospect of a deadlocked convention until the Illinois senator, with 118 votes to Buchanan's 168, dramatically threw in the towel (a fact he would never let Buchanan forget), allowing Buchanan to go over the top on the 17th ballot with a surge of 296 votes. [31]

At last, after 12 years of speculation that he might someday lead the national ticket, Buchanan was the presidential nominee of the Democrat party. He entered a general election campaign where he was by far the oldest of the other ticket mates, perhaps confirming for the 65-year nominee that his time was past: running mate and Douglas supporter John Breckinridge of Kentucky was 35; Republican presidential nominee and celebrated explorer John Fremont was 43; while Fremont's running mate William Dayton of New Jersey was 49.

Fremont would prove a refreshingly blunt candidate, contending in his letter of acceptance that the "design of the nation" had always been to "avoid giving countenance to the extension of slavery."

"The influences of the small but compact and powerful class of men interested in slavery who command one section of the country and wield a vast political control as a consequence in the other, is now directed to turn back this impulse of the revolution and reverse its principles," Fremont proclaimed.

Boldly Fremont charged that the extension of slavery was the "object of the power which now rules the government." Preventing that extension, Fremont promised, would give birth to an explosion of free labor, "the natural capital which constitutes the real wealth of this great country." [32]

Fremont's campaign would prove passionate and romantic, designed especially to appeal to the young idealists of the North.

Buchanan's campaign, by contrast, was from the start plodding and defensive. He complained in his acceptance letter that the issue of slavery had "too long distracted and divided the people of this Union and alienated their affections from each other."

From there he revealed to the country and his fellow politicians a stunning vision utterly devoid of any kind of reality: his absurd, eccentric hope that everyone would be better off if they would just stop talking about slavery altogether.

"Most happy would it be for the country if this long agitation were at an end," he bizarrely asserted, letting the world know that it was not slavery itself that bothered him, but the debate about slavery. "During the whole progress it has produced no practical good to any human being, whilst it has been the source of great and dangerous evils." [33]

Buchanan added that, if elected, he would serve only a single term. He may have made the unneeded vow because he saw himself as a patriarchal figure above the machinations of getting elected to office and then having to maneuver for re-election. But it is also possible that Buchanan was simply admitting he couldn't imagine enduring a second-term campaign when he would be nearly 70 years old.

Either way, the pledge, which he would repeat upon taking office, took some of the steam out of his campaign, signaling as it did to a young country that the coming Buchanan presidency did not promise an era of vigor, but rather a four-year slough for an elderly man capping a long career and content to merely mark the calendar until his retirement. (It didn't help that Breckinridge, at one point in the campaign, was ready to personally confront Know Nothing rioters in his home state of Kentucky, an act that would have dramatically demonstrated a youthful, physical resolve utterly lacking in Buchanan). [34]

By contrast, the Fremont campaign was spirited by the promise of the future as young activists, joined by the writers Ralph Waldo Emerson and Henry Wadsworth Longfellow, pledged their energies to the cause. Others contributed financially. New Yorker Edwin Morgan gave $25,000 to Fremont; well-known publisher and political fix-it man Thurlow Weed put up half that amount. Additional contributions above the $1,000 mark came from Horace Greeley, abolitionist publisher of the *New York Tribune;* Pennsylvania insurance man Lindley Smith, and George Morey, a Massachusetts abolitionist. [35]

But Fremont's fund-raising paled when compared with the Democrats who raised more than $1 million ($10 million in today's terms) and targeted half that amount for crucial Pennsylvania. On the in-coming side of the ledger, New York financier August Belmont gave $50,000 to be used any way the Democrats deemed worthy. From the ledger's out-going column, Buchanan pal George Pitt handed out more than $70,000 in cash to keep the Keystone State in line. [36]

Buchanan, visited at his Wheatland estate throughout the fall by any number of Democrat bosses, was particularly bolstered by a system of state employee kick-backs in Pennsylvania, though he would always maintain that he didn't know anything about it. Isaac West, an inspector at the Custom House in Philadelphia, later explained how things worked: "There was a certain tax levied upon the persons connected with the Custom House," he revealed, adding that for a person with a salary of at least $1,000 annually, the tax during the Buchanan campaign was anywhere from $30 to $33.

Because Custom House employees were grateful to have a job, West added that he never heard anyone complain. "They all felt it their duty to pay more promptly than some of their [other] debts. That was the impression." [37]

Buchanan was additionally aided by a concerted effort on the part of the Democrats to smear Fremont. That Fremont was born when his mother and father were not married, had been court-martialed in the Army for not following orders, and might be a Catholic (he was in fact an Episcopalian), was all meat for the Democratic grinder. Buchanan had known Fremont and his attractive wife Jessie for years and liked them both. There is no evidence that he had anything to do with the well-coordinated character assassination, nor is there any evidence that Buchanan did anything to stop it. [38]

The Fremont smears, combined with the Pennsylvania kick-backs, worked. On the day of the election Buchanan carried Pennsylvania easily, giving him marginally enough electoral votes nationally to become the next President. A third party effort with former president Millard Fillmore serving as the nominee of the Know Nothings carried only Maryland and 21.5 percent of the national vote.

But Buchanan's victory was a subdued one, showing how toxic the Democrat pro-slavery brand had become. His 45.3 percent of the national popular vote was the lowest of any winning presidential candidate in more than three decades. His total electoral vote of 174 was additionally significantly off from the 254 won by Pierce four years earlier.

Equally notable was the sectional profile of Buchanan's victory. Fremont, who discovered as the campaign wore on that he hated the wheeling and dealing that went with it, nevertheless managed to win states like New York, Ohio, Michigan, Wisconsin and Iowa, all states that had been won by the Democrats four years before. Buchanan did indeed clinch his victory by winning his home state, but just as significant was the monolithic support he received throughout the South, where he was frankly regarded, in a way he would never admit, as slavery's best friend.

Past successful Democrat candidates Jackson, Van Buren, Polk and Pierce had won by carrying states in both the North and South, thereby being able to claim that their victories were truly national.

But Buchanan lost most of the North and in some cases decisively so: his 32.8 percent in New York was a near record-low for a Democrat and a nearly 20 percentage point drop from Pierce's 50.2 percent. [39]

As reporters in the days after the balloting sifted through the results, two trends were clear: 1. The Democrat Party had become almost entirely the party of the South. 2. The Republicans, for a first-time national effort, had done extraordinarily well and were on the verge of becoming the party of the North. With a better financed campaign and candidate in 1860, their fortunes looked entirely promising.

Buchanan, recognizing the trends, was in a bad mood on the day of his election. He complained to one friend about the way in which his opponents had used the slavery issue to their advantage. He was particularly put out by what he described as the "preachers & fanatics of New England," where he lost every state, charging that they had "excited people to such a degree on the slavery question that they generally prayed & preached against me from their pulpits on Sunday last throughout that land of 'isms.'" [40]

That night Buchanan addressed a friendly crowd at his Wheatland estate. But his remarks were hardly generous. "The people of the North seem to have forgotten the warnings of the Father of his country against all geographic parties, and by far the most dangerous of all such parties is that of a combined North against a combined South on the question of slavery."

Casting Southern whites as victims, and remarkably ignoring entirely the plight of black slaves, Buchanan continued: "With the South it is a question of self-preservation, of personal security around the family altar, of life or of death. The Southern people still cherish a love for the Union. But what to them is even our blessed confederacy, the wisest and best form of government ever devised by man, if they cannot enjoy its blessings and its benefits without being in constant alarm for their wives and children?"

Thank goodness for Pennsylvania, Buchanan exclaimed, finally finding something positive to say. Had it voted Republican, "We should have been precipitated into the yawning gulf of dissolution. But she stood erect and firm as her own Alleghanies."

He was serious. His victory to him meant a hopeful end to the anti-slavery movement, despite the fact that abolitionism had by 1856 become a permanent part of the American political scene fostering dozens of organizations, societies and newspapers, and spiriting the ranks of the new Republican party, which would send in this same election 92 members to the House of Representatives and 20 to the Senate, both historic highs.

Flights of oratory were not really in the Buchanan style. Even so, it was a victory speech, so he gave it a shot.

"The night is departing," he proclaimed near the end of his address, "and the roseate and propitious morn now breaking upon us promises a long day of peace and prosperity for our country." [41]

Chapter Three

"A Mode of Submission that is a Mockery and Insult"

Buchanan showed what an experienced Washington hand he was with the unannounced visit he made to the nation's capital in late January 1857, five weeks before his inauguration.

Four years before he had taken Franklin Pierce to task for forming his cabinet while still in New Hampshire, sensibly arguing that Pierce would needlessly offend old-time Washington pols who expected to be consulted on such matters.

Now Buchanan, holing up at the National Hotel, met with any number of Democratic bigwigs, Congressmen, administration officials and Pierce himself for back-slapping, cigars and drinks. "Mr. Buchanan's room is overrun by politicians, office-seekers and citizens," a reporter for the *New York Herald* noted. "Everybody is admitted, without distinction." [1]

On January 29 the House of Representatives held a memorial service for Preston Brooks who had died suddenly, most likely of pneumonia, several days before. The 38 year-old South Carolina Representative had made national headlines the summer before when he violently and repeatedly smashed abolitionist Massachusetts Senator Charles Sumner over the head and shoulders with a cane, outraging Northern opinion.

Now Buchanan entered the House chamber quietly by himself and was guided by a clerk to a chair below the Speaker's podium where he listened as several Congressmen paid tribute to Brooks. [2]

Buchanan returned to Pennsylvania shortly afterwards.

What exactly he accomplished during his week-long visit to Washington was not clear. But by the time Buchanan returned for his inaugural he had settled on most of his department heads. It would prove a historic cabinet that, with Georgia's Howell Cobb for Treasury, John Floyd of Virginia as Secretary of War, Aaron Brown of Tennessee as Postmaster General, and Mississippi's Jacob Thompson as Interior Secretary, was also decidedly pro-Southern, happily regarding slavery as a constitutional right, abolitionism as a nuisance and the economic good times of the Pierce years as a given.

The Southern gentlemen would be joined by three Yankees: Connecticut's Isaac Toucey as Secretary of the Navy (who was sympathetic to Southern interests); Attorney General Jeremiah Black of Pennsylvania; and Michigan's Lewis Cass as Secretary of State. Cass, at 75, was plodding. Buchanan soon discovered that he had little use for him. Given Buchanan's extensive first-hand knowledge of foreign affairs, he would have most likely found any Secretary of State wanting. But Buchanan, never a gracious loser, also resented the portly Michigander because he had been bested by him in the contest for the 1848 Democratic presidential nomination.

Southerners would also dominate Buchanan's social life in Washington. The suave Louisiana Senator John Slidell enjoyed unfettered access to the White House, and was both a major influence on administration policy and steadfast regular at every White House party. Along with Slidell, the charismatic Cobb and his wife Mary Ann; Mississippi Senator Jefferson Davis and his wife Varina; and Alabama Senator Clement and his lively wife Virginia; made up a reliable core at virtually every White House function. It was Virginia Clay, in fact, who would contend as late as 1905 that White House parties in the Buchanan era, as organized by Harriet Lane, "rose to their highest degree of elegance, to a standard indeed that has not since been approached." [3]

Harriet was already busy making preparations for her first White House party when Buchanan got what he regarded as very good news from the U.S. Supreme Court.

He had been following the case of Dred Scott, a former slave suing for freedom, as it worked its way to the highest court. In correspondence with Associate Justice John Catron, Buchanan knew that the Southern majority on the court would rule against Scott. By so doing the court would also say that slaves were protected property under the Constitution, instantly interpreted as meaning that the government really had no right to bar slavery in any territory.

Bumptiously inserting himself into the preliminary deliberations of the court, Buchanan had not only corresponded with Catron on the matter, but also Associate Justice Robert Grier, pushing him to join the Southern majority. Grier, of Pennsylvania, was uncomfortable going against the wishes of the president-elect of his own state and may have felt additional pressure recalling that he held his seat primarily because Buchanan had declined an earlier nomination from President Polk to the bench—a nomination that subsequently went to Grier. [4]

There is, to some, noting quite as suspicious as the sight of public officials whispering to one another at a public event. So it was that in front of thousands at his inaugural Buchanan was seen quietly talking with Chief Justice Roger Taney, a figure regarded by abolitionists as evil incarnate because of his pro-slavery leanings and palsied appearance.

The conversation would, in fact, become a thing of legend, with many convinced it was the exact moment when Buchanan was tipped off on how the Court was about to vote in the Scott case—and that that news was reflected in Buchanan's subsequent address. [5]

But it was more probable that Buchanan already knew about the Scott decision given that Taney and the other members of the Court had visited him the previous evening at the National Hotel.

Three days later, in a nearly inaudible voice, Taney announced the court's contentious anti-Scott decision. The fact that other members of the bench would deliver their own versions of the decision showed how important and divisive the case had become. And even though the Court spoke with some confidence in that the vote was 7 to 2 (with Grier, in the end, voting as Buchanan wished), the decision would be roundly vilified throughout the North.

Taney's unnecessary added observation, in his written opinion, that blacks were "altogether unfit to associate with the white race" and "had no rights which the white man was bound to respect," only provided a hateful edge to the decision. [6]

"The circumstances attending the present decision have done much to divest it of moral influence and impair the confidence of the country," the *New York Times,* hardly alone, editorialized in response. [7]

From Buchanan's perspective, the timing of the decision could not have been better. In his inaugural address he declared "No other question remains for adjustment because all agree that under the Constitution slavery in the States is beyond the reach of any human power except that of the respective States themselves wherein it exists. May we not then hope that the long agitation on this subject is approaching its end?" [8]

Although that question illustrated the limits of Buchanan's political imagination, he did have reason in general for optimism.

His journey from Pennsylvania had been one of uninterrupted acclaim. Traveling with Harriet Lane, nephew James Buchanan Henry, and John Breckinridge, Buchanan was greeted by tens of thousands of well-wishers between Lancaster and Washington. Arriving at Washington's Baltimore and Ohio station he was overwhelmed by an unlikely mob of well-dressed older women. Somehow he escaped and made it to the National Hotel. But even here there was danger: rotting food from a nearby sewer had created enough airborne bacteria to kill several guests, including eventually Buchanan's nephew Elliott Lane.

Buchanan soon felt ill himself. But he rallied on inaugural morning to ride down Pennsylvania Avenue in an open carriage with President Pierce, waving to the cheering throng. A correspondent for the *Baltimore American* noticed that the balconies along the avenue were filled with dozens of women who, when the procession passed, "signified their enthusiasms by waving handkerchiefs held in hands white and delicate as the first snowflakes of winter." [9]

Buchanan was sworn in at the Capitol by Taney and then escorted to a platform built specially for his address. A reporter for the *Philadelphia Public Ledger* observed that once Buchanan was seen on the stands, there came a "deafening shout from the vast human mass. It spread over the whole multitude, and it was some time before it could be quieted." [10]

In response, Buchanan bowed repeatedly.

In his address, Buchanan not only celebrated what he hoped would be an end to the national debate over slavery, he also bolstered American expansionism, pushed for using a recent surplus to pay down the national debt, and proposed increasing the size of the Navy. [11]

Speech finished, Buchanan was driven directly to the White House where he hosted an afternoon reception for more than a thousand visitors.

That night he showed up around 11 and stayed well past midnight at his inaugural ball. Guests gained entry to the event by producing enameled invitation cards that contained a medallion portrait of Buchanan. It was a crowded, glimmering event. As a 40-piece orchestra played waltzes and military tunes, more than 5,000 hungry Democrats, including ex-President Pierce and Vice-President Breckinridge, made quick work of a four-foot high pyramid cake, 400 gallons of oysters, 500 quarts of chicken salad and 1,200 quarts of ice cream. [12]

Buchanan woke up the next morning triumphant. He was President of the United States. No man in American history had ever taken so long to get to the White House, more than four decades in public office at almost every level of government, four decades of dreaming for an office that always eluded him, four decades of maneuvering that, up to now, had fallen well short of its goal.

But now he had the job: he was the most important man in America, and determined to enjoy a station he regarded as his due.

The fact that Buchanan was surrounded not only by a supportive cabinet, but Harriet (who would throw herself into redecorating the White House) and the shy James Buchanan Henry, signing on as his secretary, only made the post more pleasant. [13]

The tranquil mood matched the seemingly tranquil times. Buchanan hoped to tie up loose ends remaining from the Pierce Administration and then devote the rest of his term to stoking a blazing domestic economy and pushing the boundaries of the country westward.

One of those old Pierce matters was Kansas. Pro and anti-slavery advocates had been moving there with the contrasting hopes of creating a new state that would either be a part of or totally free from the peculiar institution. Buchanan wanted the matter settled quickly. In late March he appointed an old friend, Robert Walker, as the new territorial governor of Kansas assigned to oversee a process resulting in a constitution being drawn up and accepted by Congress as the necessary step to statehood. Because Walker was known for his honesty, the choice proved popular. "The President has knocked, it is said, the right nail on the head to secure the peace of Kansas by the appointment of Robert J. Walker to the Governorship," said the *Philadelphia Public Ledger*. [14]

But it was not an appointment made easily: "I refused two or three times verbally and once in writing," Walker later recalled of Buchanan's efforts to get him to accept the post. "But the request was renewed from time to time with great earnestness by the President, and by many friends through whom he communicated with me upon the subject." Buchanan even lobbied Walker's wife, urging her to convince her husband to take the job. Walker did not succumb until Buchanan declared that he wanted nothing more than for the people of Kansas to decide whether their soon-to-be-state would be slave or free. "I will go then," Walker told Buchanan, "in the full confidence, so strongly suggested by you, that I will be sustained by your own high authority, with the cordial cooperation of all of your cabinet." [15]

Buchanan subsequently helped Walker to write his inaugural address, which boldly stated that unless actual Kansas voters participated in the constitution process, it "Will and ought to be rejected by Congress." [16]

Shortly after arriving in Kansas in June, Walker quickly figured out that the anti-slavers were in the majority. "It was universally conceded that it could not be made a slave state by a fair vote of the people," he decided. This was not a prospect that particularly thrilled Walker. He regarded a rough equilibrium between the free and slave sates as essential to the country's well-being. A Kansas free state would distort that equilibrium in the favor of the free states, which already made up a majority anyway. "I should have preferred that a majority of the people would have made it a slave state," Walker later remarked. [17]

Even so, Walker declared that the issue must be decided by a fair vote, a decision that greatly alarmed Southern leaders. "We are betrayed," Georgia Judge Thomas Thomas told Congressman Alexander Stephens, also of Georgia. "If Buchanan retains him [Walker] for thirty days, we are ruined." [18]

Not appreciating the extent of the Southern angst, Buchanan initially stood by Walker. "The point on which you and our success depend is the submission of the constitution to the people of Kansas," the President assured Walker. "And by the people, I mean and have no doubt you mean, the actual bona fide residents who have been long enough in the territory to identify themselves with its fate." [19]

As reports from Kansas filtered back to Washington indicating that Walker was determined to play it down the middle, not favoring one factor over the other, the Southern majority in Buchanan's cabinet, which had previously assumed that Walker was for slavery being established in Kansas (otherwise, it was thought, Buchanan would not have appointed him in the first place), got nervous. Their agitation was mirrored by Democratic Party meetings in Alabama, Mississippi and Georgia in July where resolutions were passed demanding that Buchanan fire Walker. [20]

Walker, meanwhile, worried about the specter of violence between the two factions, sent a request to Washington asking for the support of 2,000 federal troops, a request that War Secretary Floyd quickly spiked. Secretary of State Cass, at the same time, cynically wondered if Walker's real goal wasn't to "Attempt to disperse the peaceable assemblies of his people at the point of a bayonet." [21]

As Cass was writing to Buchanan, the President was relaxing at a retreat in Bedford Springs, Pennsylvania. He had enjoyed the rural setting for years, hiking several hours a day and propping his feet up on the railing of the retreat hotel's front porch at night, talking with anyone who stopped by. [22]

When, by late August, Buchanan returned to Washington he found waiting for him a letter written by Yale University science professor and abolitionist Benjamin Silliman that was endorsed by 42 New England clergymen (perhaps, Buchanan must have wondered, some of the same ministers who had worked against him in the 1856 election), attacking him for his Kansas policy. The document was widely reprinted in the nation's press.

Silliman, too, was concerned about Walker's request for additional troops, but from the perspective of a free-stater who thought a show of soldiers would be used to "force the people of Kansas to obey laws not their own." Buchanan responded in a written statement that was also released to the press, arguing that his policy had always been to protect the would-be state of Kansas from the "violence of lawless men." His ultimate goal remained unchanged, he insisted, which was to let the people of Kansas decide matters "for themselves and their posterity." [23]

But it was becoming increasingly clear to Buchanan that no matter how quickly he wanted to dispense with matters in Kansas, he would be burdened with the issue at least for the next year of his presidency.

Meanwhile the White House received a jolt from an unexpected quarter. Charles Stetson, president of the large Ohio Life Insurance and Trust Company, a bank with deposits exceeding $2 million, suddenly announced the suspension of payments to creditors due to the failure of clients to pay on their loans. In a public statement Stetson sought to reassure depositors that despite the suspension decision, the bank remained "solid and reliable." [24]

Naturally, Stetson's words were taken as a sure indication that the bank was in serious trouble.

When it was subsequently revealed that the bank's liabilities were in excess of $7 million, traders in New York reacted with alarm. Banks across the country called in loans and suspended payments on checks. Making matters worse was the strange connection between the panic and the Dred Scott decision: because that Supreme Court ruling cast doubt on whether the territories would be slave or free, bonds for east/west railroads collapsed, also negatively impacting the nation's banks. In response, depositors at other banks, mostly in the East, withdrew funds, starting a national run. The big Bank of Philadelphia was characterized as being in a "precarious position." The Bowery Bank, East Bank and Grocer's Bank, all in New York, closed their doors. Things looked equally dicey in Boston and Baltimore. [25]

By late September hundreds of small businesses, primarily up and down the East coast, had gone belly up, resulting in substantial unemployment. The crisis took on an added ethnic flavor when unemployed Irish laborers gathered in Tompkins Square in New York and attacked anyone who looked or sounded German on the theory that the city's merchants, accused of hoarding bread, were nearly all German.

When New York Mayor Fernando Wood vowed to find jobs for the men, protest leader George Campbell angrily issued the kind of blanket condemnation that neither the obsessively political Wood nor Buchanan could understand: "Put not your trust in politicians, nor yet in any man who is their tool," he declared. "Trust yourself." [26]

Back in Washington, Buchanan wondered if a stronger tariff policy might help matters. In an era when the federal government rarely attempted to manage the economy, no one expected Buchanan to help the banks. And he didn't. But Buchanan did axe a series of public works programs—exactly the opposite response that modern day Democratic presidents would take during times of economic trouble—on the theory that additional federal spending would only add to the problem. He additionally ordered a company of federal troops to be prepared to back the District police in the event of a riot.

The financial panic even, in a bizarre moment, reached into the White House. On November 23, a Washington resident barged into the President's office with a claim that the government owed him money. He handed Buchanan several documents to read. When Buchanan stalled, the man became enraged. Buchanan then told him to leave. When the man refused, Buchanan responded "Then I will go," and walked into James Buchanan Henry's office. [27]

Despite such distractions, Buchanan continued to focus his attention on Kansas. Repeatedly he had promised that great things should be expected from the upcoming constitutional convention in Lecompton, Kansas. That convention, Buchanan was sure, would speed up the statehood process by scheduling a vote deciding whether Kansas should adopt a constitution allowing for slavery. But the convention proved a fiasco. Pro-slavery men pushed through a constitution to their liking, refusing to let voters have a say on it one way or the other. The convention did draft a pro-slavery article that actually would be submitted to a popular vote, but it, too, was a sham: even if the article was defeated by the voters, the constitution would still recognize slaves already in Kansas as property.

By late fall Walker had begun to have grave misgivings that the statehood process, under current conditions, could realistically move forward. His increasing doubts confirmed for his Southern detractors that Walker was the problem and needed to be removed. Buchanan still insisted that he was in Walker's corner, yet it was clear that most of the members of his cabinet wanted to get rid of him and were dropping word with reporters that Walker's days were numbered. The *New York Tribune* on November 8 ominously observed that the administration was "seriously perplexed as to what course it shall pursue regarding Governor Walker's conduct." [28]

Whatever doubts Buchannan may still have had regarding Walker were probably finally resolved eight days later when his long-time trusted adviser Robert Tyler bluntly urged him to remove Walker "without hesitation." [29]

In his message to Congress shortly thereafter, Buchanan claimed that it was "Far from my intention to interfere with the decision of the people of Kansas, either for or against slavery." Walker returned to Washington and met with Buchanan, arguing with him over the legitimacy of the Lecompton constitution. On December 15 he submitted his resignation. "It is no longer in my power to preserve the peace or promote the public welfare," Walker said, convinced that Buchanan had pulled the rug out from under him. [30]

Buchanan's acceptance of Walker's resignation coupled with his refusal to criticize the activities of the Lecompton men, who subsequently won a bogus state vote that was boycotted by anti-slavery residents, outraged Northern Republicans. But this time Buchanan was also under attack from Northern Democrats, particularly Illinois Senator Stephen Douglas, who felt, among other things, that in dumping Walker, Buchanan had placed Democrats in a precarious position going into the 1858 midterm elections.

"By God, sir, I made James Buchanan, and by God, sir, I will unmake him," Douglas had famously declared. Once again Douglas reminded the world that had it not been for his withdrawal as a candidate at the 1856 Democratic convention, Buchanan would probably not now be president. [31]

A break between the two most powerful Northern Democrats in the country would not only be bad for the party, but ruinous for an administration that would need every vote it could get in Congress in the wake of anticipated Republican gains in the coming midterm contests.

When Douglas, in early December, visited Buchanan in the White House, the President bluntly remarked that he was tired of hearing about Kansas. Once voters there finally passed on a constitution, he said, the subject would be done with. Douglas thought this was a shockingly ignorant take on events and urged instead that Buchanan save himself and his presidency by disowning Lecompton altogether and starting the ratification process all over. Douglas added that he was determined to oppose the Lecompton constitution, even if that meant attacking Buchanan.

Annoyed, Buchanan replied: "Mr. Douglas, I desire you to remember that no Democrat ever yet differed with an administration of his own choice without being crushed." Buchanan additionally reminded Douglas that the result of divisions among the Democrats during Andrew Jackson's presidency had only made Jackson stronger. Douglas then pointed out to Buchanan that he was no Andrew Jackson. [32]

Douglas shortly appeared on the Senate floor and in an address in which he never attacked Buchanan personally provided a way out of the Lecompton disaster for Northern Democrats, arguing that opposition to that proposed constitution was not a sign of being disloyal to the party, but rather one of standing up for principle "If this constitution is to be forced down our throats in violation of the fundamental principle of free government under a mode of submission that is a mockery and insult, I will resist it to the last," Douglas declared.

"I have no fear," he added, "of any party associations severed." [33]

Concluding, Douglas was gratified to see and hear the response from the Senate gallery where visitors in violation of Senate rules give him a standing ovation.

At the White House, Buchanan, facing a solid bloc of Republican opposition as well as break-away Douglas Democrats, now made a decision that would have a devastating impact on his presidency. Ignoring the growing public resentment towards the Lecompton constitution, Buchanan would dig in, determined against all odds to ramrod it through an increasingly unenthused Congress.

Chapter Four

"We Had a Merry Time of It"

"Mr. Buchanan, with the most astounding duplicity and inconsistency, violated his pledges to the people of Kansas and joined the ranks of their enemies," the *Ohio Repository* newspaper charged as 1858 dawned, reflecting general public disappointment with the President over Kansas. [1]

On February 2, Buchanan gave his critics even more reason to revile him when he urged Congress to accept the Lecompton constitution, even though a second vote in Kansas had since resulted in the popular rejection of that document.

From Massachusetts, the *Springfield Daily Republican* described Buchanan's message as a "disgrace to the man who wrote it and to the nation which he represents before the world." Buchanan's embrace of the Lecompton document, added the *Philadelphia North American,* was "so evidently the work of a mind determinedly defending the wrong, as to destroy all the credit that the President had before possessed." [2]

Many things about Buchanan's stubborn advocacy of the Lecompton constitution got by him, most obviously that the document, forged by a minority, refuted his earlier stated commitment to majority rule. But politically, Buchanan also failed to appreciate how his Kansas actions were now helping the opposition party.

The Republicans, charged the Buchanan-friendly *Kalamazoo Gazette,* regarded the Kansas controversy as "all they have to go into the next presidential campaign upon—and hence they have no desire" for a "present settlement of the Kansas difficulties." [3]

On March 6, Missouri Representative Francis Blair, Jr., in Washington, predicted: "The opinion here is that we shall beat Lecompton in the House." Blair, a recent convert to the Republican Party, could clearly see that the ongoing controversy was damaging Buchanan and Democrats in general. Daily, through angry debates, constituent letters, and newspaper editorials, House members recognized that Lecompton had emerged as a nationwide firestorm. Even though Administration supporters in the Senate finally approved the admission of Kansas with the Lecompton constitution by a vote of 33 to 25, Republican House members combined with rebellious Northern Democrats to pass a substitute measure calling for an entirely new public vote on the constitution. [4]

To mitigate further humiliation of Buchanan, Indiana Democrat William English proposed a new bill promising that if the voters of Kansas would ratify the Lecompton constitution as is, they would be given a land grant of about 4 million acres and put on the fast track for statehood.

For Congressional reporters the prolonged spring debate proved nothing if not entertaining: during one late evening session, Buchanan's friend, South Carolina Representative Lawrence Keitt, always sitting on a pin, tried to choke muscular Pennsylvania Representative Galusha Grow, leading to a general brawl of several dozen Northern and Southern congressmen that also saw Pennsylvania Representative John Covode, known as "Honest John," carrying a heavy spittoon into the battle, and an elderly Southern member losing his wig in the fracas. At other times the prolonged proceedings were simply frustrating. On April 5, the Washington correspondent for the *Philadelphia Public Ledger* reported: "Appearances are, at present, adverse to the adjustment of this disagreeable question. Members have taken their ground for or against the Lecompton constitution, and will be slow to recede from it." [5]

Not until late April did both chambers pass the English bill. Buchanan quickly hailed the vote as a personal triumph, telling a crowd of supporters: "The best interest of the country were involved in the long contest which has so happily terminated. I hope and believe the result will tend to promote the peace and prosperity of our glorious Union." [6]

Buchanan's "victory" speech was only the latest evidence that he really had no strong feelings one way or the other on either the Lecompton constitution or how exactly Kansas became a state. He had simply and incautiously embraced the document as a required step in bringing statehood to Kansas. Technically, of course, he was correct. But in ignoring the outrage over how that constitution came into being, Buchanan had seen the trees but not the forest.

As Buchanan delivered his remarks, 19 year-old Washington resident James Powers was awaiting execution in the City Jail for the shooting murder of another young man named Edward Lutts. The Powers-Lutts trial had galvanized much of Washington, not only because testimony revealed that Powers, who had gotten in a fight with Lutts at a summer 1857 Sunday school picnic, was singularly determined to murder him, but also because it was clear that once Powers was convicted he would be hanged, a sentence rarely meted out in the Washington Criminal Court. Several days before the scheduled execution, local Reverend Timothy O'Toole met with Buchanan and asked him to commute Powers'sentence to life. Buchanan was troubled by the case and remarked "If you can show me an extenuating circumstance, I will grant it." As there was no such circumstance, on the contrary dozens of witnesses had testified to having seen Powers shoot Lutts in a Washington tavern, Buchanan instead granted Powers a respite of eight days so that he could prepare himself spiritually for what Buchanan called the "the awful changes which await him." Buchanan additionally told O'Toole that the Powers case saddened him, remarking "Nearly all the murders and other crimes of violence of late in the District of Columbia have been committed by such young men." Eight days later Powers was hanged in the yard of the City Jail. [7]

Republicans had nothing to say in response to Buchanan's actions in the Powers affair. But the President's insistence on pushing through the Lecompton constitution had compelled party members and leaders to rethink their larger policy goals. Regarding the very existence of slavery, William Goodell, a New York abolitionist and Republican supporter, remarked "We must admit it, to its fullest extent, or we must deny it altogether."

"By the former, we should surrender all the states to slavery. By the latter, we should deny its legal and constitutional right in any of the states," Goodell continued in a letter to Maine Representative Israel Washburn. "We have no tenable right or abiding middle ground." [8]

It was a theme most persuasively given voice to during the summer by Abraham Lincoln, running for the U.S. Senate in Illinois against Stephen Douglas.

In widely quoted remarks delivered at the close of the Illinois Republican State Convention in Springfield, Lincoln eloquently proclaimed: "A house divided against itself cannot stand. I believe this government cannot endure permanently half slave and half free. I do not expect the Union to be dissolved. I do not expect the house to fall. But I do expect it will cease to be divided. It will become all one thing, or all the other." [9]

Lincoln's "all one thing or the other," which sounded a lot like Goodell's letter, coming as it did in the summer of 1858, dramatically encapsulated the overarching Republican fall campaign, declared Illinois Republican Congressman William Kellogg, who called the speech a "most able vindication of our doctrines and the fundamental principles...I would esteem it *the* speech of the campaign." [10]

The subsequent Lincoln-Douglas debates, with Lincoln frequently attacking Buchanan, and Douglas reduced to what was for him an uncomfortable defense of the President (who was actually hoping for a Douglas defeat), proved a political sensation. Indiana Congressman Schuyler Colfax, a rising figure in national Republican circles, said as much when he reported to Lincoln on August 25: "I have been absent from my house at South Bend nearly a month campaigning in my district & speaking every day, but have not been an inattentive spectator of the great contest in your state. Everywhere, the deepest interest is felt in it." [11]

Just as important to the fortunes of the still-growing party were the dozens of other well-organized and well-funded Republican congressional campaigns taking place throughout the North, particularly in New Jersey, New York and Pennsylvania where Republicans expected to make dramatic gains.

Unlike Buchanan, Vice-President John Breckinridge at least tried to provide a rationale for voters to support administration-friendly candidates, warning one Kentucky gathering that the goal of the Republicans in recent months had evolved into "broader and deeper resistance to the administration." If successful, Breckinridge warned, the Republican agenda would be clear: "To prevent any more slave states into the Union and ultimately abolitionize all the states." [12]

It hardly helped the Democrats' cause that Buchanan had become such a figure of criticism and ridicule. Several Republican newspapers in Indiana went so far as to claim that Buchanan had penned a letter to home state Congressman English, his spear-carrier during the debate over the Lecompton constitution, noting that he was facing opposition in his primary and telling English to get the word out that "by giving you a clear track, they [English's primary foes] will gain my favor and may expect to be provided for in a suitable manner." [13]

The letter was a forgery. But to many Buchanan detractors in an atmosphere thick with memories of his rank interference in the Dred Scott decision as well as his betrayal of Robert Walker, anything seemed possible.

"The youth of our land are looking forward," proclaimed William Pennington in New Jersey, a recent convert to the Republicans and candidate for Congress. "But when they look now to that seat once held by Washington, they see one there who deceived the people and is now again attempting to deceive them by cajoling them."

Pennington, who in a surprise turn of events, would end up becoming the next Speaker of the House, additionally characterized Buchanan's approach to government as one of "say as I do [and] there won't be a whimper of dissatisfaction."

Then, crisply capturing the spirit of rebellion spreading across the North, Pennington added: "No, there will not be a whimper, but there will be thunders of outraged public sentiment." [14]

Jefferson Davis, speaking in Boston's Fanueil Hall on October 11, did his best to stanch the Republican flow, warning "Men may be goaded by the constant attempt to infringe upon rights and to produce enmity, and in the resentment which follows it is not possible to tell how far the wave must rush. I therefore plead to you now to arrest a fanaticism which has been evil in the beginning and must be evil in the end." [15]

But the trend was too powerful to halt. In October, the pivotal states of Pennsylvania, Indiana and Ohio voted overwhelmingly Republican for Congress.

Buchanan later claimed to Harriet Lane that he had been anticipating the dreadful results for the last three months, and "was not taken by surprise as to the extent of our defeat."

Meeting on election night in the White House with a small gathering of friends, Buchanan said, "We had a merry time of it, laughing among other things over our crushing defeat. It is so great that it is almost absurd." [16]

Zachariah Chandler, the Republican Senator from Michigan and, like Colfax, also an emerging national voice, had a more studied take on the Democratic defeat: "They could control their party, but could not sacrifice its principles & hold the people." Chandler added a thought that Buchanan would have found bewildering: "The Republican Party is founded upon the principles & success of the old party [the Democrats] having abandoned their principles." [17]

Final Republican mid-term wins in November, for Buchanan, confirmed the worst: although the Democrats retained control of the Senate, 36 to 26, they lost an epic 26 seats in the House. The destruction was greatest in New York, where the Republicans picked up 8 new seats; Pennsylvania, with a gain of 11; New Jersey, with 4 new seats; and Massachusetts, with 3.

The decline of Democratic fortunes in these states tracked the same downward trend charted in Buchanan's 1856 election, where his percentage of the vote on average had dropped by nearly 10 percent from Franklin Pierce's 1852 vote. If the current trend continued, the once-vibrant Northern base of the Democratic Party was at risk of extinction in 1860.

Young Republicans across the country rejoiced over the results. Organization, high principle and more effective fund-raising than was evident during John Fremont's losing presidential campaign of two years ago all combined for victory and a new sense of purpose.

"I trust to God there will be no more dallying, no more backing down, no more Fremont experiments," buoyant Republican supporter George Talbot enthused to Congressman Washburn after the election. [18]

But the conservative *New York Sun* provided a sobering thought for the ecstatic Republicans as well as a damning take on Buchanan's performance in the White House when it argued that in the final analysis the big 1858 Republican win was "not so much the result of party organization as the consequences of the mistakes or misconduct of the present administration." [19]

Chapter Five

"An Instinct in Such Matters Created by Long Experience."

Just one month after his reversals in the 1858 election, Buchanan was ready to plunge headfirst into a new controversy when he proposed, in his second annual message to Congress, that the United States purchase Cuba.

"The truth is that Cuba, in its existing colonial condition, is a constant source of injury and annoyance to the American people," he said. By purchasing the island nation, Buchanan added in an afterthought obviously intended to tweak abolitionists, "The last relic of the African slave trade would instantly disappear." [1]

The proposal was not made in a void. Buchanan worshipped in the church of Manifest Destiny, the notion famously celebrated by newspaperman John O'Sullivan proclaiming that the U.S. had a right to "possess the whole of the continent which Providence has given us." [2]

Worried about an ongoing civil war in Mexico, Buchanan also proposed the creation of a temporary U.S. protectorate over the northern states of Chihuahua and Sonora, which historian Allan Nevins would later describe as a "proposal for war and seizure." [3]

Buchanan additionally supported filibusterer William Walker's attempts to invade Nicaragua, and asked Congress for authority to send in the Army and Navy to keep open a transit route from the Gulf of Mexico to the Pacific.

In all ways imaginable, Buchanan regarded Latin America as an accessible playground for the U.S., a pliable continental swath that

Americans could influence and control with little regard to the rights or feelings of the people or governments there.

The task of advancing the President's Cuban proposal in the Senate fell to the durable John Slidell, a long-standing devotee of invading the island nation. Brandishing charts and maps, Slidell, beginning in January 1859, championed legislation that would give Buchanan $30 million to be used in the acquisition of Cuba. Slidell imaginatively argued that the purchase of Cuba was a natural outgrowth of American expansionism. The "law of our national existence is a growth we cannot disobey," he exclaimed, telling his colleagues that as Britain was in India, and France was in Africa, the U.S. should be in Cuba. [4]

It wasn't just Slidell who swung into action on this one. To Buchanan's pleasure, his pals came out of the woodwork in favor of his proposal.

"If Spain be indisposed to sell, I would seize Cuba," Mississippi Senator Aaron Brown told an enthusiastic gathering of Tammany Hall Democrats in New York. Brown went on to note that the U.S. had tried to negotiate before with Spanish officials over Cuba—always unsuccessfully. "I have grown weary of this thing, of having young, proud, glorious America knocking at the door of Spain and asking for admission. It is our policy not to ask justice, but to demand it, because it is our right." [5]

Democratic Representative Samuel "Sunset" Cox of Ohio, so named because he once delivered a lengthy treatise on the wonders of a sunset, tried a different tack, announcing that the purchase of the island would make Cuba "co-equal with New York and Ohio in a common league for the commonweal." South Carolina Congressman Lawrence Keitt, never before known to have been concerned about the plight of slaves in the U.S., brought up the subject of current slave laws in Cuba and remarked "No matter how stringent or even savage they may be, they would be immediately relaxed under the influence of our system." [6]

Others were not so sure. The *Richmond Enquirer* regarded the proposal as "most derogatory" to national interests. The *New York Times* was less bothered by the idea of the proposed purchase itself than Buchanan's participation in it. "The proposal is the work of an old and desperate politician," the paper said. [7]

In fact, it soon became clear that the hoped-for appropriation of $30 million was not even close to the likely $100 million asking price for the island. Instead, the $30 million was intended to simply be used in any manner Buchanan might see fit to cajole Spain into finally selling. But what Buchanan would never publicly reveal were his real plans for the money: to create a slush fund for bribing Spanish political leaders in return for their support of the purchase. [8]

"What do you propose to do with this $30 million?" Michigan Republican Zachariah Chandler asked Slidell, before going on the attack. "It is a great corruption fund for bribery and for bribery only." [9]

The *New Orleans Bee* agreed, remarking that "The country is far from reposing in the President that unlimited confidence which could alone justify the entrusting of $30 million to his discretion." [10]

And there were other considerations: Senator John Thompson of Kentucky reminded his colleagues that Buchanan descended from a Scotch line and that giving $30 million to a man of such lineage was foolhardy. "I never knew a Scotchman when he had got a grip upon anything and had it in his grasp, who would let it go." [11]

Although Slidell had originally hoped for a quick vote, he could see the lay of the land after a month of debate when New York Republican William Seward, in a classic display of legislative foot-dragging, decided that Slidell's proposal deserved not a "debate of an hour in the morning for one morning, or two or three, but it has got to be discussed from the beginning to the end, through and through, up and done, come whatever it will." [12]

In other words, Seward was prepared to filibuster. Just short of three months after he proposed it, Buchanan's plan for Cuba was dead. Citing a lack of support, Slidell withdrew his bill on February 26.

Buchanan may have been angry over the way in which the proposal had been received in the Senate, but his defeat was quickly blown off the front pages by a Washington shooting taking place the following afternoon.

The gun shots rang out across the street from the White House on the southeast corner of Lafayette Square. The assailant was Buchanan's former secretary and friend, New York Democrat Congressman Dan Sickles, ironically one and the same who had previously pushed Buchanan into the Ostend Manifesto, the clumsy attempt to acquire Cuba by purchase or invasion.

Sickles' victim was Philip Barton Key, the District Attorney of Washington and son of Francis Scott Key, author of the *Star-Spangled Banner.*

Sickles accused Key of having an affair with his attractive 22 year-old wife Teresa. He shot him three times, resulting in the District Attorney's instant death and Sickles' arrest later that afternoon. Buchanan was told of the shooting within minutes by a breathless White House page named John Bonitz who witnessed the killing.

"I was afraid this would happen," Buchanan responded, before warning Bonitz, a recent immigrant from Germany, that he, too, might be arrested. He handed the young boy a roll of dollars, and, strangely, a new razor as a presidential memento, and urged him to get out of town as quickly as possible. [13]

Buchanan's actions may have seemed odd. Bonitz was under no threat of arrest and Buchanan knew it. Instead, the President was responding impulsively. Unaware that over a dozen other people had also seen Sickles shoot Key, Buchanan wanted to remove from the prosecution's reach the one person he thought was the witness. He additionally decided to write a quick note of support to Sickles. Just as when he had blatantly lobbied the members of the Supreme Court during the Dred Scott proceedings, Buchanan would see no reason to observe legal niceties in the Sickles' trial now, staying in touch with Sickles' defense team and monitoring its progress.

The reasons for his actions were many.

His affection for Sickles was great. Sickles and his wife Teresa frequently invited Buchanan to their mansion on the other side of Lafayette Square, one of the most popular homes for the young and connected in Washington. Buchanan reciprocated by inviting the couple to the White House.

Buchanan knew and to a certain extent was bemused by the fact that Sickles lived on the margins of the law. He liked that Sickles was a man's man who romanced any number of women before and during his marriage to Teresa, patronized prostitutes, and did what he wanted when he wanted. For his part Buchanan was always certain of his own aptitude and intelligence, but never of his masculinity. Hanging around Sickles was like a shot of testosterone for the old man.

And then there was Teresa.

Buchanan had fallen in love with her when she was only 18 and he was 64. She had been married to Sickles for just over a year at the time and was depressed due to her husband's lack of attention. In despair she turned to Buchanan who, taking in the young girl's large brown eyes, olive skin, and small body, was soon smitten with a woman unlike any of the wealthy dowagers he usually courted. [14]

That nothing ever came of the romance, if indeed it could even be called that, was seen by the fact that Buchanan and Sickles remained close, raising the possibility that Sickles knew of Buchanan's infatuation with his wife, but let it continue because he didn't view the old man as a threat. Sickles also undoubtedly took Buchanan's measure: he knew he loved to flirt but rarely, if ever, followed through. At the same time, Sickles, always on the lookout for career advancement, wanted to maintain his friendship with the man who would be president. [15]

To make this melodrama even more complicated, Teresa, beginning in the winter of 1858, brought her new love interest Key to the White House for afternoon visits with the President. Teresa and Key had, in fact, first met at Buchanan's inaugural ball the year before. There would soon be rumors that the amorous Key, unknown to Buchanan, had even made love to Teresa in the White House.

Both Sickles, and indirectly, Buchanan, would eventually discover that they had been duped by Key, who knew how to play the political game when he had to: originally lobbying James Knox Polk in 1845 for the D.A. position, Key made sure to remind the Democrat President that he had "done everything in my power to promote the success of the Democratic Party." [16]

Key also regularly took advantage of the influence and prestige of his uncle, Supreme Court Chief Justice Roger Taney, who successfully leaned on Polk to appoint his nephew and repeated the ritual eight years later with President Franklin Pierce.

When Buchanan came into office, Key decided to play a new card. Meeting Sickles at a Washington party and knowing that the New Yorker was close to Buchanan, he asked him to put in a good word for his re-appointment. Sickles agreed. But not long afterwards Key began his months-long flirtation with Teresa, a flirtation that shortly turned into a genuine affair.

By the end of 1858 Key had secured a two-story ramshackle home in an impoverished Washington neighborhood where, usually wearing a top hat, vest, broadcloth coat and pantaloons, he was an object of curiosity to the more modestly attired residents. In an upstairs bedroom he and Teresa would make love, always in the afternoon. [17]

Because Key, as a result, was increasingly spending less time in court and was marginally effective on the days when he did show up, losing more cases than he won, word soon got to Buchanan that the District Attorney was no longer up to his duties. Buchanan, in response, began to give serious consideration to replacing him with hard-working Robert Ould, the assistant District Attorney. [18]

Buchanan may or may not have known that Key and Teresa were meeting clandestinely, but he could easily see from their body language when they visited him at the White House or when he saw them together at different Washington parties, that Key and Teresa were more than just idle friends. At the same time, Buchanan worried that Sickles was not paying enough attention to his wife and was far too trusting of Key, who always seemed to be available to escort Teresa to this or that function when Sickles was otherwise preoccupied in Congress.

What Buchanan's many enemies in the press would do if all of these sordid details regarding his role in the scandal should ever become known was too much to imagine. Buchanan was at risk of looking like a john, a seducer of young married girls, or a sad old man who had been made a fool of by Dan and Teresa Sickles, not to mention Philip Barton Key. [19]

The atmosphere in the immediate aftermath of Key's murder was like so much political theatre: Washington Mayor John Barrett, California Senator William Gwinn, and even Robert Walker, Buchanan's former man in Kansas, escorted Sickles to jail. John Slidell and Buchanan's Attorney General, Jeremiah Black, came forward to offer Sickles advice. [20]

Once behind bars, Sickles was additionally visited by an endless number of top Democrat Congressional leaders. Even Vice-President John Breckinridge stopped by.

When White House legal advisers, unaware of Buchanan's compromised role in the scandal, suggested to him an offer of assistance to Ould, who would be prosecuting Sickles and was in over his head facing off against a defense team composed of some of the most successful lawyers in both Washington and New York, Buchanan got an idea. [21]

He summoned a friendly reporter for the *New York Herald* to the White House in order to put matters in perspective. Compliantly, the reporter ended up filing the following ludicrous dispatch regarding any conceivable White House attempt to help Ould: "The President has expressed his surprise at this singular attempt to draw him into an interference with the usual course of justice." [22]

Buchanan's manipulation of the *New York Herald* served his immediate purpose. But his larger goal of securing Sickles' acquittal was done by others. In a time when murdering the paramour of a man's wife was almost always regarded as an act upholding the sanctity of marriage by all-male juries (it was referred to as "dishonoring the family bed"), Buchanan soon realized that Sickles was a cinch for acquittal.

And the fact that Washingtonians were also soon openly discussing the likelihood that Buchanan would pardon Sickles on an off chance that he might be convicted only helped the defense. If Sickles was going to be set free by the President anyway, why even bother to find him guilty?

By mid-April it was obvious that the trial was going all the way of the defense. A happy Buchanan on Saturday night, April 16, ambled over to the home of Jefferson Davis where he encountered the Senator's wife, Varina. "The only person I have seen in high spirits for some days is Mr. Buchanan, who paid me a very long and very pleasant visit yesterday," Varina wrote the following day to Jefferson, who was taking care of business back at their plantation in Mississippi, adding "Thank goodness he did not mention the everlasting Sickles trial." [23]

Ten days later the Sickles jury deliberated for just over an hour before delivering a verdict of "Not Guilty." Sickles was cheered loudly in the courtroom, outside the courthouse and on the street as he proceeded to a friend's house for a night of drinking and good cheer. [24]

In the following weeks, Buchanan resumed his friendship with Sickles, who, although he was now shunned by many both in Congress and Washington high society, was still a welcome presence at the White House. Teresa, meanwhile, had been sent back to New York, where she would soon be forgiven for her transgressions by Sickles.

It had been a long and exhausting spring. At the urging of Cabinet members who thought he needed a change of scene, Buchanan decided to take his most extensive trip outside of the nation's capital since becoming president.

He would bring along with him Treasury Secretary Jacob Thompson as he traveled to North Carolina, stopping on May 31 just outside of Raleigh. There, Governor John Ellis, standing with Buchanan on the back platform of the president's rail car, surveyed a large group of young women waiting expectantly behind the train. He began to remark "I have the honor to present to you the President of the United States. As the train is behind time, he will not have the time to go among you and…"

At this point Buchanan, showing remarkable agility for a man of his age, jumped from the platform remarking "Oh, yes I will, though," before greeting what a reporter described as "pretty maidens who blushed and laughed a great deal." [25]

In Raleigh more than 2,000 people turned out to greet him. Bluntly, Buchanan brought up the topic of disunion, a topic that Southern leaders had been more openly discussing in the wake of the 1858 election. "These threats were not spoken of when I was a young man, they were not spoken of twenty years ago, not that I was young twenty years ago," the President said.

A man in the crowd yelled out: "I knew you 20 years ago and you were certainly not very young at that time."

"I know I was not," Buchanan amicably responded before continuing, "Let this Union cease to exist, let the sovereign sister states be separate, let intestine wars arise, and liberty upon earth is gone forever." [26]

He spent that evening in Raleigh, hosting a late night reception with city leaders before enduring a day of relentless heat on June 1 as he and Thompson traveled by coach along a dusty trail to Chapel Hill. There, on the following day, Buchanan was given an honorary degree from the University of North Carolina. Introduced by a student who had just been given an award for writing the best composition in his class, Buchanan delivered a speech that was at a minimum strange. [27]

"The great merit of composition, in my humble judgment, consists in short, pointed sentences," Buchanan said to an audience that may have expected him to expound on more weighty matters.

"The author who writes your long sentences involves himself in too many difficulties," Buchanan continued. "One distinct idea presented in a distinct manner has more potency and more power than the sentence of a book in which everything under the sun is brought together, according to the style of many of our modern writers."

Buchanan also revealed, for no particular reason, that he had little respect for readers who skimmed a book's index, rather than reading its entire contents.

After his speech, Buchanan shook hands with the students, once again flirting with a gathering of young women, before retiring for the evening. He was up early on June 3, returning to Raleigh where he benignly observed "The man who moves from North Carolina to any other state always leaves his heart at home." [28]

Edward Hale, the captain of the Wilmington Light Infantry, called out three cheers for both Buchanan and Cuba, declaring that if the island nation could not be acquired one way, "it would be the other."

Buchanan responded diplomatically: "Fighting is altogether out of the question," he protested. [29]

That evening Buchanan rested at the plantation home of former North Carolina Congressman Weldon Edwards near the town of Ridgeway. The 71 year-old Edwards, a wealthy grain and hay farmer, had 80 slaves, divided equally by gender. It would have been impossible for Buchanan to not encounter one or several of those slaves, especially as Edwards also used them for servants in his house. If so, Buchanan never said anything about the experience. He remained pro-slavery, even when, as a man of the North, confronted with the rare experience of actually meeting a slave. [30]

Buchanan returned to Washington the following day. His meandering 500-mile plus journey proved well covered in the nation's papers. But when an editorial appeared in the *Pittsburgh Post* suggesting that the trip had really been the first salvo in a Buchanan re-election campaign for 1860, Buchanan slapped the idea down.

"My determination not, under any circumstances, to become a candidate for re-election is final and conclusive," he declared in a statement.

"My best judgment and strong inclination unite in favor of this course." To long-time friend and Philadelphia Port Collector Joseph Baker, Buchanan righteously proclaimed that the *Pittsburgh Post,* in saying that he would be a candidate again, essentially was charging with him "gross inconsistency & hypocrisy. Besides, the imputation is calculated to impair my influence in carrying out the remaining measures of my administration." [31]

That didn't mean he wasn't interested in the 1860 election. On the contrary, Buchanan viewed the coming contest as a referendum on his presidency. And he was certain that the voters would rally to any candidate he anointed as his worthy successor. When Robert Tyler expressed concern about which party would carry crucial Pennsylvania, Buchanan responded in a letter that would eventually prove incorrect on two important counts: forecasting that William Seward, and not Abraham Lincoln, would be the Republican nominee, and that the Democrats would easily hold onto Pennsylvania. "I have an instinct in such matters created by long experience. I perceive certain symptoms of triumph in Pennsylvania in 1860," Buchanan said. [32]

Buchanan had no way of knowing it at the time, but his letter to Tyler was written on the outer edge of a coming campaign year that would see virtually everything he stood for crushed to dust and defeat.

Chapter Six

Symptoms of an
Incurable Disease

As Buchanan was finishing his letter to Robert Tyler, a gray-haired man with a look of haunted wildness was in the last hours of preparing for what would prove to be a sensational attack on a federal armory some sixty-five miles northwest of Washington.

"Moral suasion is hopeless," the 59 year-old John Brown would remark after he led a small posse of 18 white and black men over an Baltimore and Ohio Railroad bridge, invading the Harper's Ferry armory after midnight on October 17.

"I don't think the people of the slave states will ever consider the subject of slavery in its true light until some other argument is resorted to than moral suasion," Brown later declared. [1]

Brown's idea was simple: by seizing hostages from slave-holding families in the area and getting the word out that his actions were being done in the name of abolitionism, thousands of slaves would rally to his cause. That cause, of course, was much larger than the liberation of slaves in just northern Virginia. Brown envisioned an uprising taking place across the South that would violently and finally put an end to all slavery in the U.S.

By all accounts Brown was a fanatic. And his plan was senseless: how could less than two dozen men seizing a single federal armory inspire a regional slave uprising, particularly when those slaves were under the control of armed owners supported by sympathetic local law enforcement? Even more, how many Virginians still remembered the failed 1831 rebellion inspired by the slave Nat Turner in Southampton County, some 230 miles to the south? Certainly tales of that rebellion, told and retold, had become part of the state's lore and a valuable lesson to anxious slaveholders to always be vigilant.

Brown never really concerned himself with such questions and may have simply hoped to make a dramatic statement designed to shock slave owners into rethinking what they were doing. But the fact that he and his men would suddenly be in control of the armory, which contained an arsenal of weapons valued at more than $1 million, meant that he was at least for the moment dangerous.

In the early morning darkness, Brown and several of his men forced a slow-moving B&O train to come to a halt on the bridge. One of Brown's men shot and killed a baggage master. "You no doubt wonder that a man of my age should be here with a band of armed men," Brown told conductor Andrew Phelps upon detaining him. "But if you knew my past history you would not wonder at it so much." [2]

Even though Brown would hold other hostages inside a brick building normally used to house fire engines, he inexplicably allowed Phelps to go on. When the conductor arrived in Monocacy, Maryland, 24 miles to the east, he telegraphed the B&O office in Baltimore reporting that abolitionists were in possession of the "arms and armory of the United States." The message concluded: "They say they have come to free the slaves and intend to do so at all hazards." [3]

Reading Phelps' message, the young B&O President John Work Garrett informed the White House of the attack.

"Your dispatch has been received and shall be promptly attended to," Buchanan wired back by mid-day, disclosing that he was ordering three companies of artillery, backed by nearly one hundred Marines, to retake the armory. Garrett subsequently urged Buchanan to think about a stronger response: Brown's men, he said, were at least 700 strong. [4]

These were hours of wildly varying reports.

Typographers at the *Richmond Dispatch* that afternoon laid out a front-page story for the next-day edition estimating that up to "two hundred and fifty whites, followed by a band of Negroes," were in control of the armory. A reporter for the *New York Times* put the number at 600 "runaway Negroes" and another 200 white men. [5]

By afternoon, Buchanan held a hastily-arranged meeting with War Secretary John Floyd, who had first received Garrett's initial message, and two men destined for Civil War legend: Brevet Colonel Robert E. Lee and Lieutenant J.E.B. Stuart of the First Cavalry.

Stuart had actually been in an antechamber of Floyd's office, waiting to see the Secretary and show him his invention, a mechanism for attaching a saber to a belt, when an aide to the Secretary told him that Floyd needed Lee's help. Stuart, in response, volunteered to ride into Arlington to retrieve the Colonel.

Upon their return to Washington, Lee and Stuart met with Floyd. All three men then quickly walked to the White House.

Not certain that a general slave uprising wasn't about to explode, Buchanan ordered Lee to lead the Marines with the immediate task of overcoming the insurrectionists. Stuart volunteered to ride along as an aide. At the same time, Buchanan also ordered a volunteer militia to be posted at two Washington armories.

While some of his detractors would later charge that Buchanan over-reacted to events at Harper's Ferry, what happened next was inevitable.

Lee and his men waited until daylight the following day before approaching the armory. As a crowd of more than 2,000 cheering spectators watched, Stuart approached the fire engine building holding a white flag. He was greeted at a half-opened door by Brown, who held a rifle in his hands. Stuart read from a statement announcing that upon Buchanan's orders, Lee was demanding the surrender of Brown and his men, all of whom, he promised, would be safely quartered awaiting further instructions from the President.

Brown instead asked for safe passage out of the armory. When Stuart told him that was impossible, Brown said he preferred to die at Harper's Ferry.

Stuart stepped back and waved his hat to Lee, who, previously instructing his men to only use bayonets, charged the building. Although some of Brown's men shot their rifles in response, Lee's command quickly took possession of the structure. On Lee's orders Brown and his followers were then marched to the Harper's Ferry paymaster's office where it was learned that Buchanan wanted Virginia authorities to take custody of the captives. [6]

At the White House, meanwhile, Kansas had entered the discussion. The subject that had annoyed and frustrated the President for most of the first two years of his presidency returned when he learned that Brown was the same man who had led an 1856 attack resulting in the slaughter of five pro-slavery men in Kansas. [7]

Swiftly defeating the Harper's Ferry seizure made quick work of a singularly amateurish attempt at rebellion. But Buchanan could only wonder: how many other insurrectionists were similarly being planned?

The President wasn't the only one in Washington who was nervous.

In the hours and days after the attack, the District of Columbia police maintained a constant guard on all roads leading into the city in order to prevent a feared invasion of rebelling slaves from Virginia. Simultaneously, city officials locked away some 200 muskets and the requisite ammunition inside Washington's City Hall to be used to put down a rebellion. Police at the Capitol were placed on special alert as news of the insurrection among both white and black people "spread throughout Washington with great rapidity," a correspondent for the *New York Herald* observed, adding that, among whites, "fears of an outbreak have become general." [8]

City authorities additionally withdrew permits for all upcoming African-American balls and parties on the theory that any large gathering of blacks anywhere in the city might be trouble. Police officers told any African-American walking on the street to go home or risk being arrested. Meanwhile a nervous Lewis Clephane, secretary of the National Republican Association in Washington, was forced to issue an immediate denial after it was reported that he had made light of the attack on Harper's Ferry. On the contrary, Clephane protested, Brown and his followers "have met and are to meet their just deserts" for the attempted insurrection. [9]

Just to make sure that everyone understood, the National Republican Association also passed a resolution condemning Brown's "mad, wicked and absurd schemes." [10]

Clephane wasn't the only Republican caught flat-footed in the wake of the Brown raid. All of the party's most prominent leaders, including William Seward, Zachariah Chandler, Charles Sumner and Abraham Lincoln, were conspicuously quiet in the days after the attack. A columnist for the *Charleston Mercury* ventured that the Brown attack had very definitely stained the Republicans "with some odium," predicting that "their name, their principles and their purposes will come into disrepute." [11]

While Lincoln would eventually challenge Democratic critics to prove Republican complicity in Brown's mission, Massachusetts Senator Henry Wilson, addressing an excited gathering in New York, took a different tack, suggesting that the matter must be considered in a national context. The country, he said, was now in the throes of a great moral struggle between those who would propagate slavery and those "striving to suppress and restrict" it. The Harper's Ferry seizure showed how far people were willing to go to take a stand. [12]

That things had come to this, Wilson continued, was entirely the fault of the Democrats: "The slave party had seized upon the Democratic Party and used it for the extension of slavery on this continent." Republicans, in return, existed only to combat this power, the Massachusetts Senator said. But just as he came to the part of his speech vowing that the Republicans would fight on, the 47 year-old Wilson was forced to sit down for fear of passing out. A participant chalked the incident up to an attack of vertigo, but Wilson's sudden collapse could also be attributed to the undeniable excitement of the hour. [13]

Treasury Secretary Howell Cobb was worked up, too. Unlike Wilson, he declined the honor of personally addressing a New York audience, opting instead to have his remarks telegraphed to a group of Democrats gathered at the historic Volks Theatre in Manhattan.

In person or not, Cobb left no doubt in the minds of his audience who should be blamed for the Harper's Ferry fiasco.

Brown's attack, proclaimed Cobb in a general indictment of the Republican party, was the result of the "recognized leaders of a political organization which struggles with the hope of success to obtain the control of our general government and which has already possession of most of the non-slaveholding states of the Union." [14]

Interior Secretary Jacob Thompson chimed in, sending a communication to the same meeting declaring that Republican leaders "may succeed in clearing themselves from all direct connection with the late abortive attempt to incite the slaves of Virginia to insurrection, murder and plunder. But still it is impossible to deny that this attempt is the legitimate, practical working out of the doctrines and teachings of those who speak for the black Republican Party." [15]

Former President Franklin Pierce, declining to specifically name the Republicans, charged that the Harper's Ferry imbroglio was the inevitable and natural product of Northerners who "habitually appeal to sectional prejudices and passions by denouncing the institutions and people of the South." [16]

Pierce additionally forecast that the "amazing, dangerous and unconstitutional aggression on the part of the North against the people and institutions of the South which has kept up through so many years," would eventually have to come to an end, "or the relations which have been the basis of our prosperity, power and glory must be terminated." [17]

Buchanan's erstwhile mouthpiece, the *Washington Constitution,* placed the blame entirely on New Yorker William Seward, recalling the Republican's 1858 speech in which he talked of an "irrepressible conflict" between the slave and non-slave holding states. Seward's rhetoric, charged the paper, had inspired a "spirit of rebellion and treason." In a swipe at Seward as an 1860 presidential contender, the paper additionally challenged readers to imagine a President Seward's response to Harper's Ferry, a response that would most likely result in no federal attempt to smash the rebellion: "What would be left but anarchy, blood and revolution?" [18]

Years later, Jefferson Davis looked back at the Harper's Ferry insurrection and judged it "insignificant in itself and its immediate result." But the incident, he continued, "afforded a startling revelation of the extent to which sectional hatred and political fanaticism had blinded the conscience of a class of persons in certain states of the Union." [19]

That perspective was shared and given voice to by many in the South in the immediate aftermath of Harper's Ferry. Here, at last, was proof that Northern abolitionists were not only obsessed and unreasoning on the subject of slavery, but determined to stoke rebellion inside the South.

"It had the sympathy, and in many instances, the active support by the contribution of money, of the leading abolitionists of the North," charged the *Daily Picayune* of Brown's attack, describing those same abolitionists as "a class whose humanity would prompt the desolation of our states by fire and sword, the kindling of civil war, and even the disruption of this confederacy to accomplish their irrational ideas of philanthropy." [20]

Buchanan initially refrained from making any public comment on Harper's Ferry. He was to some degree even bored by it all. But he was not unaware of the political implications. Whether or not it could be decisively proven that Northern abolitionists and Republicans had directly supported Brown, it was obvious, from Buchanan's point of view, that they had created the environment that encouraged Brown to do what he did.

Brown would be executed by hanging in Charles Town, Virginia on December 2. While composing his third annual message to Congress in the days to come, Buchanan wrote out his first official comments on what had happened at Harper's Ferry. [21]

"I shall not refer in detail to the recent sad and bloody consequences at Harper's Ferry," Buchanan began, before doing just that. "Still, it is proper to observe that these events, however bad and cruel in themselves, derive their chief importance from the apprehension that they are but symptoms of an incurable disease in the public mind which may break out in still more dangerous outrages and terminate, at last, in an open war by the North to abolish slavery in the South."

Devoting a torturously long paragraph to the theory that the North had been ceaselessly picking on the South and that all such agitation should cease and desist, Buchanan was patronizing when he concluded: "This advice proceeds from the heart of an old public functionary whose service commenced in the last generation among the wise and conservative statesmen of that day now nearly all passed away, and whose first and dearest wish is to leave his country tranquil, prosperous, united and powerful." [22]

Buchanan's wish, while misguided, was nonetheless sincerely felt. But if that wish could be realized along with defeating the Republican Party, so much the better.

Daily listening to the one-sided political perspectives of the likes of Howell Cobb, Jacob Thompson, John Slidell and Jefferson Davis, Buchanan could be excused if he thought that in the John Brown affair the Democrats might have stumbled upon the key to electoral success in 1860.

Chapter Seven

"Nothing But the Basest Perjury Can Sully My Good Name."

Buchanan was forced to wait for nearly two months until his message to Congress could be officially received in the House of Representatives.

The delay was due to an unexpectedly bitter and prolonged battle to name a new Speaker, a battle which would not be finally settled until February 1, 1860, when the compromise candidate, freshman William Pennington of New Jersey, was elected.

The battle for the Speakership, like almost everything else in the wake of the John Brown raid, was played out against a backdrop of racial and sectional recrimination not seen in most previous House leadership contests.

An overwhelming majority of the Republican caucus backed John Sherman of Ohio for Speaker. A moderate who got along well with almost every faction in the House, the 35 year-old Sherman seemed like a sure bet. But his candidacy was instantly flummoxed by Southern Democrats who objected to his endorsement in a party circular of the controversial Hinton Rowan Helper's book *The Impending Crisis of the South*. Helper argued that slavery was bad for the South both socially and economically, claiming that "Slave holders and slave-breeders are downright enemies of their own section." [1]

Caught by surprise, Sherman at first denied but eventually admitted he had read Helper's book. He additionally muddied the waters when he said that even though he had given his signature to the Republican circular, he didn't necessarily agree with all of Helper's conclusions. "The ultra-sentiments in the book are as obnoxious to me as they can be to anyone," Sherman protested to his brother, William Tecumseh Sherman. [2]

Southerners had returned to Congress in an edgy, confrontational mood. Senate Democrats announced plans to conduct a thorough investigation that they hoped would reveal Republican complicity in the John Brown attack. When it was disclosed that the pro-Hinton Republican circular also called for a slave rebellion, all hell broke loose. Democrat Representative John Clark of Missouri declared "Such advice is treason; such advice is rebellion…it is an incipient movement of treason against a common country." [3]

"The blood of Southern men shed at Harper's Ferry cries to us from the ground and brands you with the acts of the poor, miserable, deluded followers of your misplaced philanthropy," Democrat Representative Lucius Gartrell said in a general indictment of House Republicans. [4]

Meanwhile Shelton Leake, Democrat from Virginia, wondered if the election of Sherman would mean elevating a man to office that "while I am here in the discharge of my duties, is stimulating my Negroes at home to apply the torch to my dwelling and the knife to the throats of my children." [5]

Finally Sherman dramatically withdrew from the contest, allowing Republicans to rally around Pennington, who had not signed the circular, although he privately agreed with its contents. The House was at last back in business. This was not good news for Buchanan who had been wondering for months what it would be like to deal with a Republican majority in the lower chamber. [6]

But if he was worried privately, Buchanan put on a good show for the public. Two weeks after the Pennington election, he invited both Republican and Democrat Congressional leaders, and practically everyone else he knew, to a massive White House party that would be attended by nearly 1,000 people. A reporter for the *New York Herald* surveyed the scene in astonishment: "Congressmen and clerks, diplomats and office-seekers, Cabinet ministers, butchers and bankers, newspaper men, printers, poets, parsons and dancing masters, diamonds and cameos, silk and muslins, the eaters of canvass back and the consumers of salt junk are all fused together." [7]

Two weeks later, in celebration of Mardi Gras, Buchanan hosted an even bigger spectacle, this time attended by more than 2,000 people.

On that same day, Buchanan wrote a letter to Robert Tyler disclosing that he had overheard rumors concerning the funding of his 1856 campaign in Pennsylvania. Was it possible that, after all, Buchanan really knew nothing about such matters? Or was he, hedging as always, simply trying to document on paper, for future Congressional investigators, an implied ignorance?

His letter suggests an unconvincing innocence: "Did New York money & influence turn things so decidedly in 1856 as they represent it?" Buchanan asked. "Is it true that any influences that were brought to bear in Penn. then made any material change in what the result might have been?" [8]

These were the same questions that John Covode wanted answers to.

A Pennsylvania Republican elected to Congress in that same 1856 election, Covode, known as "Honest John," had long heard reports of Buchanan campaign fund abuses. No fan of Buchanan, Covode was never able to act on his suspicions until the Republicans gained control of the House.

Then, with the encouragement of Sherman, Covode began to meticulously lay the groundwork for what he hoped would prove a sweeping investigation of Buchanan and his administration. He was certain that not only had the Democrats played fast and loose with large sums of cash in Pennsylvania in 1856, but that they had subsequently used government jobs as lures to win votes during the 1858 mid-term election.

Covode was additionally convinced that Buchanan had tried to bribe individual members of Congress during the 1858 debate over the Lecompton constitution. Thinking Covode was onto something, Sherman urged Pennington to call for the creation of an investigating committee that would be chaired by the Pennsylvanian.

With Sherman and Pennington behind him, Covode on March 5 announced that the committee would be made up of himself and four other members of Congress. The committee's mission would be massive, Covode declared, nothing less than exploring "whether the President of the United States, or any other officer of the government, has by money, patronage or other improper means," tried to use bribes to influence Congress or win elections. [9]

The creation of the committee won the immediate praise of the *New York Times,* which editorialized the following day that there is "undoubtedly a general conviction throughout the country that the administration of Mr. Buchanan has been profligate and corrupt beyond all precedent." [10]

Less than three weeks later the Covode Committee began taking testimony, beginning with Cornelius Wendell, long-time Democrat insider and fund-raiser, who told of large amounts of money raised and generously circulated for election purposes in Pennsylvania in 1856. He also suggested Buchanan's murky complicity: "He never went into details," Wendell said of his many conversations with Buchanan on money matters. "But we were to make satisfactory arrangements and not bother him about it." [11]

New York Customs Collector Augustus Schell, appointed to his post by Buchanan in early 1857 (against the urging of Dan Sickles), revealed that he had knowledge of up to $40,000 that had been raised for a variety of party purposes in Pennsylvania. He said he talked with Buchanan several times during the 1856 race, although, again, nothing specific was said. "The conversation was general, upon political subjects," Schell commented. But he did confirm that would-be Democrat voters were hired for federal jobs just days before the 1858 election and subsequently dismissed from those same jobs afterwards. "All were employed, I think, at the solicitation or request of candidates for Congress," Schell said. [12]

Despite the relentless probing of Covode and his fellow committee Republicans, the early testimony proved inconclusive at best. Yes, great amounts of money had been raised to carry Pennsylvania in 1856, and yes, government jobs had been handed out in return for votes. But this was hardly explosive stuff worthy of a major congressional investigation, nor was it particularly damaging to the President. The testimony confirmed the worst opinions of those who disliked Buchanan, providing proof that he was hopelessly compromised and corrupt. Those who supported Buchanan would argue that there was still no proof that he had done anything wrong personally.

Even so, as Buchanan followed the daily reports of the Covode investigation, he grew increasingly anxious. On March 28 he decided to fight back, launching a formal protest to the House and charging that the investigation had "no jurisdiction, no supremacy whatever over the Presidency."

Buchanan additionally sought to cast doubts on Covode himself, arguing that instead of the House Judiciary Committee weighing the charges of corruption against him, the House had "made my accuser one of my judges."

"To make the accuser the judge," Buchanan added, "is a violation of the principles of universal justice and is condemned by the practice of all civilized nations. Every free man must revolt at such a spectacle. I am to appear before Mr. Covode either personally or by a substitute, to cross-examine the witnesses which he may produce before himself to sustain his own accusations against me—and perhaps even this poor boon may be denied to the President."

Summoning powers beyond the earth, Buchanan theatrically added: "I defy all investigation. Nothing but the basest perjury can sully my good name. I do not even fear this; because I cherish a humble confidence that the gracious Being who has hitherto defended and protected me against shafts of falsehood and malice, will not desert me now, when I have become 'old and gray-headed.'" [13]

This was obviously overkill. Buchanan knew the difference between a congressional inquiry that was merely asking questions and an impeachment committee that really would serve as his judge. His protest instead was a roll of the dice designed to raise doubts about the objectivity of Covode's committee in the hope that future and presumably more embarrassing revelations would be questioned by a skeptical public.

Sherman responded instantly during an angry Congressional debate over Buchanan's protest, noting that the Constitution guaranteed to the House "the right to examine into anything which may affect the conduct of any pubic officer under this government, from the Chief Executive down to the little page who runs your errands upon this floor. Every one of the officers of this government is subjected to the powers of this House."

Although Sherman privately claimed a distaste for oratorical flourishes, he nevertheless on this day proved himself equal to Buchanan's windy grandiloquence, arguing that the "doctrine set up by the President of the United States in this message is the same under which Europe was governed for a thousand years—that the King can do no wrong. That is the doctrine—that the King could not be tried and executed, because the King could do no wrong. Charles I went to the block because the people of England believed the King was not above and beyond their power. So it was with Louis XVI and the French people."

His voice rising, Sherman added dramatically: "This doctrine set up by the President of the United States is, in my judgment, the very worst that has been enunciated since the foundation of this Republic—His conduct not to be inquired into!" [14]

While the normally icy Sherman appeared on this occasion to possess a surfeit of fire, the majority Republicans agreed to send Buchanan's protest to the Judiciary Committee. This was really only a symbolic and meaningless retreat as the Republicans held a majority on that committee as well. Predictably, on April 9 the Judiciary Committee slapped Buchanan down, noting that "For Congress to reach the conclusion to which the President would lead them would be to practically settle forever that impeachments are obsolete and that officers had the immunity of perfect irresponsibility." [15]

Covode now eagerly brought forward former Kansas territorial governor Robert Walker, who told committee members of his unhappy experience working with the President in 1857. Walker produced documentation showing that Buchanan had promised one thing regarding the situation in Kansas, but then embraced policies that were quite the other. He also said he was put off by Buchanan's arm-twisting during the Lecompton Congressional debate, a reference that got Covode tantalizingly closer to one of his central conceits, that Buchanan offered bribes and threats to get the Lecompton constitution approved in Congress.

But Covode was unable to complete his circle. No member of Congress came forth to testify to actually receiving a bribe or even an offer of one. No functionary could be found to confirm that money was passed from the President to a Congressman. No one had any proof at any point of Buchanan doing anything that was actually wrong or illegal.

By mid-June Buchanan must have been feeling relieved. The committee by now had interviewed more than 90 witnesses who produced a blinding amount of smoke, but no fire. Covode, however, had one final star witness: John Forney, long-time Buchanan intimate and current clerk of the House of Representatives.

Forney, thought Buchanan, could be trouble. The two men had once been friends. As the editor of the *Lancaster Intelligencer,* Forney had for years provided Buchanan favorable coverage, doing what he could to advance the older man's career. Buchanan, in return, steered business advertisers to Forney and kept him politically connected.

Things fell apart several months after Buchanan's 1856 election. Buchanan promised Forney that he could take over the management of the *Washington Union,* a Democrat paper.

But once in Washington, Buchanan was forced to backtrack when Southern leaders said they didn't trust the consummately political Forney. Buchanan then decided to give his backing to Forney as a candidate in a special U.S. Senate election in Pennsylvania, only to see him lose to Republican Simon Cameron.

Still true to his friend, Buchanan suggested naming him to Nathaniel Hawthorne's old post as consul in Liverpool. But Forney claimed to regard the job and pay as beneath him, eventually telling Buchanan, unreasonably, "I have suffered deep and bitter humiliation since you have been elected." [16]

Buchanan was beside himself, wondering what the emotional Forney, who would soon openly throw in with Pennsylvania Republicans, might do next. "I mourn over Forney," the President wrote to old friend Joseph Baker, the collector of the Port of Philadelphia. "I fear he can never return to us & yet he must feel awkward in his new associations." [17]

Forney's new friendships paid off—he was elected clerk in the Republican majority House of Representatives. Simultaneously, Forney announced himself as a decided Buchanan opponent, declaring to one Washington gathering in February 1860 that the President "has become a despot, a despot more intolerant than any ever before known in the history of this country, who has performed acts of tyranny which, if attempted in despotic France, would create a revolution."

Ominously, Forney added: "I have returned to settle accounts with him." [18]

Forney's appearance before the Covode Committee on June 11 was therefore a greatly anticipated event. Everyone, but especially Covode, who rather gently led the questioning, expected an explosion.

From Covode's point of view, Forney started out strong, claiming he was more disappointed with than angry at Buchanan. Sadly, he said his falling out with his one-time colleague and mentor "has been of the most painful nature."

He then told of Buchanan's attempt to secure employment for him, adding that Cornelius Wendell said that if he was confirmed for the consul job he would receive $10,000 in cash. Forney claimed that he rejected the offer out of hand to both Wendell and Buchanan. "I told them that I was not entitled to that much money, that an inquiry would be raised."

But, Forney added, "This offer was repeatedly made to me and repeatedly declined."

Forney went on to claim that his final break with the administration came when he was pressured by Buchanan and Attorney General Jeremiah Black to alter his pro-Robert Walker stance in the *Philadelphia Press,* a paper that Forney had established the year before. He was even told by others, he claimed, that if he adhered to the administration line he would be the recipient of a valuable postal printing contract. "That it [the offer] was done with the knowledge of Mr. Buchanan all through I have no manner of doubt," Forney said. [19]

From Covide's perspective, this was sensational stuff. Here, finally, was proof of Buchanan as the most corrupt president ever. He had offered cash as well as a lucrative printing contract to keep a potentially troublesome friend happy--and quiet.

Yet by the end of Forney's testimony, Washington reporters and the nation at large wondered: exactly where was the explosion?

As with so much of the earlier testimony, Forney's claims were just that, claims. He had proved nothing, particularly regarding the postal contract offer. On his wildest charge, the $10,000 offer for him to accept the London consul job, the whole thing rang false. Buchanan was not averse to having such a proposition made, but the idea that he would do it himself suggested an uncharacteristic recklessness. That Buchanan, in addition, would directly offer such a large sum of money to a man he regarded as not being entirely reliable and perhaps even emotionally unstable was inconceivable.

But more suspicious was Forney's claim that he refused both the money and position. It had become common knowledge in Washington that Forney, supporting five children, had significant debts. In addition, he was inordinately motivated by position. With the Liverpool Consul job he would have held a prestigious post and made valuable international connections. That he now claimed to have summarily rejected the offer, and even went so far as to call it an insult, rang hallow.

The truth was that Forney desired political influence in the U.S., and regarded anything that would require his presence out of the country for a protracted period of time as an annoying distraction.

Four days after the conclusion of the Covode Committee hearings, a report signed by only its Republican members was read on the floor of the House. It accused Buchanan of everything from encouraging election fraud to bribing editors and offering patronage in return for political favors.

But, incredibly, the report did not recommend impeachment, prompting Democrats to immediately charge that this was proof that the purpose behind the committee from the start had been only to besmirch and embarrass Buchanan. [20]

Never one to let matters die, Buchanan now turned to James Cooper Bennett for help. "I thought I should never have occasion to appeal to you on any public subject, and knew if I did, I could not swerve you from your independent course," he wrote to the publisher of the *New York Herald*. [21]

But steamed by the whole Covode Committee experience, and particularly put out that such papers as the *New York Times* and *New York Tribune* had reported committee leaks of the most incriminating nature, Buchanan hoped the much more powerful *Herald* could balance things out.

He suggested that Bennett should read both the majority and minority reports of the Covode Committee and then "do to me what you may deem to be justice." [22]

Bennett, undoubtedly enjoying his presidentially-sanctioned role as judge, responded with an editorial that must have surpassed Buchanan's fondest dreams.

"When his administration comes to be examined by an unprejudiced and capable critic, its record will be found to compare favorably with that of any of Mr. Buchanan's predecessors," the *Herald* declared on June 26. "The very same men who led the opposition against Mr. Polk now stand ready to canonize him as a saint. That will be the case with Mr. Buchanan, and history will say that his administration was characterized by eminent ability, wisdom, prudence and moderation—prime requisites for practical statesmanship." [23]

Anticipation of this purely public relations victory wasn't enough for Buchanan, who by now had also launched one more official protest against the Covode Committee itself, arguing that should the actions of the committee become a precedent, "both the letter and spirit of the Constitution will be violated."

"One of the three massive columns on which the whole superstructure rests will be broken down," Buchanan maintained. "Instead of the Executive branch being a coordinate, it will become a subordinate branch of the government. The presidential office will be dragged into the dust." [24]

Buchanan's Congressional allies declared victory. Mississippi Representative William Barksdale, a Jefferson Davis confidante, now said of the President: "He has come out of the fiery ordeal unscathed and he stands before the country today without fear and without reproach, occupying a prouder, loftier, nobler position than ever before, illustrious as ever been his services to the country." [25]

A frustrated Sherman, recording that Buchanan's final protest had been received just as the contentious first session of the 36th Congress was coming to an end, remarked that had the Presidential message come sooner, the Republicans would have had more time to officially respond. [26]

Chapter Eight

Destined to Encounter
Bitter Hostility

By the time that the Covode Committee had limped to an inglorious ending, Buchanan was preoccupied with another looming disaster: the implosion of the national Democratic Party.

Meeting for one hot and angry week in Charleston in late April, Democrats failed to agree on a nominee. Stephen Douglas led for 57 ballots, but still fell short of the two-thirds convention vote needed for nomination. To add to the chaos, delegates from South Carolina, Florida, Alabama, Mississippi and Texas took a walk after charging that the party's platform failed to sanction slavery and its extension.

From the comfort of his Sherwood Forest estate in Virginia, former President John Tyler remarked: "The severance which took place at Charleston filled me with apprehension and regret." Buchanan was also depressed: "Everything looks bad," he thought, in a note to Tyler's son Robert, "not just for the party, but for the country." [1]

That Buchanan dreaded the idea of Douglas as party nominee was one of the worst kept secrets in Washington. He had never forgiven the Illinois Senator for opposing him during the debate over the Lecompton constitution two years before and had consistently frustrated Douglas' pleas for federal patronage ever since. To Buchanan it was unthinkable that this short, rude man could someday occupy the White House, a man who didn't play by the rules, which called, at a minimum, for a Senator to follow the lead of the President of his own party.

But was a latent desire for a second term also fueling Buchanan's enmity?

Certainly the *New York Herald* hoped so, arguing as early as January that the Democrats should stick with a president who by his "wise, firm and prudent administration has won the confidence of all conservative men." [2]

On April 14, as speculation increased that he might want to try for another term (and Douglas' delegate lead grew, but not to the point of assuring victory), Buchanan set things straight, writing a letter that he asked Pennsylvania Congressman Arnold Plumer to read to the Charleston convention: "In no contingency can I ever again consent to become a candidate for the Presidency"

"My purpose to this effect was clearly indicated both in accepting the Cincinnati nomination [in 1856] & afterwards at my Inaugural address & has been repeated on various occasions, both public & private," Buchanan continued. "In this determination neither my judgment nor my inclination has ever for a moment wavered." [3]

As Democrats prepared for a second nominating convention in mid-June, this one to be held in Baltimore, party leaders looked around for someone, anyone, besides Douglas. Former President Franklin Pierce, Mississippi Senator Jefferson Davis and even current Democratic convention chairman Caleb Cushing were all mentioned. But the most intriguing prospect was found in Buchanan's own White House: the handsome 39 year-old John Breckinridge, Buchanan's loyal and long-suffering vice-president.

Breckinridge had put in a frustrating service to Buchanan over the course of the last three and a half years. Buchanan, obsessed with the fact that he was in his declining years, regarded Breckinridge's mere presence as an unwelcome reminder of his mortality. While his door was open to drinking buddies Treasury Secretary Howell Cobb, Louisiana Senator John Slidell, and New York Congressman Dan Sickles, Buchanan insulted Breckinridge—who was heavily invested in the Southern gentleman's code—by requiring him to first run by Harriet Lane the reason why he desired any meeting with the President.

This condescending and belittling treatment was the result of resentments rooted in the 1856 Democratic convention that nominated the Buchanan-Breckinridge ticket. Buchanan grumpily noted that as a delegate Breckinridge had seemed to be for everyone but Buchanan, voting first for Franklin Pierce and then, after Pierce's chances for re-nomination disappeared, Stephen Douglas. Buchanan also knew that there was a genuine and ultimately successful draft movement on the floor of the convention to nominate Breckinridge for the second spot, the likes of which Buchanan, who won his nomination instead as a reward for decades of unexciting bureaucratic service, could never have inspired.

There were even some Democrats who had daydreamed about getting rid of Buchanan altogether and naming Breckinridge to lead the ticket. Clearly, on just a personal level, the young Breckinridge was a more well-liked and popular man among many of the party faithful than the senior Buchanan. And Buchanan knew it. [4]

Looking back, Breckinridge realized by 1859 that it was almost impossible for Buchanan, given his paranoia, suspicions and resentments, to have treated him with any degree of respect. Nonetheless his complete isolation as Vice-President still came as a surprise.

Yearning to once again be his own man, Breckinridge won a U.S. Senate seat (which he would not formally occupy until 1861) from Kentucky in 1859, while still serving as vice-president. When, in the spring of 1860, Breckinridge subsequently began to hear speculation from disconsolate Democrats that he might make, as a border Democrat, for a perfect party nominee, he could only laugh, maintaining that his only goal was to serve the people of his state in the Senate once his miserable term as vice-president came to a close.

But in more ways than Breckinridge at least publicly acknowledged, a presidential candidacy made no small amount of political sense. He was admired and respected by leaders in both the Northern and Southern wings of the party, an exciting and captivating speaker, and confident enough to go his own way when he felt the need: during the Congressional debate over the Lecompton constitution, as Southern Democrats were providing Buchanan lockstep support, Breckinridge openly wondered whether Congress had the right to dictate the manner in which a would-be state could adopt a constitution. [5]

Even more, Breckinridge was no fire-eater. He was anything but a slavery enthusiast and deplored talk of Southern secession. Despite his apostasy on such matters, Southern leaders at the Charleston convention thought Breckinridge was a substantial improvement over Douglas and should declare his candidacy. The thinking worked this way: if Breckinridge could get the support of an overwhelming majority of the Southern delegates, and add to that the solid backing of New York, where New York City Mayor Fernando Wood was known to be friendly (although Wood himself was at the same time engaged in a battle for control of that delegation), he would end up with more delegates than Douglas. That lead, in turn, might be transformed into a pro-Breckinridge stampede later in the balloting, when all of the other candidates, besides Douglas, had fallen by the wayside.

But the pro-Breckinridge strategizing had one obstacle to overcome: Breckinridge, who noted that he had already pledged himself to former Treasury Secretary James Guthrie and could not go back on his word.

After Charleston, Southern leaders once again asked Breckinridge to either run openly for the Baltimore nomination or, short of that, at least not oppose the efforts of others to win the nod for him. These supporters additionally argued that Breckinridge's previous endorsement of Guthrie applied only to the Charleston convention, not the upcoming meeting in Baltimore. [6]

Breckinridge may have been tempted to make a full-fledged try for the nomination. But not for the first time he found himself at the mercy of Buchanan, who even though desperate to find someone to beat Douglas at Baltimore, was still pointedly not supporting Breckinridge. Could the Vice-President throw his hat in the ring when the very President he served was either openly unenthused about him or on the verge of endorsing someone else? Breckinridge worried that Buchanan might be secretly hatching a plot to embarrass him.

"The President is not for me, except as a last necessity," Breckinridge told his friend James Clay, "that is to say not until his help will not be worth a damn; meanwhile I suffer the imputation of being his favorite." [7]

Despite his doubts about Breckinridge, Buchanan was horrified by the prospect of a general election contest between Douglas and Abraham Lincoln, who surprised almost everyone in May by beating out favorite William Seward for the Republican nomination in Chicago. [8]

Trying to salvage Democratic prospects, Buchanan encouraged both Cobb and Davis to make the race. When neither took the bait, it became clear to Buchanan, still failing to rally behind Breckinridge, that Douglas' Baltimore nomination was almost inevitable, particularly after the delegates in Baltimore agreed to a simple majority, rather than two-thirds vote for the nomination.

As soon as Douglas won, dissident Democrats, including, incredibly, convention head Cushing, headed out the door to convene a break-away meeting in another part of Baltimore. Making short work of it, they named Breckinridge on June 25 as their presidential nominee and Senator Joseph Lane of Oregon as his running mate.

The sudden birth of the Breckenridge-Lane ticket to lead the new National Democratic Party (Douglas was officially the nominee of the Democratic National Party) was additionally complicated by yet one more slate in the field: John Ball and Edward Everett, running as the presidential and vice-presidential nominees of the newly formed Constitution Party. Bell, most recently a U.S. Senator from Tennessee, and Everett, former U.S. Senator from Massachusetts, had little organizational or grassroots support. But in a contest now divided by four candidates, the Bell-Everett ticket had the potential of taking votes away from both Breckinridge and Douglas, particularly in the upper Southern states.

Breckinridge was startled by his National Democratic Party win. He would have been happy and even excited to be the nominee of the regular party, but was greatly troubled by the prospect of running a campaign based on dividing that party. Visiting Breckinridge in his Washington home, Davis and Cushing urged him to accept the break-away nomination. Davis made the argument that Douglas, upon seeing that he had no support in the South, would probably soon withdraw from the general election anyway.

This was a farfetched notion, and Breckinridge knew it. There was no way that Douglas, after two previous attempts to win the Democratic nomination, would quit the race, no matter what his Election Day odds. Even so, and against his own better judgment, Breckinridge succumbed to the pleadings of Davis, Cushing and others, agreeing to become a full-fledged candidate for the National Democratic Party. "I trust I have the courage to lead a forlorn hope," he sardonically remarked. [9]

Breckinridge's nomination was endorsed by former Presidents Tyler and Pierce. But what about Buchanan?

As he prepared to make his intentions known, Buchanan was visited by Wood. Buchanan had long since ceased having any use for the New York Mayor, a disillusionment that probably had its roots in the 1856 election when Wood clumsily toyed with Buchanan and Douglas, offering both his support before the convention, and then, after the convention, sought to turn Buchanan against Dan Sickles, after Sickles failed to generate sufficient support for a Wood gubernatorial bid. Since then Buchanan had simply grown weary of the Mayor's ceaseless internecine manipulations, manipulations that to Buchanan, a serial manipulator himself, seemed unimportant and trivial.

Now Wood told Buchanan he would be happy to organize Democrats in New York for Breckinridge but hoped in return that Buchanan would fire several prominent pro-Douglas party men from their current federal posts in New York. Buchanan, who showed his disregard for the Mayor by repeatedly calling him "Alderman Wood," declined the offer, remarking that he could not afford to "turn the last days of my administration into a slaughterhouse." Buchanan then pulled on a rope connected to an outer bell, which summoned an aide, and coldly remarked "Mr. Wood wishes to leave—show him out." [10]

Finally on July 9, as he greeted a gathering of Breckinridge-Lane supporters at the White House, Buchanan came to the aid of his vice-president, but in the most circuitous, nonsensical way possible.

"They have served their country in peace and war," Buchanan said of Breckinridge and Lane. "They are statesmen as well as soldiers, and in the day and hour of danger, they will be ever at their post."

The President then mostly forgot about Breckinridge, embarking upon a lengthy, complicated and officious reason for his endorsement that couldn't possibly have been of interest to anyone but himself.

He strangely claimed that because the convention that nominated Douglas had discarded the cherished two-thirds voting requirement, it really wasn't a Democratic convention at all. "And no Democrat, however devoted to regular nominations, was bound to give the nominee his support; he was left free to act according to the dictates of his own judgment and conscience," Buchanan said.

"If the convention which nominated Mr. Douglas was not a regular Democratic convention, it must be confessed that Breckinridge is in the same condition in that respect," Buchanan continued, obviously relishing this pointless arcana.

"The convention that nominated him, although composed of nearly all the certain Democratic states, did not contain the two-thirds, and therefore every Democrat is at perfect liberty to vote as he may think," Buchanan happily declared.

This was an endorsement?

To make the waters even murkier, Buchanan added that while he was supporting Breckinridge, no one should interpret that support to mean active opposition to any Douglas campaign in any individual state. [11]

Buchanan's endorsement address, if it could even be called that, bewildered both the Breckinridge and Douglas campaigns. "The question is whether the friends of Breckinridge or those of Douglas are more annoyed at his quasi-endorsement of both," the delighted pro-Lincoln *Springfield Daily Republican* remarked. [12]

Given a new opportunity a week later, Buchanan still declined to issue a clear rallying cry for his vice-president, remarking generically instead in a public letter to a New York Democrat that he had high hopes for the new generation and wished a local volunteer party effort "prosperity & usefulness," but saying nothing about Breckinridge. [13]

Breckinridge, by now expecting nothing from the President, officially opened his campaign in Kentucky, on July 18. He returned the favor by saying nothing about Buchanan.

Not so Douglas, who on July 31 in Concord, New Hampshire, charged that during the Lecompton debate Buchanan "claimed the right" to control his vote. "The President told me that if I did not obey him and vote to force the Lecompton constitution upon the people against their will, he would take off the head of every friend I had in office." [14]

A printed version of Douglas' remarks was sent to Buchanan by William Browne, the editor of the *Washington Constitution*. Buchanan read the extract and suddenly discovered that he could, indeed, speak clearly when needed: "I never held any such conversation with Judge Douglas, nor any conversation whatever affording the least color or pretext for such a statement," he protested.

"It is not in my nature to address such threatening and insulting language to any gentleman," Buchanan continued, unintentionally comically adding: "Besides, I have not removed one in ten of his friends and not one of his relatives." [15]

Douglas wasn't done with Buchanan. Invading Harrisburg on September 7, he excoriated Buchanan for naming Cobb to head the Treasury Department, a man whose protective policies "worked against Pennsylvania's interests." [16]

The following day in Reading, Douglas reminded listeners (as he had been reminding almost everyone for the last four years) that by bowing out of the 1856 nomination contest he had effectively made Buchanan president and Breckinridge vice-president. "I expected that the candidates before the Charleston and Baltimore convention would feel bound in honor to treat me as I treated them," Douglas added, ignoring for the moment that neither Buchanan nor Breckinridge had been actual candidates at either convention. [17]

Buchanan was annoyed by Douglas' barbs, as well as the fact that he had the nerve to campaign in Pennsylvania, which he rightly regarded as crucial to victory in 1860. Republicans, too, recognized the importance of the Keystone State, fanning in to organize it for Lincoln. Enjoying the split between the Democrats, Lincoln aide David Davis, in Scranton, assured the Republican nominee that Pennsylvania was "safe, without question. Entirely so."

A Pennsylvania win would be attached to likely wins in New York, Ohio, Indiana and Illinois. "You will be elected President," Davis predicted to Lincoln. "There is no longer any doubt of it in my mind." [18]

Eventually even Buchanan's nemesis, John Forney, weighed in: "That Pennsylvania will vote for Abraham Lincoln on the first Tuesday in November is as certain as fate." [19]

A Lincoln victory, of course, was precisely what Buchanan's Southern friends (at least those still wanting to keep the South in the Union) dreaded the most, repeatedly declaring throughout the fall that such a result would force the South to secede.

In late September, a reporter for the *New York Herald* travelled to the small town of Crawfordville, Georgia to interview the influential former

Congressman Alexander Stephens. Asked if Lincoln's election now seemed certain, Stephens answered "I can conceive of no other result."

What then?

"Undoubtedly, an attempt at succession and revolution," Stephens replied.

Reminded by the reporter that Breckinridge, currently the Southern favorite in the campaign, had said he was against secession, Stephens said it was for that reason that the Vice-President "would probably be the first man the dis-unionists would have to hang." [20]

Stephens' gloomy outlook was hardly singular. A reporter for the *Memphis Daily Appeal*, covering a Jefferson Davis speech in that city on September 22 (during which Buchanan's name was booed), noted that Davis thought it would be "self-disgrace or self-degradation for any Southern man" to either accept office or live under a Lincoln Administration. At a Breckinridge rally in New Orleans, Mississippi Governor Albert Brown declared, "Whenever the government shall be in the hands of Abraham Lincoln, the Union will be dissolved." Former Virginia Governor Henry Wise, at a Norfolk Breckinridge gathering, said Lincoln's election could only mean one thing: war.

"I stand ready," Wise declared, "to draw the sword of defense." [21]

Election results on October 10 for state offices in Pennsylvania, Ohio, and Indiana—traditionally an indicator of presidential voting in November—previewed the coming Republican triumph. In a quick note to Seward, who had been vigorously campaigning for the Republican ticket around the country, Lincoln remarked: "It now really looks as if the Government is about to fall into our hands. Pennsylvania, Ohio and Indiana have surpassed all expectations, even the most extravagant." [22]

Buchanan, meanwhile, suddenly responded to the urgency of the situation, lending his support to a far-fetched plan that would see Breckinridge and Douglas form fusion tickets in certain Northern states in a united front against Lincoln. On October 17, Franklin Pierce, usually more of a realist than Buchanan, even publicly suggested that Breckinridge and Douglas should simultaneously drop out of the race in favor of an entirely new Democrat ticket made up of Guthrie for president and former New York Governor Horatio Seymour for vice-president. "It's not too late to retrieve our fortunes and defeat sectionalism," Pierce thought. [23]

Buchanan, who claimed to be doing what he could for Breckinridge in Pennsylvania, had been in politics for too many years to not recognize an irreversible trend. As expected, Pennsylvania, Ohio and Indiana all went for Lincoln on November 6. And so did virtually the rest of the North, giving the Republican nominee 180 electoral votes, six more than Buchanan won in 1856.

Because Buchanan liked to study the post-election tallies, he couldn't help but notice the curious similarities between Lincoln's 1860 vote and his in 1856. Both Lincoln and he had won the solid backing of a single region: in Lincoln's case, the North; in Buchanan's case, the South. And both were minority winners, Lincoln with only 39.9 percent of the national vote, compared to Buchanan's 45.3 percent.

Buchanan undoubtedly appreciated that neither Lincoln nor he, at the top of their tickets, did much for those running below. The Republicans won 5 new seats in the Senate, but lost 9 in the House with Lincoln, while Democrats running with Buchanan lost 6 Senate seats, but gained 35 in the House.

The numbers, to the unimaginative Buchanan, suggested that he and Lincoln were the same kind of politicians cut from the same cloth: barely popular party warhorses winning plurality votes in a time of doubt, fear and crisis.

There is no reason to believe at this moment in both of their careers that Buchanan discerned anything particularly extraordinary or special about Lincoln. And if he had, Buchanan, who had a long history of regarding all of his opponents, direct and indirect, with contempt, probably wouldn't have admitted it anyway.

On election night Pennsylvania Republican Senator Simon Cameron had wired Lincoln, enthusiastically reporting: "Penn. Seventy-thousand for you. New York safe. Glory enough." [24]

It couldn't have thrilled Buchanan to see the Democrats lose Pennsylvania. Even worse, Lincoln had won both a higher popular vote and percentage of the vote in Pennsylvania than Buchanan had four years before. It would take 76 more years, or until 1936, for a Democratic presidential candidate to win again in Pennsylvania.

Buchanan was depressed by a result he had done much to bring about himself, but stubbornly refused to take it personally (Republicans would subsequently win the White House in 1864, 1868, 1872, 1876 and 1880, partly due to memories of Buchanan's calamitous presidency). Buchanan maintained, instead, that Lincoln's victory was nothing more or less than the consequence of long-simmering regional forces. It was not, Buchanan insisted, a referendum on his presidency.

"Every discerning citizen must now have foreseen serious dangers to the Union from Mr. Lincoln's election," Buchanan would later write. "After a struggle of many years, this had accomplished the triumph of the anti-slavery party over the slaveholding states, and established two geographical parties inflamed with malignant hatred against each other." [25]

Buchanan's task for the next four months until Lincoln took the oath of office would be to somehow stop an angry country from tearing itself apart.

Frequently melodramatic, Buchanan this time was right on the mark when he sized up the mood of both Northern Republicans and Southern Democrats and remarked of himself in the third person: "He knew that whatever course he might pursue, he was destined to encounter their bitter hostility."

"No public man," Buchanan added, "was ever placed in a more trying and responsible position." [26]

Chapter Nine

Looking the Danger
Fairly in the Face

One week before Lincoln's election, Buchanan received a curious message from Lieutenant General Winfield Scott.

Wordily entitled, "Views Suggested by the Imminent Danger of Disruption of the Union by the Secession of One or More of the Southern States," Scott's communication noted that a number of federal forts, including Forts Jackson and Phillip on the Mississippi River, Fort Monroe in Virginia, and both Forts Moultrie and Sumter in the harbor of Charleston, South Carolina, were at risk of invasion.

"In my opinion," said Scott, the Commanding General of the U.S. Army, "all these works should be immediately garrisoned as to make any attempt to take any one of them, by surprise or coup de main, ridiculous."

With the sudden presence of federal troops, Scott predicted, "the danger of secession may be made to pass away without one conflict of arms, one execution or one arrest for treason." [1]

But the 74 year-old general, admired for his bluntness, added that if the conflict did not pass and secession and anarchy followed, it might be necessary to carve the nation up into four geographical entities for more effective administration. In an accompanying cover letter to Secretary of War John Floyd, Scott additionally noted that there were presently only five companies that the Army could use for garrisoning the eight forts he thought the most vulnerable.

No message could have been better framed to annoy Buchanan.

Buchanan noted that because Scott's communication had made the rounds from the General's New York office to Floyd's Washington office, others must have read it also, making him wonder whether the General's ruminations did the "most harm in encouraging or provoking secession." By so openly discussing the federal government's vulnerabilities, thought Buchanan, Scott may have actually inspired "disunion demagogues" into thinking that "they might secede without opposition from the North."

That Buchanan, by inference, was suggesting the presence of such demagogues within his own War Department went unsaid.

At the same time, Buchanan felt that with his suggestion that the forts might be attacked by Southerners, Scott had needlessly maligned otherwise patriotic men in the region in a manner certain to "excite their indignation and drive them to extremities."

Strategically, Scott's worries were well-placed. Buchanan was uncomfortably aware that the security of the forts was at all times vulnerable. But the General's blustery state of alarm, coupled with his sensational proposal to slice the country into pieces, prompted Buchanan to greatly disregard what he characterized as Scott's "strange and inconsistent" ideas. [2]

But put off as he was by Scott, Buchanan still couldn't help wonder: What if those crazy secessionists actually did try to attack one or several of the forts?

That Buchanan didn't give more immediate attention to the question, although he had Scott's report copied in duplicate for members of the Cabinet, was due to a distracting rush of events beginning on the night of Lincoln's victory. [3]

As the election results, late in the evening, were received in Washington, local Democrats simmered. "There is no place in the United States where the people—the office holders, for nearly everyone has an office—feel it more disastrously," a *New York Herald* reporter noted of the Washington establishment's response to Lincoln's triumph. "When it was announced that he was elected, curses loud and deep went up from infuriated individuals," the reporter added. [4]

Nearly 200 men, many starting out at Brown's Hotel at Pennsylvania Avenue and Sixth Street NW, unofficial headquarters for Southern Democrats, marched drunkenly to local Republican headquarters on Indiana Avenue. There they shot guns, threw rocks, smashed windows and once inside broke lanterns, demolished furniture, and tore down banners bearing Lincoln's name. Some of the rioters also wanted to burn the building down, and most likely would have tried had not the local police arrived and put an end to things. [5]

Buchanan made no public comments about the incident, which was well covered in the Washington press. But he was forced to make a statement after South Carolina Congressman Lawrence Keitt excitedly told a crowd in Columbia that not only would his state soon "cut the bonds of this accursed Union," but that once the deed was done, Buchanan would telegraph his approval. [6]

It was widely known that Keitt and Buchanan were close. Perhaps, people wondered, the South Carolinian knew something that no one else did. Buchanan, alarmed, quickly denied Keitt's claim, but he declined to say anything at all about the larger issue of secession.

Whether or not Buchanan was prepared to talk about secession publicly, the subject was about to consume him privately.

Preparing his fourth annual message to Congress, Buchanan asked Attorney General Jeremiah Black to research whether federal or state laws were determinative when the two government entities were in conflict. Additionally, Buchanan wondered, did a President have the constitutional right to "defend the public property (for instance, a fort, arsenal and navy yard) in case it should be assaulted?" [7]

Black spent the next three days looking for answers before, on November 20, reporting back bleak findings: "Within their respective spheres of action, the Federal Government and the government of a state are both of them independent and supreme, but each is utterly powerless beyond the limits assigned to it by the Constitution."

In other words, thought Black, there was little that Buchanan could actively do once a state seceded.

By the same token, the Attorney General was certain that Buchanan had the right to defend or take back any federal property arbitrarily seized by a state. Previous Congressional acts, said Black, gave to the President "the sole responsibility of deciding whether the exigency has arisen which requires the use of military force; and in proportion to the magnitude of that responsibility will be his care not to overstep the limits of his legal and just authority."

But Black also cautioned Buchanan that if a state government had already thrown in with the secessionist cause, the presence of federal troops "would be out of place, their use wholly illegal."

In those circumstances, "to send a military force into any State, with orders to act against the people, would be simply making war upon them," Black asserted. [8]

Several days after receiving the Attorney General's paper, Buchanan, in a White House meeting, idly observed: "South Carolina has not written to me on the subject, she has not notified me that she wishes to retire from the confederacy, but she means to make me, to make myself, draw the first blood, and then drag the other Southern states into the disunion movement with her." [9]

Meeting with his cabinet almost daily throughout the last half of November, Buchanan admitted that the prospects for an amicable settlement of regional differences were hourly diminishing. "I see no gleam of sunshine yet," he glumly replied when friends asked him how things were going. [10]

On November 24, Buchanan was additionally depressed after reading a blunt letter from former South Carolina Senator and *Charleston Mercury* owner Robert Barnwell Rhett, predicting South Carolina's secession, and adding: "It is in your power to make this event peaceful or bloody. If you send any more troops into Charleston Bay, it will be bloody." [11]

Buchanan, exasperated, now confronted War Secretary Floyd. Were the forts in the Charleston Harbor safe from attack, he asked.

"I will risk my reputation," Floyd airily responded. "I will trust my life that the forts are safe under the declarations of the gentlemen of Charleston."

"That is all very well," an unimpressed Buchanan responded. "But pardon me for asking you—does that secure the forts?" [12]

Five days later, Buchanan held in his hands a second warning and/or threat from South Carolina. This time it came from Governor William Gist, in the final days of his term of office, who sent a letter to Assistant Secretary of State William Trescot that made its way to Buchanan. If Buchanan finally decided to send reinforcements to the Charleston Harbor, "The responsibility will rest on him of lighting the torch of discord, which will only be quenched in blood," Gist declared. [13]

As Buchanan was trying to absorb this most recent threat, senators and representatives were arriving in the city for the December 3 opening of the Second Session of the 36th Congress. "Washington is already filling up," noted a correspondent for the *New York Tribune*, "notwithstanding the cry of disunion." [14]

In his private White House office decorated with maps and worn furniture, Buchanan worked on his message to Congress, smoking cigar after cigar. He could not help but note that the looming crisis was making a wreck of his cabinet. His once-amiable department heads were now spending their days yelling at one another. Secretary of State Lewis Cass, along with Attorney General Black and Postmaster General Joseph Holt advocated a hard line against the would-be secessionists.

Buchanan habitually ignored Cass, regarding him in this case particularly as an alarmist. But Black and Holt, respectively 50 and 53 years old, were younger men with more energy, devoted to the Union, and more than capable of forcefully making their points of view heard. Both men were furious with the South for, in their view, pushing things to this point, giving their arguments the sort of sharp edge that must have been startling for the normally complacent Buchanan to hear.

At the same time Buchanan was also listening to Treasury Secretary Howell Cobb, Secretary of War Floyd and Interior Secretary Jacob Thompson. Buchanan was particularly comfortable, socially, with Cobb and Thompson, giving both men an emotional advantage with him when they urged that he not say anything that might further anger the South Carolinians and push them into an even more implacable state of mind.

Buchanan could live with the divisions within his Cabinet, although he admitted that he liked it more when everyone was getting along. What really depressed him was observing a simultaneous hardening of attitudes in Washington society: "There was no longer any social or friendly intercourse between the pro-slavery and anti-slavery members," Buchanan would later recall. [15]

Alfred Iverson of Georgia noticed the same thing. "There are Republican Northern Senators upon that side. Here are the Southern Senators on this side," Iverson said on the floor of the Senate. "How much social intercourse is there between us? You sit upon your side, silent and gloomy. We sit upon ours with knit brows and portentous scowls." [16]

Buchanan finished work on his message in time for the opening of Congress. It would be a message greatly informed by Black's November 20th opinion. It would also prove a document that was the very worst thing Buchanan ever advanced, the low point of a low presidency, a virtual declaration of resignation and retreat. [17]

Buchanan opened his communication by proclaiming that the "country has been eminently prosperous in all of its material interests," a vast improvement since the panic of 1857. "Our harvests have been abundant and plenty smiles throughout the land," he said.

Then he jumped feet first into the secession discussion, declaring that the "long continued and intemperate interference of the Northern people with the question of slavery in the Southern states has at length produced its natural effects."

"The different sections of the Union are now arrayed against each other," Buchanan said, "and the time has arrived, so much dreaded by the Father of his Country, when hostile geographical parties have been formed."

Buchanan's allusion to George Washington was old—he had said the same thing many times before, most conspicuously during his 1856 election night victory speech. Equally tired was his repeated observation: "How easy would it be for the American people to settle the slavery question forever and to restore peace and harmony to this distracted country."

All that was necessary to make that happen, Buchanan yet again declared, was for the Northern states to leave the Southern states to themselves so that they could "manage their domestic institutions in their own way."

With these passages, Buchanan revealed once again that he was a man with one idea, and that he was perfectly willing to beat that idea to a bloody pulp.

But what Buchanan said next was new, at least for him: his rejection of the notion that any state at any time had a constitutional right to leave the Union.

This declaration, ironically, placed him firmly in the mainstream of Lincoln Republican thought.

"In order to justify secession as a constitutional remedy, it must be on the principle that the federal government is a mere voluntary association of states, to be dissolved at pleasure by any one of the contracting parties," Buchanan said. "If this be so, this confederacy is a rope of sand, to be penetrated and dissolved by the first adverse wave of public opinion in any of the states."

To allow the people of one state to arbitrarily leave the Union, Buchanan continued, would be to "hazard the liberties and happiness of the millions composing this Union."

"It is not pretended that any clause in the Constitution gives countenance to such a theory," he added.

"The framers of the national government," Buchanan asserted, "never intended to implant in its bosoms the seeds of its own destruction, nor were they at its creation guilty of the absurdity of providing for its own dissolution."

But did this mean that the people of any state were without redress against "the tyranny and oppression of the federal government"?

Buchanan thought not.

"The right of resistance on the part of the governed against the oppression of their governments cannot be denied," he asserted.

But secession was not an "inherent constitutional right."

"Let us look the danger fairly in the face. Secession is neither more nor less than revolution," Buchanan flatly stated. "It may or may not be a justifiable revolution, but still it is revolution."

Buchanan would have been wise to stop here. He had made a strong Union speech and not only condemned secession, but argued that it was impractical, irrational and not allowed under the Constitution, something no one could have imagined him doing just a month earlier. But he pushed on, and this was where he fell into a morass from which he would never be able to extricate himself: he said he could find nothing in the Constitution giving to Congress the "power to coerce a state into submission which is attempting to withdraw or has actually withdrawn from the confederacy."

"The fact is that our Union rests upon public opinion and can never be cemented by the blood of its citizens shed in civil war," Buchanan declared. "If it cannot live in the affections of the people, it must one day perish. Congress possesses many means of preserving its conciliation, but the sword was not placed in their hand to preserve it by force." [18]

Buchanan's presentation of both the unconstitutionality of secession and the impotence of the federal government to prevent it was, of course, based entirely on his and Black's interpretation of the literal Constitution. The Constitution said nothing about the right of states being able to leave the Union at will. The Constitution also said nothing about the federal government having the authority to force a seceded state back into the Union at will.

But in making points which would be hashed out over the decades by legal scholars, Buchanan missed the social, political and even spiritual context of the moment. [19]

Americans in both regions (not all Southerners, by any means, were pro-secession) were anxious and looking for reassurance from their President that life was going to go on and that secession was not only unconstitutional, but that any and all attempts to leave the Union would be dealt with decisively. But Buchanan's message (which was more of a legal thesis), instead of providing hope, did just the opposite: it greatly contributed to a national sense of confusion and dispair.

Even though it was true that the federal Army did not at the moment have the ability to resist active secession, or rebellion, in just one state, let alone several, Buchanan's message argued a much larger conceit: no matter how many men it had or how well-armed they were, the federal government lacked the *authority* to prevent or reverse secession militarily.

This was surely a document of defeat. But how to explain it? There are three possible answers:

1. Buchanan was a traitor and as such was signaling his support of secession to the South by letting it know that it could do what it liked without fear of Union retribution. There were many in the North who believed just that, particularly Congressmen who soon contemplated launching impeachment proceedings against the President. While the evidence that Buchanan had, throughout his presidency, favored the South was beyond doubt, the evidence that he was actively involved in supporting secession or was in any way not ultimately devoted to the Union and its security is nonexistent.

2. Buchanan was a patriot and hoped that letting the South know that the Union was militarily incapable of stomping out secession might actually serve to slow down the secession process. After all, if there was no imminent threat of action from the North, why did the South need to act in such haste? This made sense and is an option that historians have generally disregarded in favor of deciding that the message really showed that Buchanan was a bumbling incompetent. Buchanan knew when he wrote his message that he was talking to a bifurcated audience. He needed to give something to both the North and the South. Declaring secession unconstitutional was exactly what the North wanted him to say. But what about the South? What could Buchanan say in the same address that might make the South happy? More aware than probably any other Northerner of the South's paranoia and its obsession with Northern (and hence, in this case, Union) might, Buchanan thought a frank admission of the limitations of the federal government might possibly calm and even to some extent placate Southern leaders. And maybe, it was a long shot, that calm would forestall secession.

3. Buchanan had no real reason one way or the other for his assertion of Union impotence. He simply thought it was all interesting stuff and, like his multi-layered and ultimately meaningless Breckinridge endorsement statement of the previous summer, mentioned it in the spirit of a pointless academic exercise.

It was known that many hands were involved in the drafting of the message. Jefferson Davis, among others, was brought in several times to look over and offer his input on several passages (he also returned to the White House after the release of the message to ask Buchanan what went wrong). But the final author was Buchanan and the document's constitutional ruminations belong to him only.

Discarding the idea that Buchanan was a traitor leaves readers with the notion that, yes, Buchanan felt he was being helpful with his admission of Union military impotence, and also that he thought the whole exercise highly fascinating.

Ironically, if Buchanan's ultimate goal was to bring the country back together, he achieved precisely that, if even for the moment, with the North and South united in the message's condemnation.

"No state paper so remarkable has ever appeared from a Chief Executive in this country—perhaps in any country," despaired Harriet Beecher Stowe, the author of the historic *Uncle Tom's Cabin*. Congressman John Sherman, still nursing a grudge against Buchanan since the failure of the Covode Committee, observed: "The Constitution provided against every possible vacancy in the office of the President, but did not provide for utter imbecility." Said Massachusetts Congressman Charles Francis Adams, Sr: "If there was any way of impeaching him, it would really deserve to be considered. But he may yet be indicted for treason." [20]

In the Senate, the normally jovial John Hale of New Hampshire weighed in. "I think the country did expect from the President some exposition of a decided policy. And I confess that, for one, I was rather indifferent as to what that policy was that he recommended. But I hoped it would be something, that it would be decisive."

Added Hale: "He has utterly failed in that respect." [21]

But it was William Seward, soon to be Lincoln's Secretary of State, who had the most memorable take on Buchanan's message. In a quote soon to be repeated from coast to coast, Seward proclaimed that Buchanan's message proved at least two things: "That no state has the right to secede unless it wishes to," and that "it is the president's duty to enforce the law, unless somebody opposes him." [22]

Some of this reaction was predictable. Buchanan knew that nothing he did would satisfy the likes of Stowe, Sherman, Adams, Hale and Seward. But it was the response of Southern leaders that really startled him. Texas Senator Louis Wigfall declared that the message was proof that Buchanan "will precipitate the very issue which he seems intent to avoid," adding that secession was now inevitable. Jefferson Davis, in a Senate debate on the message, said it was now more apparent than ever that the North and the South would soon be at war. He added that "when that declaration of war is made, the state of which I am a citizen will be found ready and quite willing to meet it." [23]

On December 8 Treasury Secretary Cobb resigned. He disjointedly told Buchanan that he was not leaving because of "anything you have said or done" but because Buchanan's views on the constitutionality of secession made it impossible for him to continue in his job. Whatever reason Cobb gave, his sudden exit spoke volumes. Predicting that posterity would record the Buchanan administration "as the last administration of our present Union," Cobb promptly boarded a train for Charleston to support the secession cause. [24]

It was now clear to the man who thought he was the South's biggest friend that he had few real friends there at all. Howell Cobb, John Slidell, Jefferson Davis, Lawrence Keitt, Clement Clay, among so many of his closest associations, had all either left his side, or signaled that they would soon.

Nursing a cold in his private upstairs quarters at the White House, Buchanan was finally becoming receptive to the pleas of his Northern cabinet members who urged a get-tough policy with the South.

Chapter Ten

"This I Cannot Do. This I Will Not Do."

If trying to withstand the outrage sparked by his December 3rd message wasn't enough, Buchanan in the last weeks of December was doing his best to keep an eye on Robert Anderson.

The Army Major, in command of the federal forts in the Charleston Harbor, had sent a message on December 20 to Adjutant General Samuel Cooper expressing alarm over the fact that Fort Sumter, Fort Moultrie and Castle Pinckney had become the singular focus of attention in the national secession debate. Anderson hoped that "events may take such a turn as soon to relieve me from the dangerous position my little command is now in." [1]

Painfully aware that the forts, or rather federal control of them, were symbols of Yankee oppression to the increasingly paranoid South Carolinians, Anderson was also certain that at the first opportune moment his men would be attacked by what he called the "authorities of South Carolina." The result, he added, would be a rout of the feds. [2]

A West Point graduate who had served in the Black Hawk and Mexican-American wars, Anderson had been ordered only a month earlier by Secretary of War John Floyd to take command of the three forts. [3]

Initially well-received by the South Carolinians, Anderson, privately sympathetic to the Southern point of view, had almost overnight become the face of the enemy after the December 20 ordinance of secession. To make matters worse, the Major never really knew where he stood with Washington as he tried to figure out the true meaning of any number of inscrutable messages sent to him by Floyd. On December 21, for example, the War Secretary informed him that it was his duty to "hold possession of the forts and harbor in Charleston" and to defend those forts if under attack. But at the same time, revealing a lack of confidence in Anderson's ability to withstand a protracted assault, Floyd told Anderson that if under attack "it will be your duty to yield to a necessity and make the best terms in your power." [4]

Floyd had earlier even gone so far as to advise Anderson to centralize his command in only one fort in order to increase his powers of resistance. [5]

Studying the Floyd-Anderson correspondence, Buchanan saw danger lurking in the Charleston Harbor. But because he continued to believe that the South Carolinians would never actually attack any or all of the forts, Buchanan couldn't understand Anderson's proposal to move his men into a single fort. What Buchanan did understand was that he was being boxed in by events. A Washington correspondent for the *Daily Picayune* of New Orleans on Christmas Eve astutely predicted that any federal effort to reinforce Anderson would incite the South Carolinians to action. But at the same time should the South Carolinians successfully seize any or all of the forts, Buchanan would almost certainly be "exposed to censure" in Congress. [6]

Christmas Day was obviously a lousy one in Washington. "There is no hilarity in the national capital in these times," a Washington-based reporter for the *Charleston Mercury* observed. [7]

But there was a lot of anger.

That morning the *Washington Constitution*, supposedly the Administration's mouthpiece, came out for secession. Even though it wasn't the first time that the paper's editor, William Browne, had differed with Administration policy, Buchanan decided he had had enough. "I have defended you as long as I can against numerous complaints," Buchanan wrote in response to Browne, officially severing his ties to the publication (Buchanan also made sure to yank all government patronage from the *Constitution,* causing the paper to go out of business several weeks later). [8]

As Buchanan was dumping Browne, Anderson had decided to make a dramatic move: transfering his entire force from the vulnerable Fort Moultrie to the more secure Fort Sumter. When, on the next day, that move was was completed, Anderson reported to Cooper: "We have one year's supply of hospital stores and about four months' supply of provisions for my command." The Major added: "The step which I have taken was, in my opinion, necessary to prevent the effusion of blood." [9]

Anderson's actions galvanized the North. By transporting his men to Fort Sumter, said the *Springfield Daily Republican* of Massachusetts in a typically jubilant response, the Major had rendered Fort Moultrie "useless to the South Carolina rebels...he completely checkmated them and defeated the scheme by which they hoped to get easy possession of all the forts." [10]

Thousands of people in Boston, Philadelphia, New York and Chicago took to the streets to cheer Anderson. For the first time, they also brought with them American flags of varying sizes as a symbol of their recently discovered devotion to the Union.

"My God, are misfortunes never to come singly?" Buchanan exclaimed to Jefferson Davis after hearing of Anderson's move, certain that it would unnecessarily irritate the South Carolinians. [11]

Trying to trace how things had come to this, Buchanan angrily confronted Floyd, who instantly denied that he had ever meant for Anderson to abandon Fort Moultrie. In turn Floyd, by wire, demanded that Anderson explain himself, noting: "There is no order for any such movement." [12]

Anderson's response was swift: "I abandoned Fort Moultrie because I was certain that if attacked my men must have been sacrificed, and the command of the harbor lost. I spiked the guns and destroyed the carriages to keep the guns from being used against us." [13]

In a separate message, Anderson also reported that since the move to Fort Sumter, his men had observed an armed steamer transporting South Carolina soldiers to both Fort Moultrie and Castle Pinckney. [14]

All of this now threatened to turn into a full blown public relations disaster for Buchanan. If he backed Anderson, Southerners would accuse the President of treachery. But if he condemned Anderson, Buchanan would be flailed throughout the North for once again caving into the South.

Buchanan had plenty of reasons to be put out by the whole affair. A bureaucrat with an obsessive need to be on top of both the small and big things in his administration, Buchanan was dumbfounded that something this important could have happened without his knowledge. Even more, because Buchanan continued to believe that he could prevent the South Carolinians from initiating any kind of military action by promising to never take any kind of action against them, he knew Anderson's move worked at a cross-purpose to that goal and would be viewed as a violation of his "hands-off" military policy, even though what Anderson did was entirely defensive in nature.

The entire matter symbolized for Buchanan his precarious position, which in the final days of 1860 was centered on only one goal: trying to prevent a war, a war that would turn Americans against Americans and soak the soil of both the North and the South in the blood of its sons. "The President may have determined to do no act which would open the temples of Janus and close the doors to peace, even if it should result in a temporary abandonment of the forts," thought the *Philadelphia Public Ledger*, one of the very few major papers to see merit in Buchanan's passivity. "At this time any unnecessary irritation might ruin the hopes of all who desire to preserve the Union. The application of force would be fatal." [15]

Buchanan would years later ask Joseph Holt, who would become his Secretary of War on January 18, to offer a defense of his stand. Holt complied, writing: "He might have acted far otherwise than he did. He might have blustered and threatened, but this would have been incompatible with his personal character and the dignity of his exalted office and would have excited only derision with the secessionists." [16]

While Buchanan was still trying to take in the many ramifications of the Anderson controversy, he got word that the new South Carolina Governor, Francis Perkins, had admitted that he had ordered a military force to take possession of the now-abandoned Castle Pinckney and Fort Moultrie. That very afternoon a delegation of South Carolina commissioners arrived at the White House and demanded that Buchanan pull all federal forces from the harbor.

Buchanan fumed, but told the commissioners diplomatically that he needed time to think before officially responding. While all of this was going on Secretary of War Floyd dramatically exited from the White House. In leaving, Floyd told Buchanan that he was resigning in protest of Buchanan's refusal to withdraw altogether from the Charleston Harbor.

That refusal, Floyd proclaimed, "Invites a collision and must inevitably inaugurate civil war."

"I cannot consent," Floyd added, "to be the agent of such calamity." [17]

Speaking at the Exchange Hotel in Richmond two weeks later, Floyd condescendingly described Buchanan as a "good old man," before recalling his final conversation with the President. "I was sorry to part from him, God knows, because he has done what has seldom been done: he has inspired during four years an affection in my heart. But when he left I could not help cocking my eye and say 'God speed you, old man, to the North.'" [18]

This was all entertaining stuff, but Floyd's narrative sidestepped the primary reason for his departure: his fear that he was about to be indicted on charges of malfeasance in office for presiding over a generous $500,000 system of payouts to friendly government contractors.

Welcome though Floyd's departure may have been to the pro-North members of the cabinet, the resignation of yet a third department head in the last 21 days left many with the feeling that Buchanan's presidency was spectacularly imploding. "Whether justly or not, there is a want of confidence in the cabinet," Theodorus Bailey Myers, a Buchanan supporter in New York, confided to Harriet Lane. Myers added that he was increasingly suspicious of a "powerful clique at work in Washington who seek for a temporary dissolution of the Union with the hope of a reorganization to cure the existing evil." [19]

The remaining supporters of Buchanan in the North, such as Bailey, would shortly feel better about things when they finally learned of his response to the South Carolina commissioners. Besides demanding the removal of all federal troops from the Charleston Harbor, the commissioners, with a healthy dose of impertinence, had also let it be known that they would not even talk to Buchanan until every last soldier was gone. [20]

Further pushing their luck, the commissioners additionally suggested that Buchanan should compile some sort of official explanation, which very much sounded like a demand for an apology to Buchanan's Northern cabinet members, as to why he had allowed Anderson to move his men to Fort Sumter in the first place. [21]

There were different ways of looking at the commissioners, but the blunt Edwin Stanton, who became the new Attorney General on December 20, held the most pointed, telling Buchanan that they were nothing more than traitors unworthy of a presidential audience. In fact, snapped Stanton, "they should be arrested." [22]

However they should be received, the commissioners' message provoked a heated but greatly needed debate within Buchanan's cabinet. On the one side, Interior Secretary Jacob Thompson, Navy Secretary Isaac Toucey and Treasury Secretary Phillip Thomas argued in favor of abandoning Charleston Harbor. Holt, Stanton, and Black (who became the new Secretary of State on December 17), took the opposing view. The debate went on for hours, well into the late evening. But by the time it was over, the Northern faction had prevailed. Exhausted, Buchanan wrote out a final response to the commissioners. In it, he asserted that although he had never ordered Anderson to centralize his command at Fort Sumter, under no circumstances would he now consider telling the Major to withdraw entirely from the Charleston Harbor. "This I cannot do," Buchanan declared. "This I will not do." [23]

He concluded by disclosing to the commissioners that he had in his possession a dispatch documenting South Carolina's recent seizure of a federal arsenal in Charleston, a seizure that netted the Southerners some $500,000 in arms and equipment. Buchanan then delivered his knock-out punch: "Whilst it is my duty to defend Fort Sumter as a portion of public property of the United States against hostile attacks, from whatever quarter they may come, by such means as I possess for this purpose, I do not perceive how such a defense can be construed into a menace against the city of Charleston." [24]

Newspaper reports of Buchanan's reply to the commissioners sent his stock soaring in the North, even among the many who had long since despaired that he would ever do anything right.

"If the President only holds," the usually critical *New York Tribune* declared on New Year's Day 1861, "everything may be well yet." [25]

Chapter Eleven

The High Standards of
Illustrious Predecessors

The debate within the White House over Buchanan's response to the South Carolina commissioners not only revealed serious fissures within the administration, but fissures within the fissures.

A starting point would have to be the demand from the South Carolina commissioners that they would not enter into any meaningful negotiations with Buchanan until he ordered the removal of all federal troops from the Charleston Harbor.

That demand sparked the beginning of a tumultuous 48-hour period of debate inside the White House. Buchanan, who in responding to the ceaseless pressures of the last month may have been nearing both a physical and emotional collapse, told his cabinet that he was seriously thinking about ordering Robert Anderson to move his troops back to Fort Moultrie as part of a larger effort to keep the South Carolinians pacified. Black, Stanton and Holt were already worried that Buchanan would additionally concede to the commissioners that Congress had no constitutional power to make a state stay in the Union. But the idea that Buchanan might also actually order Anderson to return to Fort Moultrie both alarmed and enraged all three men. To send Anderson's command back to Fort Moultrie, declared the always-blunt Stanton, would be treason, making Buchanan, by implication, subject to hanging.

"Oh, no!" Buchanan responded, perhaps wondering if in a season of things coming generally unglued, such an ending was not entirely impossible. "Not as bad as that, my friend—not so bad as that!" [1]

Both Stanton and Black soon became convinced that there was no hope for Buchanan. Stanton visited Dan Sickles, whose powers of endurance after his sensational trial for murder the year before were virtually unequaled, declaring in despair "Something must be done." [2]

For his part, Black had decided that that "something" would be his resignation, telling Stanton of his decision to leave before delivering the bad news to Buchanan himself. Stanton promised that if Black really did go, he would follow, and probably so would Holt as well. Black, dreading such a meeting with a man he had known and admired for decades, subsequently told Buchanan on December 30 that he felt he had no other choice than to leave. Buchanan, perhaps thinking of Jefferson Davis, John Slidell, Howell Cobb and Lawrence Keitt (the line continued to grow) responded by accusing Black of abandoning him.

Black wasn't in the mood for this and told Buchanan instead "There is no storm of popular indignation I would not breast by your side, no depth of misfortune into which I would not descend provided you had a course to defend." [3]

But, Black insisted, Buchanan's proposed letter to the South Carolina commissioners "sweeps the ground from under our feet, it places you where no man can stand with you, and where you cannot stand alone." [4]

Buchanan surprised Black by agreeing with the substance of his remarks and explaining that he was only trying to humor the South Carolinians in the hope of thwarting an outright war. He then prevailed upon Black to stay, astutely forecasting the likely effect of his resignation. "If you go, Holt and Stanton will leave, and I will be in a sorry attitude before the country." [5]

Referring to his letter to the commissioners, Buchanan instructed Black to "modify it to suit yourself." Black did so, with Stanton's help, and all three men—Black, Stanton, and Holt—decided, at least for the present, to stick with the President. [6]

At the same time that he, with some impatience, was trying to keep his newly-constituted cabinet together, Buchanan was also working with Holt and General Winfield Scott on what would turn out to be a disastrous plan to resupply Anderson's command. On January 5 the civilian vessel *Star of the West* would leave New York headed for the Charleston Harbor loaded with supplies and 250 troops. But before the ship arrived at its destination, Jacob Thompson read of the mission in Buchanan's one-time mouthpiece, the *Washington Constitution*. By wire, he tipped off South Carolina Governor Francis Perkins.

When the *Star of the West* pushed into the outskirts of the harbor four days later, the South Carolina militia was ready, shooting at it from batteries off the nearby Morris Island and forcing the vessel to retreat back north. Although Anderson had since communicated to Washington that he wasn't actually in need of resupply, the failed mission of the *Star of the West* emerged as a new point of contention within the administration.

Thompson, for one, claimed an outraged surprise and abruptly resigned, becoming the fourth member of the cabinet to leave in the last month. Buchanan wondered about the surprise part, reminding Thompson that he was sitting in attendance at the very cabinet meeting where the mission had first been discussed. And he was still sitting there when Buchanan concluded "It is now all over and reinforcements must be sent." How could Thompson now claim to be surprised by the *Star of the West* mission? What exactly, Buchanan sarcastically wondered, did Thompson think the President had meant when he uttered the words "reinforcements must be sent"? [7]

The Thompson resignation and subsequent appointment of New Yorker John Dix as Treasury Secretary (replacing pro-South Phillip Thomas, who resigned on January 11 using a dispute with Buchanan over loan policy as his pretext) made it official: the Buchanan cabinet was now made up entirely of men who urged Buchanan to take a stronger Union line.

While these various White House skirmishes showed that the executive branch was in the throes of combustion and change, Congress, Buchanan later contemptuously charged, was inert, doing nothing to "preserve the Union by peaceful measures or to furnish the President or his successor with a military force to repel any attack which might be made by the cotton States."

"It neither presented the olive branch nor the sword," Buchanan added. [8]

Excluded from this sweeping but largely accurate Buchanian indictment was John Crittenden, who was, in fact, trying to do something. "I trust there is not a Senator here who is not willing to yield and to compromise much in order to preserve the government of the Union of the country," Crittenden optimistically declared as he, too, tried to find a solution to the crisis. [9]

No stranger to tackling thorny challenges, the 73 year-old Crittenden had served as President Millard Fillmore's attorney general, painstakingly helping to broker the famous Compromise of 1850 which recognized Southern slavery, admitted California as a free state and organized the Utah and New Mexico territories with no restrictions on slavery. Now Crittenden visited the White House and told Buchanan that he thought he could make magic happen again, a magic that would rob secession of its purpose through the adoption of a series of amendments to the Constitution.

Those amendments would primarily prevent Congress from abolishing slavery where it existed; require that slave owners be compensated whenever fugitive slaves were harbored by abolitionists; prohibit slavery north of the Missouri Compromise line and protect slavery in territories south of that line. A final Crittenden proposal would lock it all in by declaring that none of the above amendments could be changed by subsequent amendment.

The Senate committee set up to sift through Crittenden's proposals, judged by its membership alone, was promising. William Seward, Stephen Douglas and Jefferson Davis were among the thirteen members, although Davis, increasingly skeptical about the value of keeping the Union together, acknowledged that he was "not very hopeful of a good result." Douglas, however, was classically optimistic and won applause from the Senate gallery when he declared "I am ready to act with any party, with any individual of any party, who will come to this question with an eye single to the preservation of the Constitution and the Union." [10]

A larger committee composed of thirty members was formed in the House devoted to the same mission.

Although Davis eventually, if reluctantly, vowed to support the committee's compromise proposals, he understandably said he would do so only if the committee Republicans did the same. But Seward and his fellow party members wavered, unwilling to do anything until they received a signal one way or the other from President-elect Lincoln. These maneuvers, evidence to Buchanan of the general unreliability of Congress to deal with the crisis in any realistic manner, also made him wonder about the mysterious Lincoln. Who was he and what was he thinking?

Buchanan could write a book, but never did, about his first-hand experiences with presidents. He knew Andrew Jackson to be hot-headed, but ultimately receptive to reason. Polk was stubborn and, thought Buchanan, not really up to his job, but still the two men managed most of the time to get things done. Pierce was more skilled in the political arts than was generally recognized, and in response, Buchanan girded his loins accordingly. But Lincoln—here was a different creature altogether, dedicated to containing slavery and an abolitionist sympathizer, which surely must have meant he was unrealistic dreamer, yet somehow enough of a practical politician to have won a contentious presidential election. A man of the earth, Lincoln had worked a farm, chopped wood and rode horses. Buchanan hadn't done a day of physical labor in his adulthood and rode in carriages led by teams of horses. Lincoln was preternaturally eloquent, more capable of making words and ideas flow beautifully in a dozen memos a day than Buchanan was laboring on a state speech for weeks. Lincoln inspired. Buchanan, with party hacks behind him doling out favors, compelled.

Hoping for answers, Buchanan listened when he was visited by Duff Green, the long-time Democratic insider and editor, who, more than thirty years earlier had precipitated the most embarrassing chapter of Buchanan's political life when he asked Buchanan to explain whether or not he had suggested that Henry Clay's support in the House balloting for the presidency in 1825 could be purchased if Andrew Jackson offered him a post in his cabinet. Buchanan may have through the years held a grudge against Green for the letter he wrote demanding answers, but what Green had to say now was too important to let such ancient resentments get in the way. Essentially Green, who had known Lincoln for years, told Buchanan he thought the President-elect was a reasonable man who, if he could be made to understand that the Crittenden proposals were the last best hope for the Union, might be willing to issue a public statement of endorsement. That endorsement, in turn, would provide cover for Seward and the Republican members on both the Senate and House committees to also support the proposals. Green additionally suggested that he might even be able to coax Lincoln into coming to Washington before his inaugural and, with Buchanan, issue a joint statement in favor of the Crittenden proposals.

Buchanan couldn't help but be intrigued. He instructed Green to go to Springfield and talk to Lincoln, adding that if Lincoln did decide to come to Washington he would be "received with all the respect due to the President-elect." [11]

Meeting with Lincoln at the end of December in Springfield, Green explained Crittenden's proposals, including the need for the amendments to be ratified by either the voters in the states or their legislatures. Lincoln, Green reported to Buchanan, seemed receptive. The President-elect, in a draft of a letter, pointed out that while he did not want any more amendments to the Constitution, he recognized that "questions of such amendment rightfully belong to the American people." He would do nothing, Lincoln vowed, to impede that process. [12]

Lincoln then indicated to Green that he would be willing to give him a formal letter for public release endorsing the Crittenden proposals before Green returned back east. Green must have felt that he was single-handedly on the verge of saving the Union. He sent a quick message to Buchanan on December 28 to tell him of the promising news and also let him know that once he received Lincoln's letter, he would transmit its contents by telegram to Buchanan. [13]

There was only one catch: Lincoln had decided to run the matter by Illinois Senator Lyman Trumbull, his sometimes campaign manager in the 1860 election. The excessively cautious Trumbull most likely advised Lincoln to steer clear of the entire matter, suggesting that aspects of the proposals were at variance with the 1860 Republican Party platform. Green left Springfield without the letter and on January 7 wrote to Lincoln, expressing regret that the President-elect had been unable to embrace Crittenden's proposals.

It is unclear to what degree Buchanan really hoped for any kind of a positive response from Lincoln. He thought Republicans were generally unreliable anyway, so Lincoln's actions, or lack thereof, probably didn't surprise him. But Buchanan also knew that without Lincoln's assistance, the Crittenden proposals were doomed.

At the same time that Buchanan was getting zero help from one soon-to-be president in Illinois, he was getting an abundance of it from a former president in Virginia who lauded him for pursuing "a wise and statesmanlike course" in response to the secession crisis. [14]

John Tyler was unique in that as late as January 1861 he was a prominent Southerner leader opposed to secession. Like Buchanan, he loved the South, but treasured the Union. He additionally believed that Northerners and Southerners could still work out their differences within the Union. Not for him the dramatic exits of Howell Cobb and Lawrence Keitt. Instead, Tyler thought that some kind of a border state pro-Union conference could serve as a positive bulwark against Deep South secession.

Writing to the *Richmond Enquirer* to make that idea public, the former president was subsequently startled when state lawmakers in Richmond appointed him as just the man to head up such a conference. [15]

Tyler thought that at the age of 70 he was too old to co-ordinate what would soon be widely known as the Peace Conference, a task certain to be exhausting. Even more, he noted that the Virginia lawmakers had expanded his proposed border state conclave to include every state of the Union. This considerably complicated matters. Mississippi, Florida, Alabama and Georgia had all, by mid-January, joined South Carolina in exiting the Union. They would obviously be no-shows at Tyler's conference. That, in turn, meant that the proceedings stood to be dominated by the representatives from the Northern states.

But, reservations aside, Tyler thought the effort important enough to at least give it a go, arriving in Washington on January 24 to confer with Buchanan. There Tyler encountered an irritated president who, noting the December South Carolina seizures of Fort Moultrie, the Customhouse and U.S. Post Office, among other federal properties in South Carolina, complained that the South had been "perpetuating acts of useless bravado which had been quite as well let alone." [16]

While always respectful of Tyler, Buchanan was also exhibiting a new-found resolve to the former president and anyone else who would listen, particularly in response to the wide-spread rumors of a Southern-organized coup set to take place in Washington before or on Lincoln's inaugural. "If I live until the 4th of March, I will ride to the capitol with Old Abe whether I am assassinated or not," Buchanan publicly vowed. [17]

Stanton, for one, still wasn't sure Buchanan got it. "I believe that an effort to establish a provisional government in the name of the Southern

Confederacy of Washington will be made before the 4th of March, and there is great reason to apprehend it will be successful," he confided to long-time friend Salmon Chase, soon to be named as Lincoln's Treasury Secretary. Stanton added that Buchanan "does not believe and cannot be made to believe the existence of this danger." [18]

Stanton was somewhat relieved by the mid-January arrival of more than 1300 soldiers ordered to Washington by Buchanan upon General Scott's advice. The presence of the soldiers had the effect Buchanan hoped for: locals, at least for the present, stopped worrying about an immediate rebel invasion. On February 11, the Washington correspondent for the *Boston Evening Transcript,* happily eyeing the soldiers, reported "The battle is now fought, the day is won, and the Constitution still stands." [19]

But Scott was still worried about the counting of the electoral vote on February 13: would Southern militants on that very day attack the Capitol? Scott ringed the building with soldiers and was greatly relieved to see the process come off without a hitch. In the Senate chamber, Vice-president Breckinridge gallantly announced Lincoln, the man he had run against for president, as the winner.

While Lincoln's electoral vote was in the process of being certified, the President-elect was on his way to Washington, greeted by hundreds of thousands of well-wishers along the way in Indiana, Ohio, Pennsylvania and New York. Jefferson Davis was also on the road. Elected unanimously as the provisional President of the Confederate States of America by members of the newly formed Confederate Provisional Congress, Davis arrived in Montgomery to declare that all the Confederacy really wanted was to live in peace alongside the United States.

Buchanan remained skeptical, asking Tyler if there was any Confederate plan in the offing to attack Fort Sumter. Tyler checked with his Southern sources and reported back, somewhat curiously, to Buchanan: "I am happy to say that the reply, received a moment ago, leaves me no ground to fear for any early disturbance." [20]

On the evening of February 21 Buchanan needed Tyler's help yet again regarding the annual military march in the District of Columbia honoring George Washington's birthday. Not finding him at the Willard Hotel, he instead left a note for the former president asking "Ought the federal troops now in Washington to parade tomorrow with local volunteers? I thought if this were done it might arouse the susceptibilities of the Southern members of the Peace Conference." [21]

Upon finding the note, Tyler dashed off a quick response advising against the parade.

But when, on the following morning, Buchanan cancelled that parade, he enraged General Scott, who already had his troops lined up to march. Sickles, getting word that the parade was called off, ran to encounter Buchanan in the War Department, who was just then in conversation with Holt, and noted "There are ten thousand people out on the streets of Washington today to see the parade which was just announced. I have just heard that it has been countermanded, and the report is exciting great indignation." Buchanan sighed and turned to Holt: "Go ahead with the parade." [22]

Tyler may have been disenchanted by Buchanan's parade reversal, but he had other things on his mind as the watered down Crittenden proposals finally worked out by the Peace Conference were sent to Congress where they were summarily ignored. A depressed Tyler stopped by the White House at the end of February to visit with Buchanan. It would be the last time the two men would meet. Tyler then returned to Virginia where he, too, would soon throw in with the secessionist cause.

By the final week of February, a pall had been cast over Washington. All was calm, but the prospect of something terrible continued to beckon. As he met with his cabinet on February 24, Buchanan was handed a card telling him that Lincoln and his wife Mary had arrived for a courtesy visit. "Gentlemen, Uncle Abe is in the Red Room below," Buchanan announced. "Let us not keep him waiting." [23]

Buchanan would later say that his initial meeting with Lincoln and their subsequent ride together in the inaugural parade "convinced me that he was a man of a kindly and benevolent heart." Harriet Lane was less sanguine and entirely unimpressed with Mrs. Lincoln. Even so, at Buchanan's orders, Harriet arranged to have a large dinner prepared for the Lincolns that would be waiting for them after the new President's swearing in. [24]

At the end of February a delegation of local officials stopped by to greet Buchanan. It proved an oaccsion for Buchanan to once again trot out his ghosts of the past. He had first arrived in Washington exactly forty years ago, he said, but didn't think any of his visitors were old enough to have been adults then. After yet one more trip down memory lane, Buchanan added that he had always liked the people of Washington who had consistently treated him "with the utmost kindness and respect." [25]

On March 1 Buchanan was in a comparatively more peevish mood responding to a Congressional inquiry asking him to justify his January order bringing 1300 troops into the city. "At the present moment, when all is quiet, it is difficult to realize the state of alarm which prevailed when the troops were first ordered to this city," he noted of the general Washington mood two months previous. "This almost instantly subsided after the arrival of our first company, and a feeling of comparative peace and security has existed both in Washington and throughout the country."

"Had I refused to adopt this precautionary measure, and evil consequences, which many good men at the time apprehended, had followed, I should never have forgiven myself." [26]

This Republican-inspired inquiry, in the form of a resolution, was the final evidence Buchanan needed to prove that all the second session of the 36th Congress really wanted to do was cast him in a bad light. As Inauguration Day approached, he was grateful for many things, primarily that the country was still not at war. But he undoubtedly felt a special glee knowing he would never again have to deal with the likes of Republicans John Sherman, "Honest John" Covode, Zachariah Chandler and Schuyler Colfax—all men he regarded as dangerous demagogues irresponsibly willing to advance their own partisan agendas even if it meant the destruction of the Union.

On March 4, Buchanan, in his carriage, pulled up in front of the Willard Hotel to pick up Lincoln. "My dear sir, if you are as happy in entering the White House as I shall feel on returning to Wheatland, you are a happy man indeed," Buchanan said upon greeting Lincoln.

Lincoln was diplomatic, if wordy. Denying that he would enter the White House with very much pleasure, he added "I assure that I shall do what I can to maintain the high standards set by my illustrious predecessors who have occupied it." [27]

At least 100,000 people watched Buchanan and Lincoln ride down Pennsylvania Avenue. General Scott, near the Capitol grounds, saw in every face a potential assassin.

One of Lincoln's young aides, John Hay, looking on from a distance as Buchanan rode and talked with Lincoln, couldn't help but wonder "what momentous counsels were to come from that gray and weather-beaten head." He later found out from Lincoln himself. Buchanan, never one to let the big things get in the way of the small, had revealed to the President-elect the inner workings of the White House kitchen and pantry, additionally advising him that the "water at the right-hand well" was "better than that at the left." [28]

Arriving at the Capitol, the two men walked arm-in-arm into the building where members of both chambers rushed to greet them. Inside the Senate, Breckinridge was swearing in the new Vice-president, Hannibal Hamlin. Charles Francis Adams, Jr., temporarily working as a journalist, observed the scene, and could not help but be impressed by Buchanan. "In spite of the wry neck and dubious eye, the outgoing President was, to my mind, undoubtedly the more presentable of the two; his tall, large figure, and white head looked well beside Mr. Lincoln's lank, angular form and hirsute face." [29]

Buchanan and Lincoln then walked out onto a wooden platform overlooking a crowd of some 30,000 people. The inevitable Stephen Douglas sat nearby and even held Lincoln's hat as the new President began his address. For the first time Buchanan now heard Lincoln speak, taking in the graceful flow of his words. "We are not enemies, but friends. We must not be enemies" Lincoln said. "Though passion may have strained, it must not break our bonds of affection. The mystic chords of memory, stretching from every battlefield and patriot grave to every living heart and hearthstone all over this broad land will yet swell the chorus of the Union when again touched, as surely they will be, by the better angels of our nature." [30]

Buchanan looked down at his boots throughout most of the address, applauding occasionally. When Lincoln finished speaking and a reporter asked for his reaction, Buchanan said he did not "understand the secret meaning" of the address and would have more to say after reading it for himself later. [31]

Was Buchanan's response petty? Did the phrase "secret meaning" imply that Buchanan thought Lincoln was obscuring through eloquent sentences some sort of dark agenda? Probably not. Lincoln's address presented both a moral and poetic way of looking not at just secession, but the mosaic of the American union. He said most of what Buchanan had been trying to say for months, but in a more compelling, understandable manner. The speech would be reprinted in its entirety in virtually every newspaper in the country the following day. Buchanan needed to read it, to take it apart and decipher it word for word, as perhaps only one lawyer could with an important document written by another.

Returning with Lincoln to the White House, where he at last bade the new President goodbye, Buchanan felt a strange sense of satisfaction. It was funny and unexpected, given the rancor of the last four years, not to mention the unyielding stress of the last four months. But still it was a feeling, something he could not deny, all of which was why Buchanan so needed to read Lincoln's speech quietly and carefully by himself, away from the tumult of the crowd.

Was it possible, Buchanan wondered, that this romantic figure from the plains of Illinois, the hero of the young Republicans who had so derided Buchanan, had in fact just ratified the Buchanan presidency?

Chapter Twelve

The Most Amazing of Fossils

Buchanan returned to a welcome in Lancaster that must have bolstered his spirits after his final, depressing months in Washington. A 34-gun salute, ringing church bells, a two-mile parade and some 3,500 people greeted him.

"I do not intend referring to the political affairs of our country," Buchanan announced upon his arrival. "My public acts have been committed to the pages of history, and time alone can decide whether they have been right or wrong."

Playing to his audience, Buchanan added: "If, however, any of these have been displeasing to the residents of Lancaster, I respectfully beg your pardon." [1]

The welcoming reception seemed a precursor of happier times for Buchanan. And initially a spirit of good cheer prevailed at Wheatland as Buchanan re-acquainted himself with old friends, many of whom enjoyed the multi-course dinners he hosted while simultaneously putting a dent in his wine stock.

But very soon Buchannan found himself contemplating a somber task: somehow he must correct what he regarded as wildly inaccurate and unfair popular impressions of his presidency, in particular its chaotic end. [2]

In fact, one week after his arrival at Wheatland, Buchanan told *New York Herald* publisher James Gordon Bennett that his presidency should actually be regarded as a success in both domestic as well as foreign affairs, except for what he characterized as the "sad events which have recently occurred." [3]

His determination to change negative public views of his presidency was colored by no small amount of defensiveness. A week after writing to Bennett, as Lincoln and the rest of the nation contemplated a probable Confederate attack on Fort Sumter, Buchanan told John Dix "It is probable that an attempt will be made, as you suggest, to cast the responsibility on me. But I always refused to surrender the fort and was ever ready to send reinforcements on the request of Major Anderson." [4]

When the Confederates in mid-April did in fact finally attack Sumter, Buchanan took it personally, proclaiming to his nephew, James Buchanan Henry, that the Confederate government was "repeatedly warned by my administration that an assault on Fort Sumter would be civil war, and they would be responsible for the consequences." [5]

Sullenly, the ex-president tasked Henry and a few other trusted friends with helping him to gather material for what he viewed as his final great challenge, a lengthy and exhaustive defense of the final angry weeks of his term of office that he would call *Mr. Buchanan's Administration on the Eve of Rebellion*. That Buchanan decided to focus on just the tail end of his presidency, rather than the entire four years, indicated that he knew how his actions, or lack thereof, in that period of time had been interpreted across the country, that in some quarters he was regarded as, at best, a hopeless boob, while in other quarters, nothing less than an outright traitor. Surely, there was a lot to explain.

Buchanan came to the work with reluctance, having hoped to find a writer who would do it for him. When several candidates for the job expressed interest but were in one way or another unable to be a part of the project, Buchanan decided to do it himself, writing what would become the first presidential memoir in history.

"I think it is now time that I should not merely defend, but triumphantly defend myself," Buchanan declared to his nephew, who was accustomed to his uncle's large view of himself. A thorough explanation of his presidential decisions and actions, thought Buchanan, would comprise "not merely a good defense, but a triumphant vindication of my administration." [6]

A triumphant vindication: those words, that phrase, would become Buchanan's mantra as he committed to paper arguments that, from a reader's point of view, would prove dreadfully tedious, all oddly written in the third person. "You advise me to keep quiet, which I shall do for the present," Buchanan told former Pennsylvania Congressman George Leiper in December 1861 as he steeped himself in his writing. "I shall bide my time, under a perfect conviction that my administration cannot only be satisfactorily defended, but triumphantly defended." [7]

Buchanan's quest for historical redemption was not really far-fetched. Ex-presidents, even those leaving office under a cloud of opprobrium, tend to be viewed more positively after a certain amount of time has passed, passions have cooled, and the limitations of successor presidents are revealed. John Adams and Thomas Jefferson, both of whom left office with large swaths of the American people despising them for their partisanship, would in their retirement years enjoy a national veneration as their real accomplishments in office were more fully studied and appreciated. In the 20th century Harry Truman and Gerald Ford experienced the same phenomenon.

But one of the problems for Buchanan was that any potential glow of warm recollection in the immediate years after his presidency was always dimmed by the real-life adventures of his former cabinet members who had gone over to the other side, continually reminding a war-intense North of what a safe haven for would-be secessionists his presidency really was.

Ex-Vice President John Breckinridge illustrated what Buchanan was up against. Serving briefly in the U.S. Senate after Buchanan returned to Pennsylvania, he opposed Lincoln's call for troops after the attack on Fort Sumter, was castigated in his native Kentucky for so doing, and finally joined the Confederacy where Jefferson Davis named him a brigadier general. He would prove an excellent commander in the field, eventually becoming the Confederacy's Secretary of War.

Ex-Treasury Secretary Howell Cobb served as both the president of the Confederate Provisional Congress and, by 1861, was a brigadier general in the Confederate Army. Ex-Interior Secretary Jacob Thompson was a lieutenant colonel in the same army and would be appointed by Davis as a secret envoy in a plot conspiring with Northern Peace Democrats against Lincoln in the 1864 presidential election. The redoubtable former Secretary of War John Floyd, meanwhile, became a Confederate brigadier general, serving Davis as disastrously as he had Buchanan, and becoming in the opinion of one historian "arguably the worst general the Confederacy would ever have." [8]

Even Buchanan's close social friends kept alive public associations with the Confederacy. Lawrence Keitt represented South Carolina in the Provisional Southern Congress and served as a colonel with the 20ᵗʰ South Carolina Volunteers before dying from a gunshot wound in Virginia. John Slidell was appointed by Davis as a special commissioner to France where he would unsuccessfully try to secure French recognition of the Confederacy.

Buchanan's long-time colleague Robert Tyler also joined the Confederacy, serving in a sub-cabinet post under Davis, as did his brother, John, Jr. Their father, ex-President Tyler, would be elected to the first Confederate Congress, but died in June 1862 before taking his seat.

Buchanan watched the travails of these former Cabinet members and friends from the safe distance of Wheatland as he continued to wrestle with his past. His struggle was only made more searing by the traumas of the present: William Jewett, a wealthy and eccentric Colorado gold miner, visited Buchanan at Wheatland and, in September 1862, expressed sympathy in the *New York Tribune* for the manner in which Buchanan was still negatively regarded by the general public nearly two years after his presidency. Jewett's salvo prompted an editorial in the same paper, charging that Buchanan was worse than two of history's most famous traitors, Judas and Benedict Arnold, adding that Buchanan was undoubtedly fearful of the "verdict which history must pronounce on the pusillanimous, perfidious close of his inglorious public career." One month later Buchanan was back in the news when he wrote a lengthy letter to the *Daily National Intelligencer* disputing charges made earlier in the same paper by Lieutenant General Winfield Scott that he had underused the military as a means of preventing secession. Buchanan's letter was defensive and self-serving: "After a careful retrospect, I can solemnly declare before God and my country that I cannot reproach myself with any act of commission or omission since the existing trouble commenced," he wrote, inspiring a wicked cartoon that appeared at the end of November in *Harper's Weekly* (which undoubtedly enjoyed a larger circulation than his letter to the *Intelligencer)* portraying Buchanan as an old woman proclaiming: "Oh! T'wasn't me, t'was [John] Floyd and them others that done it." In December Senator Garrett Davis of Kentucky offered a resolution stating that because Buchanan "from sympathy with the conspirators and their treasonable project," failed to prevent secession, he should "receive the censure and condemnation of the Senate and the American people." [9]

Davis's resolution went nowhere, but served as a reminder of how unforgiveable for many people Buchanan's presidency had become.

Buchanan hardly made things better (at least for himself) by failing to understand why he was so despised. He had always had a more than healthy respect for himself and out of that naturally concluded that once his book was released, and the American people truly understood things from his point of view, his popularity would be restored.

As a result he increasingly lived in a world of his own. Visiting Bedford Springs, Pennsylvania in the summer of 1863 he socialized with what he described as "several naughty secession girls from Baltimore." He told Harriet that he treated them "playfully," remarking "I love them so, that it would be impossible for me to be part from them, and that the shocking idea has never once entered my head of living in a separate confederacy with them." [10]

It was all, to Buchanan, a joke. But what the general public, in the middle of a war seeing the death of hundreds of thousands of young men would have thought of Buchanan happily flirting and kissing "secession girls" can only be imagined.

If tone deaf to such nuance, Buchanan nevertheless remained politically astute. He recognized, by 1864, that Lincoln had become a popular president and that the Democrats were hopelessly split in response. He observed that the party was irreconcilably divided between two factions: pro-war Democrats who wanted to see the war more swiftly executed and Peace Democrats (joined by former President Franklin Pierce) who doubted both the moral and Constitutional validity of the struggle and urged a settlement with the South. "The Democratic party is not yet prepared to act with power and unanimity," Buchanan judged. "They would, at the present moment, divide, should they attempt to erect a platform." [11]

Those divisions were clear at the summer 1864 Democratic convention in Chicago where Pierce's name was cheered by Peace Democrats and Buchanan's name was never mentioned at all. [12]

Trying to paper the party's differences over, the delegates approved a hybrid ticket. General George McClellan (relieved by Lincoln as general in chief of the Union armies for his unsatisfactory command) was nominated for president and Peace Democrat Congressman George Pendleton for vice-president.

Buchanan was unimpressed, remarking to his nephew: "The convention was neither more nor less a ratification meeting of the decree of the people." He added that although McClellan "would not have been my first choice," he could live with the ticket. [13]

It proved to be a surreal general election campaign. Andrew Johnson, the surly Democrat Senator from Tennessee, joined Lincoln as vice-president on the newly-constituted National Union Party ticket. McClellan, meanwhile, in accepting the Democratic nomination, disavowed the party's Peace Democrat-dominated platform—a move that Buchanan liked. "Peace, although a great blessing and greatly to be desired, would be too dearly purchased at the expense of the Union," Buchanan said of the platform, "and I, therefore, like the letter of General McClellan." [14]

After Lincoln won a triumphant re-election in November, Buchanan thought McClellan should count his blessings. "If one seriously asks himself the question, in what condition would the Democratic party be, with all the terrible difficulties and embarassments surrounding it, had it been successful, he will find grounds for consolation in defeat." [15]

The National Union Party victory, thought Buchanan, provided Lincoln with a splendid opportunity. "Now would be the time for conciliation on the part of Mr. Lincoln," Buchanan said, guessing that the Confederate government might be receptive to a "frank and manly offer" leading to a peaceful settlement of the war. [16]

The idea, of course, was naïve during a time when the Union was nearing all of its military goals and the geographic borders of the Confederacy were shrinking daily. When Union soldiers, in February 1865, pushed into Charleston, Buchanan claimed delight: "This city was the nest of all of our troubles," he told George Leiper. "For more than a quarter of a century the people were disunionists and during this whole period have been persistently engaged in inoculating the other slave States with their virus." [17]

A blur of events in the spring of 1865 saw the Confederacy collapse and Jefferson Davis, with a few remaining associates, fleeing Richmond. Lincoln visited the ransacked, defeated capital of the recent rebellion, cheered by one-time slaves and sitting for a moment in Davis's chair inside the former Confederate statehouse.

The war was over and Americans in Washington, Springfield and Lancaster, among a thousand other places, rejoiced. But Lincoln's assassination several days later revealed a darker spirit. Angry crowds gathered in Buffalo outside the home of former President Millard Fillmore, forgetting that he had been a war enthusiast. Noticing that the ex-President had failed to display either an American flag or black bunting to memorialize Lincoln's death, some in the crowd threw black paint on his front porch. In Concord, New Hampshire, more than 400 people taunted ex-President Pierce outside his residence, only retreating after he emerged and, noting that Secretary of State William Seward had also been brutally assaulted on the night of Lincoln's shooting, said that he felt a personal fondness for the "hearths and homes of the two most conspicuous families of the republic." [18]

Buchanan was spared such indignity at Wheatland, although some townspeople would have liked to repeat the antics played out at Buffalo and Concord. But when journalist William Flynn suggested to Buchanan that he "write a few lines on the death of Mr. Lincoln, which will soothe the bitter extremists of the Lincoln party against you and against your friends," Buchanan declined. [19]

"I deeply mourn his loss, from private feelings, but still more deeply for the sake of the country," Buchanan said of Lincoln's death. Yet he said he could not bring himself to offer consolation to either a shattered nation or the dead president's family. "I have weighed your suggestion with care, but regret to say that I cannot agree with you," Buchanan told Flynn, displaying only the latest evidence of his lack of imagination as a politician. "Such an act would be misrepresented." [20]

The country-wide cathartic outpouring of grief upon the death of Lincoln sobered Buchanan, who watched the slain president's funeral car go by as he sat silently in a buggy at the Lancaster depot. Hundreds of thousands and soon millions of people lined the tracks from Washington to New York to Albany to Cleveland to Columbus to Indianapolis to Chicago and finally Springfield. Poems and songs were written and performed in Lincoln's honor, lengthy eulogies delivered. Portraits of Lincoln appeared everywhere in schools, churches, restaurants and taverns.

By the time he was buried, nearly three weeks after the assassination, Lincoln the President had evolved into Lincoln the martyred saint who gave up everything for the Union cause, an iconic, towering figure who would in time surpass every other president in the hearts of his fellow Americans, winning also the scholarly praise of generations of historians who would come to regard him as the country's greatest president.

Whether he liked it or not, Buchanan would forever be linked to Lincoln in the national memory. The worst and the best president, fired through eternity by fate and fortune. There is no evidence that Buchanan ever disliked Lincoln. On the contrary he possessed a grudging admiration for him. But it was an admiration informed by the respect that one successful politician has for another. Although Buchanan made a point of publicly backing Lincoln in his conduct of the war, the other things that Lincoln stood for, his initial determination to contain slavery and subsequent successful move to end it altogether impressed Buchanan less. Despite the enormous social, cultural and political upheaval experienced by the country between 1861 and 1865, Buchanan remained essentially the same person he was before the war, forever lost in a pre-secession, pre-emancipation world where slavery was a permanent institution that no one could, or should, do anything about.

With Lincoln suddenly gone, Buchanan was, if anything, even more uneasy for the future of the country. He had no illusions that Andrew Johnson would be a successful president, regarding him as a bumptious sort far below the Southern social order once so elegantly personified by his close friends Jefferson Davis, Howell Cobb and John Slidell; all men who thrived in an aristocratic world that would always and forever be closed to the class-conscious Johnson. Just weeks after Lincoln was buried, when Johnson clumsily enraged Radical Republicans by abruptly implementing his own less severe version of Reconstruction, Buchanan wrote: "I begin to doubt seriously whether President Johnson will do, but still hope for the best." [21]

Democrats contemplated a return to power if Johnson abandoned the National Union Party and returned to the party of his heritage, the

Democratic Party. But Johnson saw more advantage in trying to keep the Republicans and conservative Democrats who made up Lincoln's winning coalition together, delegating William Seward in 1866 to use the newer party to promote the election of pro-Johnson candidates to Congress.

When delegates to the National Union Party met in the summer of that year in Philadelphia to lay the groundwork for what they hoped would be a triumphant mid-term election, Buchanan worried about the large array of issues confronting the gathering, which included suffrage for ex-slaves and benefits for Civil War veterans. He hoped instead that the delegates would confine themselves to the question of admitting to Congress senators and representatives from the Southern states. [22]

The delegates did indeed end up calling for a full Southern representation in Congress and seemed to get the National Union Party's fall 1866 campaign off to a good launch, but Johnson shortly destroyed nearly any chance for electoral success by embarking upon a much-publicized, disastrous tour of the Northern states. Throughout the journey Johnson was heckled, responding to his detractors in an increasingly vituperative manner that led some observers to question his mental stability. [23]

Buchanan was among the many who regarded Johnson's trip as counterproductive. "It would have been better had he rested on the issue as it was made by the Philadelphia convention," he judged. [24]

No one was surprised when Johnson's candidates were routed at the polls in the fall of 1866. But by then Buchanan was in hot water himself with the publication of his memoirs. *Mr. Buchanan's Administration on the Eve of the Rebellion* was, in the end, nothing more than a tired rehash of all the key rhetorical points he had made during his final months as president, written in a coldly bureaucratic manner. "He gives scarcely any new information and dwells upon old squabbles," the *New York Times* quoted one reviewer. A columnist for the *Christian Examiner* read the book and remarked: "Mr. Buchanan is the most amazing of fossils. Throughout this book no language is pathetic enough to express Mr. Buchanan's regrets for the sorrows and humiliations of the Democratic party, while of the tremendous tragedy of the war—its victories, its sacrifices, its heroes, its martyrs, and its wonderful and glorious results—there is from beginning to end, literally, not a word." The *New York Herald* was equally unenthusiastic: "His vindication is at best but a quibbling apology for his lack of earnest patriotism, his lack of moral courage and his secession proclivities." [25]

If the response to his memoirs was not proof enough that Buchanan's quest for vindication would go unsatisfied, a profile published in the best-selling book *Lives of the Presidents of the United States of America* in 1867 by author John Abbott signaled future academic condemnation.

"Mr. Buchanan was hopelessly bewildered," Abbot wrote of the ex-president's time in office. "He could not, with his long-avowed principles, consistently oppose the States-Rights party in their assumptions. As President of the United States, bound by his oath to faithfully administer the laws, he could not without perjury of the grossest kind, unite those endeavoring to overthrow the republic."

"He therefore," added Abbott, "did nothing." [26]

The profile went on to list the number of ways in which Buchanan had failed the country: his pro-Southern sympathies, support of the compromised Lecompton constitution, and unwillingness to stamp out the secession movement. Reading it, Buchanan feigned indifference: "This is a repetition and concentration of all the slanders which were in circulation against myself during the first years of the war." [27]

He could not know, but perhaps at least now surmised, that there would be more of this sort of thing to come, a verdict that would eventually see Buchanan consistently listed at the very bottom of every leadership and performance ranking compiled by scholars in the generations to come. [28]

Increasingly closing himself off from the world around him, Buchanan received some joy in his private life when Harriett Lane married Baltimore businessman Henry Johnston. When the couple gave birth to their first child, a boy, Buchanan warned Harriett, perhaps reflecting on his own childhood: "Be not too indulgent, nor make him too much of an idol." [29]

He was 77 years old in the spring of 1868 and felt it. After taking a tumble on the front steps of his Wheatland home, he reported to his son-in-law: "My hand is still so weak and swollen that I cannot carve, and it is but a few days since I ceased to have the meat on my plate cut up for me. And to add to all of this, my left eye is now as black as if I have been fighting with shillelahs at Donnybrook Fair." [30]

He rallied for a while before, in May, catching a cold from which he never recovered. On May 31, still dreadfully trying to make his point, he told Lancaster attorney Hiram Swarr: "I have always felt and still feel that I discharged every public duty imposed on me conscientiously. I have no regret for any public act of my life, and history will vindicate my memory." [31]

He died the next morning, leaving behind a will that generously gave Wheatland to Harriet and Henry Johnston, not to mention various sums of money to an assortment of relatives and friends.

In Washington, President Johnson wondered if he should do more than just send out a standard memorial release hailing a fallen leader, asking Secretary of the Navy Gideon Welles if a visit to Lancaster might be in order. "The suggestion did not strike me with favor, and I expect I showed my feelings in my looks," Welles later confided to his diary. When it became apparent that Johnson thought better of the idea, Welles wrote: "There have been Presidents whose obsequies I would have gone farther than Lancaster to have attended, but there is, on my part, no heartfelt grief nor reverence for James Buchanan which calls for this effort; his feeble and erring Administration was calamitous to the country." [32]

Meanwhile in Lancaster local residents as well as visiting delegations of public officials from New York, Philadelphia and Baltimore, provided their own public response to Buchanan's passing. As church bells tolled, several thousand people silently lined the streets of the city while a hearse bearing Buchanan's coffin was transported from Wheatland to the nearby Woodward Hill Cemetery. The coffin was soon bathed in wreathes of ivy and laurel.

Obituary notices appearing in newspapers across the country on and shortly after the day of Buchanan's funeral were surprisingly harsh. The New Orleans *Daily Picayune* said Buchanan's temperament was "cold and his manners, although habitually well-bred, for he was even stately in his courtesies, attracted no warmth of affection." The *Cincinnati Daily Gazette* said of his presidency: "Imbecility—to use no harsher term—was enthroned at the White House...and the great mass of the Northern people were alike unable to inspire the Chief Magistrate with patriotism or even with an appearance of energy." The always-critical *Chicago Tribune* was bitter to the end: "He never had a guiding principle. During his fifty years of public life there was no policy that he did not both oppose and support. More than half the years of his public life were devoted to intrigue for his elevation to the Presidency. This desolate old man has gone to his grave. No son or daughter is doomed to acknowledge an ancestry from him." [33]

It was a sign of how truly enduring the general condemnation of Buchanan was that on the day before his funeral two routine Congressional resolutions related to his passing were unexpectedly subject to debate. The first resolution, by Pennsylvania Democrat Congressman George Woodward, an old Buchanan friend, benignly paid tribute to the "purity of his private character, the ability and patriotic motives which illustrated his long career of public service, and the dignity which marked the retirement of the latter years of his life."

The second resolution asked merely that a committee be formed to attend Buchanan's funeral.

Both of the resolutions were standard Congressional responses to the death of a head of state. But John Farnsworth was disgusted. "I suggest to the gentleman from Pennsylvania that he modify those resolutions a little," the Illinois Republican said to Woodward.

Farnsworth, who had served as a Union brigadier general in the Civil War, maintained that Woodward could not "expect to get a unanimous vote of the House commending the 'patriotic motives' which animated Mr. Buchanan at all times in his public career. For one, I certainly cannot vote ay."

"Neither can I," chimed in Representative James Mullins, who risked his life during the war as a Tennessee Unionist.

Continued Farnsworth: "I am willing the grave shall bury the man's faults, and to speak only well of him now that he is dead. But when the gentlemen asks me to vote that the motives of Mr. Buchanan were always patriotic and pure, he asks me to vote what I believe to be a falsehood, and I cannot do it."

Not to be outdone, Buchanan's ancient foe Thaddeus Stevens (who himself would be dead at the age of 76 in another two months), asked Woodward to "strike out the words 'the ability and patriotic motives which illustrated his long career of public service,' and let the resolution be adopted without it."

Woodward refused. "If the House will strike out the general allusion to the patriotic motives of Mr. Buchanan they can do so, but I cannot consent to it myself," he protested.

House members then took up a motion to "lay the resolutions on the table." By an overwhelming vote of 74 to 46 that motion was agreed to.

Later in the afternoon the members decided to take the matter back up. On an 80 to 16 vote, indicating that negotiations on the matter had taken place off the House floor, they agreed to a substantially more watered-down resolution that said nothing about Buchanan being a patriot, but instead meaninglessly sent him off into history simply as "one who has held such imminent public station." [34]

Sources

PREFACE NOTES

[1] Virginia Clay-Clopton, *A Belle of the Fifties—Memoirs of Mrs. Clay of Alabama* (Tuscaloosa: University of Alabama Press, 1999), 119; The Parker residence was at 375 North C Street, see *Boyd's Washington and Georgetown Directory 1860* (Washington: Taylor and Maury, 1860), 122.

[2] John Bassett Moore, *Works of James Buchanan, Volume XI, 1860-1868* (New York: Antiquarian Press, 1960), 7-43; John W. Quist and Michael J. Birkner, *James Buchanan and the Coming of the Civil War* (Gainesville: University Press of Florida, 2013), 170.

[3] "The President and the Crisis," *New York Times*, 5 December 1860, p.1.

[4] "News and Gossip from Washington," *Springfield Daily Republican*, 8 December 1860, p.4; Glyndon G. Van Deusen, *William Henry Seward* (New York: Oxford University Press, 1967), 244.

[5] Sara Agnes Pryor, *My Day—Reminiscences of a Long Life* (New York: Macmillan Company, 1909), 153-54.

[6] Among the books that have repeated the erroneous tale: Nancy Scott Anderson and Dwight Anderson, *The Generals: Ulysses S. Grant and Robert E. Lee* (New York: Random House, 1994), 175; Bruce Catton, *The Coming Fury—Volume One* (New York: Doubleday and Company, 1961), 140; Walter Brian Cisco, *Wade Hampton: Confederate Warrior, Conservative Statesman* (Washington: Brassey's, 2005), 54; Chris DeRose, *The Presidents' War—Six American Presidents and the Civil War That Divided Them* (Guilford, Connecticut: Lyons Press, 2014), 120-21; Otto Eisenschiml, *The Civil War: An American Iliad* (New York: Mallard Press, 1991), 3; Ernest B. Ferguson, *Freedom Rising—Washington in the Civil War* (New York: Vintage Books, 2004) 17-18; Doris Kearns Goodwin, *Team of Rivals—The Political Genius of Abraham Lincoln* (New York: Simon & Schuster, 2005), 294; Katherine Macbeth Jones, *Ladies of Richmond: Confederate Capital* (Richmond: Bobbs-Merrill Publishing, 1962), 27; C. Brian Kelly, *Best Little Stories from the Civil War* (Nashville: Cumberland House, 1998), 8; Maury

Klein, *Days of Defiance: Sumter, Secession and the Coming of the Civil War* (New York: Vintage Books, 1999), 139; Philip Shriver Klein, *President Buchanan* (Newtown, Connecticut: American Political Biography Press, 2010), 375; Margaret Leech, *Reveille in Washington, 1860-1865* (Alexandria: Time-Life Books, 1980), 26; George Fort Milton, *The Eve of the Conflict: Stephen A. Douglas and the Needless War* (New York: Octagon Books, 1963), 511; William Seale, *The President's House—A History, Volume One* (Washington: White House Historical Association, 1986), 358; Elbert B. Smith, *Presidency of James Buchanan* (Lawrence: University of Kansas Press, 1975), 144; Hudson Strode, *Jefferson Davis: An American Patriot: 1808-1861* (New York: Harcourt Brace and Company, 1955), 37; Walter Sullivan, *The War the Women Lived* (Nashville: J.S.Sanders and Company, 1995), 16; Philip Van Doren Stern, *Prologue to Sumter: The Beginnings of the Civil from John Brown to the Surrender of Fort Sumter, Woven Into a Continuous Narrative* (Greenwich: Fawcett Publications, 1961), 180; John C. Waugh, *Surviving the Confederacy: Rebellion, Ruin and Recovery—Roger and Sara Pryor During the Civil War* (New York: Harcourt, Incorporated, 2002), 1-2; Richard Wheeler, *A Rising Thunder: From Lincoln's Election to the Battle of Bull Run: An Eyewitness History* (Scarborough: Harper Collins Canada, 1995), 26; Agatha Young and Agnes Brooks Young, *The Women and the Crisis: Women of the North in the Civil War Years* (New York: McDowell, Obolensky, Incorporated, 1959), 37.

[7]   The mistake is also repeated in the paper's anniversary coverage of the secession vote in 1960. Jamie Malanowski, "The Government Disintegrates," *New York Times*, 19 December 2010, opinionator.blogs.nytimes.com; accessed 28 April 2014; "That Fateful Day in South Carolina," *New York Times*, 18 December 1960, p.60.

[8]   Eric H. Walther, *The Fire-Eaters* (Baton Rouge: Louisiana State University Press, 1992), 173.

[9]   *Journal of the Convention of the People* (Columbia: R. W. Gibbs, 1862), 37-49.

[10]   "A Brilliant Wedding," *Washington Evening Star,* 2 May 1860, p.3.

[11]   Ibid.

[12]   "Marriages," *Daily National Intelligencer*, 5 May 1860, p.1; "Marriage in High Life," *Harper's Weekly*, 12 May 1860, p.295; "From Washington—A Marriage in Fashionable Life," *New York Times*, 2 May 1860, p.5; "News From Washington," *New York Herald*, 3 May 1860, p.3.

[13]   Mary Elizabeth Parker Peabody to Amanda Bouligny, 16 October 1860, Bouligny-Ganin Family Papers, MSS 361, Folder Number 16, Williams Research Center, Historic New Orleans Collection.

[14]   Clay-Clopton, *A Belle of the Fifties*, 47.

[15]   Ibid.

[16]   Waugh, *Surviving the Confederacy* (New York: Harcourt, Incorporated, 2002), 324-333.

[17]   Ibid., 338-39.

[18]   "Charleston Convention," *New York Times*, 1 May 1860, p.1; "The Charleston Convention," *New York Herald*, 1 May 1860, p.1.

CHAPTER ONE NOTES

[1]   David Black, *The King of Fifth Avenue—The Fortunes of August Belmont* (New York: Dial Press, 1981), 77; "The Weather at Washington—The President's Levee," *Springfield Daily Republican*, 26 January 1859, p.2; "Personal," *Harper's Weekly*, 28 November 1857, p.758.

[2]   Mary Black Clayton, *Reminiscences of Jeremiah Black* (St. Louis: Christian Publishing Company, 1887), 106-07.

[3]   Despite the dirty handkerchief incident, Hawthorne seemed to like Buchanan, noting that he "takes his wine like a true man, loves a good cigar, and is doubtless as honest as nine diplomats out of ten." James O' Donald May, *Mr. Hawthorne Goes to England—The Adventures of a Reluctant Consul* (Burlington: New Forest Leaves, 1981), 113, 116.

[4]   Frank Blair to Martin Van Buren, 13 February 1860, Martin Van Buren Papers, Reel 34, Series 2.

[5]   "Notabilities at Washington," *Boston Saturday Evening Gazette*, 20 March 1858, p.1.

[6]   George Ticknor Curtis, *Life of James Buchanan—Fifteenth President of the United States, Volume II* (New York: Harper & Brothers, 1883), 16-17.

[7]   David Dixon Porter, *Incidences and Anecdotes of the Civil War* (New York: D. Appleton & Company, 1885), 11.

[8]   James Buchanan to Harriet Lane, 8 January 1849, Papers of James Buchanan and Harriet L. Johnston, Reel 1; Thomas Balcerski, "Harriet Rebecca Lane Johnston," academia.edu, accessed 9 May 2014.

[9]   Stevens, at 68, could not have been more different from Buchanan: blunt, humorous, eloquent, dedicated to the cause of the abolitionists, Stevens lived with an African American woman who may have been his partner and was actively involved in the underground railroad system providing a route to freedom for escaped slaves. "The War in the Enemy's Country," *New York Times*, 4 October 1856, p.2; Thaddeus Stevens to Edward McPherson, 19 December 1860, Thaddeus Stevens to Jeremiah Brown, No Date, 1847, both Thaddeus Stevens Papers, Series 1, Roll1; John W. Quist and Michael K. Birkner, *James Buchanan and the Coming of the Civil War* (Gainesville: University Press of Florida, 2013), 136.

10   William Salter, *James W. Grimes—Governor of Iowa and U.S. Senator, 1854-1869* (New York: Appleton and Company, 1876), 360.

11   Allan Nevins, *The Emergence of Lincoln, Volume II—Prologue to Civil War, 1859-1861* (New York: Charles Scribner's Sons, 1950), 360.

12   Beverly Wilson Palmer, *The Selected Letters of Charles Sumner, Volume Two* (Boston: Northeastern University Press, 1990), 38-40.

13   Talk of a coup in Washington, with or without Buchanan's participation, was widespread in the winter of 1860-1861. Ohio Representative James Ashley suggested to Ohio Governor Salmon Chase that the nation's capital might soon be "in the possession of Maryland and Virginia under the jurisdiction of a foreign government (meaning a Southern government) and that Lincoln's inauguration would be resisted by force." Wrote Massachusetts Congressman Charles Francis Adams, Sr.: "The people of Washington are grimly convinced that there is to be an attack on Washington by the Southerns or else a slave insurrection, and in either case or in any contingency they feel sure of being ruined and murdered." Benjamin Butler, in late 1860 a Massachusetts legislator, later claimed to have been led to a wooden shed near the edge of Georgetown by an unidentified Washington Democrat where he observed up to 100 men drilling. Butler asked if the men were practicing in order to escort Lincoln upon his arrival in the nation's capital. The man supposedly replied "Yes, they may escort Lincoln, but not in the direction of the White House." It is not known if Butler ever reported the incident, but he says he saw the man one more time: "It was in the old Capitol Prison," he said. Edward P. Miller, Jr., *Lincoln's Abolitionist General—The Biography of David Hunter* (Columbia: University of South Carolina Press, 1997), 50-51; David Hunter to Abraham Lincoln, 18 December 1860, Papers of Abraham Lincoln, Reel 12; James Ashley to Salmon Chase, 18 December 1860, Salmon P. Chase Papers, Reel 14; Charles Francis Adams, Sr., to Charles Francis Adams, Jr., 18 December 1860, The Adams Papers, Reel 550; Benjamin F. Butler, *Butler's Book* (Boston: A.M. Thayer and Company, 1892), 100.

14   The paper's notion, as the authors John Tebbel and Sarah Miles write, that "God was on its side," not only informed the *Chicago Tribiune's* treatment of Buchanan, but also its coverage of the Democratic Party in general and life in Washington, a city it regarded, until Lincoln became president, as a moral cesspool. John Tebbel and Sarah Miles Watts, *The Press and the Presidency—From George Washington to Ronald Reagan* (New York: Oxford University Press, 1985), 173; Richard Norton Smith, *The Colonel—The Life and the Legend of Robert R. McCormick, 1880-1955* (Evanston: Northwest University Press, 1997), 18; "Our Washington Letter," *Chicago Tribune*, 20 December 1860, p.1; "The Government," *Daily Constitutionalist*, 20 December 1860, p.2.

15 "The President's Defense," *New York Times*, 20 December 1860, p.1; "The President in His Own Defense," *New York Times*, 20 December 1860, p. 4; "The President's Letter to Mr. Conkle," *New York Times*, 22 December 1860, p. 4; "The Conkle Letter Again," *New York Times*, 24 December 1860, p. 4.

16 "The Bearings of American Disunion," *Economist*, 12 January 1861, p.30.

17 John B. Edmunds, Jr., *Francis W. Pickens and the Politics of Destruction* (Chapel Hill: University of North Carolina Press, 1986), 153-55; Philip Shriver Klein, *President James Buchanan—A Biography* (Newtown, Connecticut: American Political Biography Press, 2010), 375; "Narrative and Letter of William Henry Trescot, concerning the Negotiations between South Carolina and President Buchanan in December, 1860," *American Historical Review*, Volume XIII, Number 3, April 1908, p. 540.

18 Throughout his presidency, Buchanan went to great lengths to keep Bennett happy, which meant regularly tipping off the publisher on imminent administration addresses and decisions. Buchanan may have learned from the example of Franklin Pierce what could happen when Bennett was displeased. Hoping to be named Ambassador to France by then-President Pierce, Bennett became embittered when Pierce not only gave that post to another person, but did not even bother to reply to Bennett's letter asking for the appointment. Shortly afterwards, Bennett's paper began to slam Pierce regularly on both its editorial and news pages, calling him "Poor Pierce." Lincoln, undoubtedly aware of the *New York Herald*'s treatment of Pierce, sent an emissary to New York shortly after receiving the 1860 Republican nomination who promised Bennett unprecedented White House access if he would go easy on Lincoln during the general election campaign. Bennett proved amenable to the idea, and did indeed soft-pedal criticism of Lincoln in the fall of 1860. John Bassett Moore, *The Works of James Buchanan—Volume XI, 1860-1868* (New York: Antiquarian Press, 1960), 69-70; James Gordon Bennett to Franklin Pierce, 15 December 1852, Franklin Pierce Papers, Series 2, Reel 1; Joseph Medill to Abraham Lincoln, 5 July 1860, Abraham Lincoln Papers, Reel 7.

19 The official ordinance voted on by the members of the South Carolina secession convention repealed the 1788 ordinance bringing the state into the Union, noting that that union "Now subsisting between South Carolina and the other states, under the name of the 'United States of America,' is hereby dissolved." The secession vote was 169 to 0. *Congressional Globe—36th Congress, 2nd Session* (Washington: John C. Rives, 1861), 169; *Journal of the Convention of the People* (Columbia: R.W. Gibbes, 1862), 42-43.

20 "Our Washington Dispatches," *New York Times*, 21 December 1860, p.1.

21 Ibid.

22 Chester G. Hearn, *Admiral David Dixon Porter—The Civil War Years* (Annapolis: Naval Institute Press, 1996), 34-35; Richard S. West, Jr., *The*

Second Admiral—A Life of David Dixon Porter, 1813-1891 (New York: Coward-McCann, 1937), 100-01; Howard K. Beale, *Diary of Gideon Welles, Volume II, April 1, 1864-December 31, 1868* (New York: W. W. Norton & Company, 1960), 255-56; Ishbel Ross, *First Lady of the South—The Life of Mrs. Jefferson Davis* (New York: Harper & Brothers, 1958), 72.

23   Joan E. Cashin, *First Lady of the Confederacy—Varina Davis's Civil War* (Cambridge: Belknap Press, 2006), 92-93; Lynda Lasswell Crist, *Papers of Jefferson Davis, Volume 6, 1856-1860* (Baton Rouge: Louisiana State University, 1989), 373; Moore, *Works of James Buchanan—Volume XI, 1860-1868*, 71-72.

24   Moore, *Works of James Buchanan, Volume XI, 1860-1868*, 71-72.

25   "Narrative and Letter of William Henry Trescot," p.541; "Washington Gossip," *Charleston Mercury*, 25 December 1860, p.4.

CHAPTER TWO NOTES

1   George Ticknor Curtis, *Life of James Buchanan, Volume I* (New York: Harper & Brothers, 1883), 2; Jean H. Baker, *James Buchanan* (New York: Times Books, 2004), 11.

2   Philip Shriver Klein, *President James Buchanan—A Biography* (Falls Creek: Pennsylvania State University Press, 1962), 9.

3   Ibid.

4   Curtis, *Life of James Buchanan, Volume I*, 7; Baker, *James Buchanan*, 13-14.

5   John Bassett Moore, *Works of James Buchanan, Volume II, 1830-1836* (New York: Antiquarian Press, 1960), 182.

6   Mark Hatfield, *Vice-Presidents of the United States, 1789-1993* (Washington: U.S. Government Printing Office, 1997), 181-87; John M. Martin, "William R. King: Jacksonian Senator," *Alabama Review*, Volume XVIII, Number 4, October 1965, 243-67; "Death of Vice-President King," *Mobile Daily Register*, 20 April 1853, p.2.

7   Historian/sociologist Jim Loewen contends that Buchanan was a homosexual. "There can be no doubt that James Buchanan was gay before, during and after his four years in the White House. Moreover, the nation knew it, too—he was not that far into the closet. Today I know of no historian who has studied the matter and thinks Buchanan was heterosexual." Loewen is known as a "turning history upside down" historian, and so wants Buchanan to be gay on the premise that conventional history assumes all of the U.S. presidents have been straight. Buchanan biographer Jean Baker, I think, is closer to the mark when she writes "The best speculation about the sexuality of the non-shaving Buchanan, who in his portraits has the eunichlike, endomorphic features of body and face, as well as the low hairline characteristics of asexual men with low levels of testosterone, is that he had little interest in sex." Contemporary opinion, contrary

to Loewen's undocumented assertions, accepted that Buchanan was a bachelor *and* straight. The one-time German revolutionary Fredrich Hecker claimed before a Republican gathering in the fall of 1856 that the Romans "denied to bachelors the highest honors of the Republic," not because they suspected homosexuality, but because they thought such men would be vulnerable to the wiles of presumably unscrupulous women. "If Franklin Pierce had given away so much to the slaveholders merely from the influence of the men who surrounded him, what concessions might not be expected from a bachelor if all the arts and arms of women were brought to bear upon him?" Hecker asked in reference to Buchanan. "President Buchanan in North Carolina," *Richmond Enquirer,* 7 June 1859, p 2; Jim Loewen, "Our Real First Gay President," 14 May 2012, salon. com; Baker, *James Buchanan*, 26; "German Republican Meeting," *New York Tribune,* 10 October 1856, p.1.

8   Klein, *President James Buchanan*, 56.

9   Harold D. Moser, *The Papers of Andrew Jackson, Volume VI, 1825-1828* (Knoxville: University of Tennessee Press, 2002), 359-60.

10   Daniel Webster to Henry Clay, 24 July 1827 and 22 August 1827, Daniel Webster Papers, Reel 6.

11   Moser, *The Papers of Andrew Jackson, Volume VI, 1825-1828*, 373-74; Robert Remini, *Henry Clay—Statesman for the Union* (New York: W.W. Norton & Company, 1991), 319.

12   Robert Remini, *Andrew Jackson and the Course of American Freedom* (New York: Harper & Row, 1981), 88; Merrill D. Peterson, *The Great Triumvarite—Webster, Clay and Calhoun* (New York: Oxford University press, 1987), 148; "Mr. Clay and Mr. Buchanan," *Mobile Daily Register,* 20 June 1856, p. 2.

13   Moore, *Works of James Buchanan, Volume II, 1830-1836*, 199.

14   Robert Remini, *Andrew Jackson and the Course of American Democracy, 1833-1845* (Baltimore: Johns Hopkins University Press, 1984), 397.

15   Elaine K. Swift, *The Making of an American Senate—Reconstitutive Change in Congress, 1787-1841* (Ann Arbor: University of Michigan Press, 1996), 163.

16   Remini, *Henry Clay—Statesman for the Union*, 476-77.

17   Ibid.

18   Klein, *President James Buchanan*, 142; Baker, *James Buchanan*, 32-38.

19   James Buchanan to James K. Polk, 14 September 1847, James K. Polk Papers, Reel 48; Mark E. Byrnes, *James K. Polk--A Biographical Companion* (Santa Barbara: ABC-CLIO, Inc., 2001), 22; Walter R. Borneman, *Polk—The Man Who Transformed the Presidency and America* (New York: Random House, 2009), 335.

20   Moore, *Works of James Buchanan, Volume II, 1830-1836*, 219.

21   John Bassett Moore, *Works of James Buchanan, Volume VIII, 1848-1853* (New York: Antiquarian Press, 1960), 66.

22   Robert Carlson notes that as early as 1832 when some supporters thought Buchanan might make for a good running mate with President Jackson, Buchanan had already perfected a routine in response to possible drafts that he would use whenever he felt uncertain about his prospects. First he would "Thank his friends for their interest and deny any previous knowledge of what was being planned, then refuse the draft because of well-laid plans for an immediate retirement from public office, next attribute all past successes to his constituency, and finally humbly admit that the people had already given him more than he rightfully deserved." Robert Carlson, "James Buchanan and Public Office: An Appraisal," *Pennsylvania Magazine of History and Biography*, Number Three, Volume LXXXI, July 1957, 256, 261.

23   Ibid., 265.

24   "Letters of Presidents and Ladies of the White House," *Pennsylvania Magazine of History and Biography*, Number 1, Volume XXVI, January 1902, 121-23.

25   John Bassett, *Works of James Buchanan, Volume VIII, 1848-1853* (Philadelphia: J.B. Lippincott Company, 1904), 453.

26   Buchanan was often given to overstatement, particularly when it concerned his career fortunes. But on his chances for national office in the wake of Pierce's 1852 victory he was being realistic. If Pierce, 48 years old at the time of his inaugural, proved a successful president, he would be re-elected in 1856. That would mean that Buchanan would not have another chance to make a presidential campaign until 1860, when he would be 69 years old. Moore, *Works of James Buchanan, Volume VIII, 1848-1853*, 491.

27   What most bothered critics of the manifesto was not its militaristic air, but the suspicion that Southern political leaders wanted to get Cuba in order to extend the boundaries of slavery. "The United States had better dismiss the idea of aggregating the Star of Cuba to their galaxy," Hungarian freedom fighter Louis Kossuth observed in the wake of the manifesto's release. "They will not get Cuba, at least not as long as slavery is not perfectly abolished throughout the United States." Author Conrad Black argues that Buchanan's association with the manifesto wasn't a total loser for him politically: "Buchanan, the ne plus ultra and cul-de-sac of doughface moral enfeeblement and amoral appeasement of whatever quarter complained loudest, gained support in the South, enhancing his prospects as a presidential nominee, which had narrowly been deniend him in 1852." James Buchanan to William Marcy, 22 September 1854, 6 October 1854, 8 October 1854, 3 November 1854, *Dispatches From the United States Minister to Great Britain, Volume 66, May 5, 1854 to February 2, 1855*, Microfilm Roll 62; Klein, *President James Buchanan*, 240; Amos Aschbach Etlinger, *The Mission to Spain of Pierre Soule* (New York: Oxford University Press, 1932), 342-48; Roy Franklin Nichols, *Franklin Pierce—Young Hickory of the Granite Hills* (Philadelphia: University of Philadelphia Press, 1958), 358-59;

"The Ostend Conference," *National Era*, 15 March 1855, p.42; "More of the Ostend Papers," *New York Times*, 17 March 1855, p.1; "Letters from L. Kossuth," *New York Times*, 19 March 1855, p.4; Conrad Black, *Flight of the Eagle— The Grand Strategies That Brought America from Colonial Dependence to World Leadership* (New York: Encounter Books, 2013), 207.

[28] Carlson, "James Buchanan and Public Office," 273; James Buchanan to Harriet Lane, 9 November 1855, Papers of James Buchanan and Harriet L. Johnston, Reel 2.

[29] "The Presidency," *New York Times*, 25 April 1856, p.1.

[30] Upon leaving New York, Buchanan stopped off to speak to a gathering of local merchants in Philadelphia where he presciently expanded on his view that the American experiment would eventually serve as an inspiration to democratic movements across the globe. "We are no propagandists, except by our example," he said, "and yet our example is destined in future time to carry free and liberal institutions over the face of the whole earth—peacefully, quietly, without danger, and with the approbation of the wise and virtuous in every clime." "The Presidency," *New York Times*, 25 April 1856, p.1; "Mr. Buchanan at Philadelphia," *Daily National Intelligencer*, 28 April 1856, p. 3.

[31] "The Presidential Canvas," *New York Herald*, 4 June 1856, p.1; "From Cincinnati," *New York Tribune*, 6 June 1856, p.6.

[32] Thomas Chaffin, *Pathfinder—John Charles Fremont and the Course of American Empire* (New York: Hill and Wang, 2002), 439-40; "Col. Fremont's Letter of Acceptance," *Baltimore Sun*, 10 July 1856, p. 1.

[33] "Mr. Buchanan's Letter of Acceptance," *Baltimore Sun*, 20 June 1856, p.1.

[34] On September 29, Breckinridge reported to Buchanan: "It is a melancholy truth, from all I hear, that Louisville is controlled by mob law." Several weeks later Breckinridge contemplated heading up a corps of as many as 200 men to stand guard at the polls there. "The image, well-publicized and managed, of a candidate for the vice-presidency standing cudgel in hand, with blooded brow, bravely defending with his life the rights of free men to vote as they chose, would be political dynamite," noted Breckinridge biographer William C. Davis. Despite threats of violence from both the Know Nothings and Democrats in Louisville, the election passed without significant incident, allowing Breckinridge to stay home in Lexington. John Breckinridge to James Buchanan, 29 September, 1856, Historical Society of Pennsylvania; William C. Davis, *Breckinridge: Statesman, Solider and Symbol* (Baton Rouge: Louisiana State University, 1974), 162-63.

[35] Buchanan did have some support in the arts: Edwin Forrest, the day's greatest Shakespearean, contributed $250 ($2,500 in today's terms) to the Democratic effort in Pennsylvania. James Rawley, "Financing the Fremont Campaign," *Pennsylvania Magazine of History and Biography*, Number 1, Volume LXXV, January 1951, 25-35; James Rees, *The Life of Edwin Forrest: With Reminiscences*

and Personal Recollections (Philadelphia: T.B. Peterson & Brothers, 1874), 307-08.

[36]   *The Covode Investigation* (Washington: Government Printing Office, 1860), 22-28.

[37]   Ibid.

[38]   Buchanan had for some years been close to both Fremont and his wife, Jessie Benton. When Fremont was 28 years old and wanted to marry the 17 year-old Jessie, he met with the vehement opposition of the man who would eventually become his father-in-law, Missouri Senator Thomas Hart Benton. According to a story that Benton himself later related, a distraught Fremont at one point asked Buchanan how a man could steal an underage girl and marry her. Supposedly Buchanan replied that the solution was to let the girl steal the man. The story is impossible to pin down, but given Buchanan's romantic passivity, it bears a ring of truth. Several years later, Buchanan, as Secretary of State, unsuccessfully urged President Polk to commute Fremont's sentence after he had been court-martialed during his service as a Lieutenant Colonel in the U.S. Army on charges of insubordination and mutiny. After Fremont resigned from the Army in protest of his conviction Buchanan was startled to learn that Jessie planned to join her husband on a long return trip to California, asking the young mother "You have two children, you have been very ill this past year. Do you think you would be a help or a burden for your husband?" Jessie ignored Buchanan's concerns and joined her husband on what must have been a difficult journey. Leslie H. Southwick, while lauding Fremont's integrity and intelligence, contends that as a leader he was a disaster: "Fremont was impetuous, not reflective, never showed an ability to work well with others. Time and again the 'Pathfinder' was impractical, and his headstrong actions resulted in either glory or a disaster." Says Fremont biographer Perol Egan of Fremont's 1856 campaign: "He was taken from rally to rally in much the same manner as a show horse making the circuit of county fairs. All of this was without meaning and pointless to him. He was accustomed to mapping out campaigns which had definite objectives. If the wind blew, it was real and carried the feel of the seasons. But in this political campaign, nothing that blew his way appeared to be touched with reality." To make things more discomfiting for the Fremont effort was a bid by the Buchanan forces to promote Millard Fillmore in the Eastern seaboard states where Fremont was the strongest, in order to decrease the Republican's total. From all accounts, such political maneuvering, while second nature to Buchanan, was nothing less than bewildering to Fremont. William Nisbet Chambers, *Old Bullion Benton--Senator from the New West* (Boston: Little, Brown and Company, 1956), 255; Mary Lee Spence and Donald Jackson, *The Expeditions of John Charles Fremont, Volume 2* (Urbana: University of Illinois Press, 1973), 292-94, 362-63, 477-83; Sally Denton, *Passion and Principle—John and Jessie Fremont—the Couple*

Whose Power, Politics and Love Shaped Nineteenth-Century America (New York: Bloombury, 2007), 153-54; Leslie H. Southwick, *Presidential Also-Rans and Running Mates, 1788-1980* (Jefferson, North Carolina: McFarland & Company, Inc., 1984), 218-24; Perol Eagan, *Fremont—Explorer for a Restless Nation* (New York: Doubleday and Company, 1977), 507-08; *The Conspiracy of Fillmore Leaders* (New York: H.F. Snowden, 1856), 1-3.

[39] Buchanan's friend Dan Sickles proved one bright spot for New York Democrats on election night, winning a Congressional seat in the Third District. It was a race that Buchanan, despite Sickles' pleas for help, declined to become involved in, indicating that he might have been put off by the way Sickles had ensnarled him in the Ostend Manifesto controversy. Buchanan's decision was a wise one: two factions of Democrats were running candidates in the race, both pledged to supporting a Buchanan presidency. Just days before the balloting, Hiram Walbridge, a young and wealthy businessman, dramatically announced he was withdrawing from the race, thereby ensuring victory for Sickles. In return Sickles pledged in writing to Walbridge not to run for re-election in 1858, a pledge he would subsequently break. Jerome Mushkat, *Fernando Wood—A Political Biography* (Kent: Kent State University Press, 1990), 54-58; Jerome Mushkat, *Tammany Hall—The Evolution of a Political Machine* (Syracuse: Syracuse University Press, 1971), 286; "City Politics," *New York Herald*, 17 October 1856, p.1; "The Democracy Uniting," *New York Herald*, 30 October 1856, p.1.

[40] Buchanan is one of the few presidential candidates in history to have won the White House while losing pivotal Ohio. Of the 53 presidential elections between 1804 and 2012, only Martin Van Buren in 1836, James Knox Polk in 1844, Zachary Taylor in 1848, Grover Cleveland in 1884, Franklin Roosevelt in 1944 and John Kennedy in 1960 have managed the same feat. John Bassett Moore, *Works of James Buchanan, Volume X, 1856-1860* (New York: Antiquarian Press, 1960), 98-99.

[41] Ibid.

CHAPTER THREE NOTES

[1] "The Latest News," *New York Herald*, 28 January 1857, p.4; "Arrival of the President-Elect," *Washington Daily Union*, 28 January 1857, p. 2.

[2] "The Latest News," *New York Herald*, 29 January 1857, p.4; "Funeral Obsequies of a National Legislator," *New York Herald*, 2 February 1857, p.4; "The Funeral Obsequies at the Capitol," *Washington Daily Union*, 30 January 1857, p. 2; "Investigating Committee—Toombs—Brooks Funeral," *New York Tribune*, 2 February 1857.

3   Virginia Clay-Clopton, *A Belle of the Fifties—Memoirs of Mrs. Clay of Alabama* (Tuscaloosa: University of Alabama Press, 1999), 114.

4   James Bassett Moore, *The Works of James Buchanan, Volume X, 1856-1860* (New York: Antiquarian Press, 1960), 105-08; Ethan Greenberg, *Dred Scott and the Dangers of a Political Court* (Lanham: Rowman & Littlefield Publishers, 2010), 65-77.

5   Historian Paul Finkelman contends that it is "extremely unlikely that Chief Justice Taney told Buchanan what the Court would decide in Dred Scott moments before the president-elect gave his inaugural address. Their public-yet-private conversation was far too brief, and Buchanan had, after all, written his inaugural address well before he gave it—and before chatting with Taney." Finkelman instead suggests that Buchanan knew which way the decision was going to go due to a February 23 letter from Grier who told him that six of the seven justices would vote in favor of declaring the Missouri Compromise unconstitutional, thus abrogating the legal framework Scott referenced to sue for his freedom. J.H. Van Evrie, *The Dred Scott Decision: Opinion of Chief Justice Taney* (New York: Van Evrie, Horton & Company, 1959), 1-48; John W. Quist and Michael J. Birkner, *James Buchanan and the Coming of the Civil War* (Gainesville: University Press of Florida, 2013), 38; Moore, *The Works of James Buchanan, Volume X, 1856-1860*, 105-08.

6   Elbert William Robinson Ewing, *Legal and Historical Status of the Dred Scott Decision* (Washington: Cobden Publishing Company, 1909), 32-49.

7   "The Personnel of the New Cabinet," *New York Times*, 10 March 1857, p.1.

8   *Inaugural Addresses of the Presidents of the United States, Volume I* (Bedford: Applewood Books, 2000), 115-20; Moore, *The Works of James Buchanan, Volume X, 1856-1860*, 105-13.

9   A reporter for the *Baltimore American* estimated that at least 150,000 people turned out to watch Buchanan's inaugural parade. "Men, women and children were seeking every available position from which a sight of the anticipated pageant could be had, and the balconies, windows and doorways were thronged to their utmost capacities. The boys were obtaining lodgements in the trees and on the awning posts, and the ladies finally commenced to mount the dry good boxes in front of the stores." "The Inauguration of the President," *Baltimore American*, 5 March 1857, p.2.

10   "Inauguration of President Buchanan," *Philadelphia Public Ledger*, 5 March 1857, p.1.

11   Historian Michael Carrafiello, noting that Buchanan's address emphasized the careful, subtle nuance of foreign affairs and diplomacy while being mostly devoid of bold domestic policy, contends that the speech "demonstrates conclusively that James Buchanan was first and foremost a diplomat. As such, he was both unprepared and temperamentally incapable of providing the kind of

strong presidential leadership that the nation desperately needed at this critical juncture in its history. Simply put: James Buchanan was tragically ill-equipped to become the nation's chief executive at a time of burgeoning crisis." Michael J. Carrafiello, "Diplomatic Failure: James Buchanan's Inaugural Address," *Pennsylvania History*, Volume 77, Number 2, Spring 2010, 145-65.

[12] Homer Rosenberger, "Inauguration of President Buchanan A Century Ago," *Records of the Columbia Historical Society, Washington, D.C.* (Volume 57/59), 119; Michael J. Carrafiello, "Diplomatic Failure: James Buchanan's Inaugural Address," *Pennsylvania History*, Volume 77, Number 2, Spring 2010, 145-65; "Inauguration Festivities," *New York Herald*, 5 March 1857, p.1.

[13] Buchanan only naturally took a paternalistic interest in his young nephew. "He is a calculating & I think a determined boy," Buchanan had said of James Buchanan Henry in a letter to Harriet in early January 1856 after the boy visited his uncle in London. "I am convinced I did him much good during his brief stay here in correcting some of his eccentricities & rubbing off some of his rough corners. He certainly has a peculiar taste in dress. His coats are either too long or too short; but his hands were always clean. He speaks French beautifully." William Seale, *The President's House—A History* (Washington: White House Historical Association, 1986), 334-36; Moore, *The Works of James Buchanan, Volume X, 1856-1860*, 6-8.

[14] "Letter from Washington," *Philadelphia Public Ledger*, 2 April 1857, p.1

[15] In the spring of 1860, long after the Buchanan-Walker relationship had soured, Walker told the Covode Committee, which was looking into corruption charges against the administration, of how Buchanan had approached him for the job, telling Walker that he considered the governorship of Kansas as the "most important position in the country, and peculiar and flattering reasons were given why I should go. It was said that I was a northern man by birth and southern man by long residence and adoption, and perhaps enjoyed the confidence of the whole nation as to my impartiality upon this question, and that possibly I could do more, from these peculiar circumstances, to reconcile conflicting elements in Kansas than any other person." *Covode Investigation* (Washington: Government Printing Office, 1860), 105; "Letter of R. J. Walker," *National Era*, 2 April 1857, p. 535.

[16] Buchanan not only helped Walker write the address and gave it his final seal of approval, he also asked Secretary Cass to look it over. Cass would remark that Kansas "Should be established by the votes of the people of Kansas, unawed and uninterrupted by force and fraud." At this point all three men, Buchanan, Walker and Cass, assumed matters in Kansas could be dealt with swiftly and that the new state would emerge reliably Democratic. George Harmon, "President James Buchanan's Betrayal of Governor Robert J. Walker of Kansas," *Pennsylvania Magazine of History and Biography*, Volume 53, Number 1 (1929),

54; Willard Carl Klunder, *Lewis Cass and the Politics of Moderation* (Kent: Kent State University Press, 1996), 297-98.

[17] Walker frankly acknowledged that he was interested in seeing Kansas become a state that would vote Democratic. "And the only plan to accomplish this was to unite Free State Democrats with the pro-slavery party, and all those whom I regarded as conservative men against the more violent portion of the Republicans." *Covode Investigation*, 107, 109.

[18] Thomas asserted that Buchanan was controlling Walker, although all of the evidence, on the contrary, indicates that Buchanan ultimately had little influence over him: "He [Walker] puts himself in thought, feeling and hope with our enemies, and that's the truth," said Thomas. "Our victory is turned to ashes on our lips, and before God I will never say well done to the traitor or to his master who lives in the White House." Harmon, "President James Buchanan's Betrayal of Governor Robert J. Walker of Kansas," 57.

[19] *Covode Investigation*, 112-13; Harmon, "President James Buchanan's Betrayal of Governor Robert J. Walker of Kansas," 61.

[20] Buchanan friend South Carolina Congressman Lawrence Keitt also came out against Walker, calling him "corrupting and debauching, tricking and bullying, wherever free-soil objects could be accomplished by these base means." "Democratic Anti-Walker Meeting," *Charleston Mercury*, 3 July 1857, p.1; "Democratic State Convention of Mississippi," *Charleston Mercury*, 8 July 1857, p.1; "Georgia," *Charleston Mercury*, 24 July 1857, p.1; "The Rumored Disturbances in Kansas," *Charleston Mercury*, 27 July 1857, p. 1; Kenneth M. Stampp, *America in 1857: A Nation on the Brink* (New York: Oxford University Press, 1990), 169.

[21] Cass was additionally worried that Walker, with all of the national attention he was getting for his Kansas work, might use his new-found prominence to advance his own political career, telling Buchanan: "We all fear that Governor Walker is endeavoring to make a record for the future." Harmon, "President James Buchanan's Betrayal of Governor Robert J. Walker of Kansas," 63-66.

[22] Buchanan spent several weeks of each summer relaxing at Bedford Springs, hiking in the daytime, smoking cigars at night on the front porch of the retreat's hotel, "cozily chatting with all who approached him on any and every subject of current interest," a reporter would observe. "Life at Bedford Springs," *Baltimore American*, 11 August 1858, p.2.

[23] A revealing example of Buchanan's leaden style of writing is seen in the following passage to Silliman: "The Convention will soon assemble to perform the solemn duty of framing a constitution for themselves and their posterity, and in the state of incipient rebellion which still exists in Kansas, it is my imperative duty to employ the troops of the United States should this become necessary, in defending the Convention against violence, while framing a constitution, and

in protecting the bona fide inhabitants, qualified to vote under the provisions of this instrument in the free exercise of the right of suffrage when it shall be submitted to them for their approbation or rejection." Stampp, *American in 1857*, 179; "From Washington," *New York Tribune*, 3 September 1857, p. 5; "President Buchanan's Reply to Professor Silliman's Memorial," *Philadelphia Public Ledger*, 4 September 1857, p.1; Moore, *The Works of James Buchanan, Volume X, 1856-1860*, 117-20.

[24] Stampp, *America in 1857*, 221-22.

[25] Scholars Charles W. Calomiris and Larry Schweikart write: "Beginning with the Dred Scott decision of March 6-7, 1857, the prospects of free-soil interests deteriorated, and uncertainty about the ultimate status of the territories grew. This reduced the territories' attractiveness to new immigrants, especially from the populous North, and recued the probability of the establishment of further settlements west of the territories or of government involvement in a transcontinental railroad through Kansas." "Washington Correspondence," *Baltimore American*, 17 September 1857, p.4; "From Washington," *New York Tribune*, 28 September 1857, p.5; "Bank Difficulties," *New York Tribune*, 28 September 1857, p.4; "The Run on the Banks of New Orleans," *Philadelphia Public Ledger*, 23 October 1857, p4; Charles W. Calomiris and Larry Schweikart, "The Panic of 1857: Origins, Transmission and Containment," *Journal of Economic History*, Volume 51, Number 4, December 1991, 807-34.

[26] "The Unemployed," *New York Tribune*, 12 November 1857, p.5.

[27] "From Washington," *New York Tribune*, 30 November 1857, p.4; Quist and Birkner, *James Buchanan and the Coming of the Civil War*, 150-51.

[28] "From Washington," *New York Tribune*, 9 November 1857, p.4.

[29] On November 16 Tyler had suggested that Buchanan find another job for Walker, perhaps appointing him to the U.S. Senate, anything to get him out of Kansas: "The more I reflect upon the subject, the stronger my impression becomes against the good faith of Governor Walker to his cause and his friend [Buchanan]. At any rate it seems he has chosen a line of action that may make a great man of him, and this outside of the Democratic party perhaps, while it could not be for the advantage of anyone else." Harmon,"President James Buchanan's Betrayal of Governor Robert J. Walker of Kansas," 85-87.

[30] In his letter of resignation, Walker additionally declared: "I was pledged to the people of Kansas to oppose, by all lawful means, the adoption of any Constitution which was not fairly and fully submitted to their vote for ratification or rejection. These pledges I cannot recall or violate without personal dishonor and the abandonment of fundamental principles; and therefore it is impossible for me to support what is called the Lecompton Constitution, because it is not submitted to a vote of the people for ratification or rejection." "From Washington" *New York Tribune*, 2 December 1857, p.3; "Letter from Washington," *Philadelphia Public*

Ledger, 18 December 1857, p.1. For an overview of the Kansas constitutional process, see *Reports of the Committees of the House of Representatives, 1859-60, 36ᵗʰ Congress, 1ˢᵗ Session, Report Number 255* (Washington: Thomas H. Ford, 1860), 1-55.

[31]   Writes Douglas biographer Robert Johannssen: "Although Douglas, as chairman of the Senate Committee on Territories, would be responsible for Kansas legislation in Congress, the President had acted without seeking his views or advice. Shocked at being so peremptorily ignored, Douglas became angry with the President." Phillip Auchampaugh, "The Buchanan-Douglas Feud," *Journal of Illinois State History Society*, Volume 25, Number 112, April-July 1932, p.11; Robert Johannssen, *Stephen A. Douglas* (Champaign: University of Illinois Press, 1997), 586.

[32]   Douglas had other reasons to dislike Buchanan. In patronage matters, Douglas, while not by any means being shut out by the Buchanan administration, nonetheless felt that the President was disregarding Illinois when it came to handing out federal jobs. Douglas was all the more outraged given his strong and active campaigning for Buchanan in the fall 1856 election. See in particular, Buchanan's summary replacement of Douglas' friend, Philip Conley, as the Port of Chicago's Collector of Customs. John Conley to James Buchanan, 21 March 1857, Stephen A. Douglas Papers, Box 6, Folder 13, Special Collections Research Center, University of Chicago Library; Johannssen, *Stephen Douglas*, 552-57; Quest and Birkner, *James Buchanan and the Coming of the Civil War*, 84-92.

[33]   *Congressional Globe—1ˢᵗ Session, 35ᵗʰ Congress* (Washington: John C. Reeves, 1857), 18.

CHAPTER FOUR NOTES

[1]   With a Midwestern, Republican and abolitionist readership, the *Ohio Repository* obviously had been disappointed in the last two administrations. But in its January 13, 1858 indictment of Buchanan it did manage to praise Franklin Pierce, if barely: "As was well remarked by a friend in our hearing a few days since, President Buchanan's Administration bids fair to render that of President Pierce respectable by contrast. When the latter began his official term, and before he became the property of the fire-eaters, his administration was marked by several acts which commended themselves to the good sense of the people of the nation. But in Mr. Buchanan's case, this has not been so. He has been, from the first, body and soul, entirely under the control of the most violent and fanatical counselors, in and out of his Cabinet." "Nine Months of Mr. Buchanan's Reign," *Ohio Repository*, 13 January 1858, p.2.

[2]   The message ends with a classic touch of Buchanan self-indulgence: "I have thus performed my duty on this important question under a deep sense of

responsibility to God and to the country. My public life will terminate in a brief period, and I have no earthly ambition than to leave my country in a peaceful and prosperous condition and to live in the affections and respect of my countrymen." "The Lecompton Message," *Springfield Daily Republican*, 4 February 1858, p.2; "The Administration," reprint of *Philadelphia North American* editorial published in the *Progressive Age and Coshocton County Local Record*, 24 February 1858, p.1.; John Bassett Moore, *Works of James Buchanan, Volume X, 1856-1860* (Philadelphia: J.B. Lippincott, 1910), 179-92.

3   "Mr. Buchanan and Kansas," *Kalamazoo Gazette*, 3 March 1858, p.2.

4   Francis P. Blair, Jr. was the son of long-time Democratic insider Francis Blair, who had left the Democratic Party in the mid-1850s primarily over the slavery issue, becoming a Republican. His brother, Montgomery Blair, had followed the same course and served as co-counsel for the plaintiff in *Dred Scott v. Sandford*. Francis Blair, Jr., like his father and brother, abandoned the Democrats in favor of the Republicans and ran for the House of Representatives in Missouri's First Congressional District that included the city of St. Louis. As a Republican, his fortunes often ran counter-cyclical to national trends: he was elected during the Democratic year of 1856, but defeated in the Republican mid-term sweep of 1858. Francis P. Blair, Jr. to George R. Smith, 6 March 1858, George P. Smith Papers, Missouri Historical Society.

5   In the time-honored tradition, the verbal confrontation between Keitt and Grow that led to their physical fight was left out of the *Congressional Globe*, undoubtedly at the request of the participants. But a reporter for the *New York Times* claims to have heard Keitt when he saw Grow on the Democratic side of the House aisle, ask: "What business have you over on this side anyway?" Grow supposedly responded: "This is a free hall," adding that he had a right to speak from any spot within the chamber. "What did you mean by that answer you gave me now?" Keitt asked. When Grow said he meant what he just said, Keitt called him a "damned Black Republican puppy." Grow then called Keitt a "Nigger driver." Fisticuffs at this point were most likely inevitable. Keitt's actions, condemned in the press, didn't seem to bother Buchanan who invited Keitt to the White House shortly afterwards. But Michigan Senator Zachariah Chandler was troubled enough by the Keitt-Grow encounter and the specter of increasing violence in both chambers to meet with fellow Senators Benjamin F. Wade of Ohio and Simon Cameron of Pennsylvania. Together the men declared that that if any of them were threatened by a Southern lawmaker they would "carry the quarrel into a coffin." Once word got out of the Cameron-Chandler-Wade declaration, the men later claimed in a joint memo, "The tone of their [Southern] insults was at once modified, and staid modified." "Detailed Account of Keitt and Grow Fight," *New York Times*, 6 March 1858, p.1; "Letter from Washington," *Philadelphia Public Ledger*, 6 April 1858, p.1; Moore, *The*

Works of James Buchanan, Volume X, 214; Simon Cameron, Zachariah Chandler, Benjamin F. Wade Memorandum, 26 May 1874, Papers of Zachariah Chandler, Reel 3.

[6] "The Latest News," *New York Herald*, 3 May 1858, p.5; "Rejoicing Over the Passage of the Kansas Bill," *New York Times*, 6 March 1858, p.1; Moore, *Works of James Buchanan, Volume X*, 214; Elbert B. Smith, *The Presidency of James Buchanan* (Lawrence: University Press of Kansas, 1975), 42-26.

[7] "Local Matters," *Daily National Intelligencer*, 19 April 1858, p.1; "Respite of James Powers," *Daily National Intelligencer*, 19 June 1858, p.3; "The Execution of James Powers," *Daily National Intelligencer*, 28 June 1858, p.3; "A Dispatch from Washington," *National Era*, 1 July 1858, p. 591

[8] In this letter, Goodell also accuses Buchanan of promoting the idea that the Constitution allowed for slavery to exist anywhere. He adds that Buchanan showed his cards during his February 2 message when he declared "Kansas is, at this moment, as much a slave state as Georgia or South Carolina." William Goodell to Israel Washburne, 19 March 1858, Papers of Israel Washburne, University Archives & Historical Collections, Michigan State University.

[9] In his June 16th Springfield speech, Lincoln traced the roots of the current Kansas crisis to three events: President Pierce's backing of the Kansas-Nebraska Act, the *Dred Scott v. Sandford* decision, and Buchanan's subsequent support of that decision. Grasping at straws, Douglas responded by charging that Lincoln was knowingly lying about Buchanan's involvement with the Kansas-Nebraska Act. "He knows Mr. Buchanan was at that time in England, representing this country with distinguished ability at the Court of St. James, that he was there for a long time before and did not return for a year or more after that," Douglas said. Douglas' response was beside the point: Lincoln never said that Buchanan had anything to do with the Kansas-Nebraska Act. He was instead trying to present a chronology of events designed to put the national Democrat leadership in the worst possible light. But even more, Douglas' defense of Buchanan, the man he had been prominently warring with throughout most of 1858, made him seem duplicitous. In a letter to Elihu Washburne, Lincoln enjoyed noting that while Douglas and his followers were "going over to the President's side" for the sake of the 1858 election, "the President himself does nothing for his own peculiar friends here." Roy P. Basler, *The Collected Works of Abraham Lincoln, Volume II* (New Brunswick: Rutgers University Press, 1953), 461-69; Roy P. Basler, *The Collected Works of Abraham Lincoln, Volume III* (New Brunswick: Rutgers University Press, 1953), 68-69; Abraham Lincoln to Elihu Washburne, 27 May 1858, Abraham Lincoln Papers, Reel 2.

[10] William Kellogg to Abraham Lincoln, 26 July 1858, Abraham Lincoln Papers, Reel 3.

11   Colfax, 35 years old in 1858, was first elected to Congress in 1854. While Lincoln in 1858 was receiving national attention for his speeches, Colfax as a speaker was no slouch. In one of his most famous addresses, delivered on March 20 in response to Buchanan's pro-Lecompton message, he remarked: "The President complains that he is tired of Kansas troubles and desires peace. How easy is it to be obtained? Not by forcing with despotic power and hireling soldiery a constitution hated and spurned by the people upon a territory that will rise in arms against it; not by surrendering the power and authority of an infant State into the hands of a pitiful minority of its citizens, who by oppressive laws and persistently fraudulent elections, have continued to wield the power under a shameless usurpation gave them; but by simply asking the people of Kansas, under your own authority, if you insist of rejecting the vote authorized by their Legislature, the simple and yet essential question—Do you desire Congress to ratify the Lecompton Constitution or the new Constitution now being framed? How easy is the pathway when justice is the guide! How rugged and devious the pathway of error, when wrong lights the road of her followers with her lurid torch, I have endeavored to show." Robert W. Johannsen, *Stephen A. Douglas* (New York: Oxford University Press, 1973), 646-47, 654; Schuyler Colfax to Abraham Lincoln, 25 August 1858, Abraham Lincoln Papers, Reel 3; *Speech of Schuyler Colfax, March 20, 1858* (Washington: Buell and Blanchard, 1858), 3-14.

12   Although Buchanan made no campaign appearances during the 1858 mid-term elections, he sought with uneven success, through the use of patronage, to influence the results by supporting Democrats who had supported him during the Lecompton Congressional debate. His efforts were particularly notable in Ohio, Indiana, Michigan and Illinois. Of those states, the Democrats lost three Congressional seats in Ohio, 2 in Indiana, and 1 in Illinois. The only Democratic victory, in Michigan's First Congressional District, which included Detroit, proved illusory: Democrat banker George Cooper beat Republican incumbent William Howard by 75 votes out of 26,171 votes cast. But a subsequent Congressional investigation threw out more than 100 Cooper ballots which were deemed fraudulent, giving the seat back to Howard more than a year after the election. "Democratic Meeting at Florence," *Louisville Daily Courier*, 28 July 1858, p. 1; David E. Meerse, "Buchanan, The Patronage, and The Lecompton Constitution: A Case Study," *Civil War History*, Volume XLI, December 1995, Number 4, 291-312

13   A search of the James Buchanan Papers housed at the Lancaster Historical Society, Buchanan's microfilmed letters, and the William English Papers at the Indianan Historical Society has produced no such correspondence. "Mr. Buchanan's English Letter," *Ohio Repository*, 11 August 1858, p.2; "Executive Interference with Elections," *Poughkeepsie Eagle*, 11 September 1858, p.3.

14   "The Ratification Meeting," *Newark Daily Advertiser*, 28 September 1858, p.2.

15   It was perhaps a lucky thing for the Republicans that Buchanan was the face and voice of the national Democrats in 1858 and not Davis. Everywhere Davis went on his fall Eastern turn, he was greeted by friendly, cheering crowds who obviously enjoyed his energetic speaking style and talent for compelling argument. In a typical example of Davis' approach, he told voters at the Palace Gardens in New York that the Republican party had become the party of division, noting "You have seen your churches divided, you have seen trade turned aside, you have seen jealousy and all uncharitableness and bickering stronger and stronger every day until you are at last thrown upon the single cord of political union between the States and that cord cannot long hold the States together." "Democratic Meeting at Faneuil Hall," *Boston Evening Transcript*, 12 October 1858, p.4; "The State Ticket Again Ratified," *New York Herald*, 20 October 1858, p.1.

16   A Washington correspondent for the *New York Herald* contended that Buchanan after the October Democratic drubbing was in "high health, hopes and spirits, with ruddy cheeks and elastic step, indicative of great strength and vigorous constitution." James Buchanan to Harriet Lane, 15 October 1858, Papers of James Buchanan and Harriet L. Johnston, Reel 1; "Our Washington Correspondent," *New York Herald*, 25 October 1858, p.5.

17   Zachariah Chandler to John Clark, 15 October 1858, Papers of Zachariah Chandler, Reel 1.

18   George Talbot to Israel Washburne, 16 November 1858, Papers of Israel Washburne, University Archives & Historical Collections, Michigan State University.

19   In an earlier editorial published by the *New Orleans Bee* in the wake of October Republican wins in Pennsylvania, Ohio and Indiana that also produced a hefty 20 percent jump in the Republican vote in Iowa over 1856, the paper squarely placed the blame for the Democratic reverses on Buchanan: "In Ohio, Indiana and Iowa there is no earthy doubt that anti-slavery was the controlling sentiment which compassed the defeat of the Democracy. The first and last of these states had voted for Fremont in 1856 and were hardly expected to join the administration now. But Indiana had been carried by Buchanan and was thought to be reliable at all times. The course pursued by the President in urging the admission of Kansas under the Lecompton Constitution made the tender-footed Democracy of the West wince somewhat; yet their allegiance would probably be unchanged had the administration quietly acquiesced in the English bill and permitted honest differences of opinion among its own supporters. But when the President undertook to compel any Democrat to abjure all personal independence and endorse whatever he might dictate; when he evinced a bitter hostility to every anti-Lecompton Democrat by systematic

persecution and eviction from office; when through his immediate organs he initiated an unrelenting warfare against Douglas and placed him under the ban of party denunciation—it was evident that the Democracy throughout the West would be greatly weakened and dispirited." "The Cause and the Remedy," reprint of *New York Sun* editorial published in the *New Orleans Bee*, 12 November 1858, p.1; "What Does it Mean?" *New Orleans Bee*, 15 October 1858, p.1.

CHAPTER FIVE NOTES

[1]   Buchanan's biographers and historians of the period have correctly noted his long-standing preoccupation with Cuba. Jean Baker says Buchanan had an "expansionist obsession of buying Cuba," and quotes Buchanan saying "We must have Cuba. We can't do without Cuba...Cuba is already ours. I feel it in my fingertips." Philip Shriver Klein writes: "Of all the elements of his Latin American policy, Buchanan personally had the most interest in the acquisition of Cuba. He had advocated its purchase since the 1830s and as president he called again for money and political support to attain the 'Pearl of the Antilles.' In 1856, Buchanan had said 'If I can be instrumental in settling the slave question...and then add Cuba to the Union...I shall be willing to give up the ghost.'" Klein subsequently notes: "'We must have Cuba,' he was in the habit of saying, but his enemies took delight in translating his statement into the words, 'We must have slavery.'" Historian Kenneth M. Stampp observes that Buchanan's endless quest to acquire Cuba was certainly in keeping with a President who would not have been elected without Southern votes and looked to the leaders of that region of the country for further support: "Southern expansionists had a most sympathetic friend in President Buchanan. His interest in the acquisition of Cuba from Spain dated back to his term as Secretary of State in Polk's administration, and he had subsequently shown empathy for the use, if necessary, of means more drastic than peaceful purchase." John Bassett Moore, *Works of James Buchanan, Volume X, 1856-1860* (Philadelphia: J.B. Lippincott Company, 1910), 235-77; *Message from the President of the United States to the Two Houses of Congress at the Commencement of the Second Session of the Thirty Fifth Congress* (Washington: James B. Steedman, 1858), 3-33; Jean Baker, *James Buchanan* (New York: times Books, 2004), 3, 43; Philip Shriver Klein, *President James Buchanan—A Biography* (Falls Creek, Pennsylvania: Pennsylvania State University Press, 1962), 324-25; Kenneth M. Stampp, *America in 1857: A Nation on the Brink* (New York: Oxford University Press, 1990), 193; John W. Quist and Michal J. Birkner, *James Buchanan and the Coming of the Cold War* (Gainesville: University Press of Florida, 2013), 120.

2   Alan Brinkley, *American History: A Survey, Volume I: To 1877* (New York: McGraw Hill, 2007), 340-41.

3   Michael P. Riccards, *The Ferocious Engine of Democracy, Volume I* (Lanham, New York: Madison Books, 1995), 136, 151, 161, 166-67, 176-77; Allan Nevins, *The Emergence of Lincoln, Volume I* (New York: Charles Scribner's Sons, 1950), 422-24. Zachary Taylor and Millard Fillmore, out of all the presidents between Andrew Jackson and Buchanan, were the most unenthusiastic about the goals of Manifest Destiny while James Knox Polk, declaring war on Mexico, was obviously the most. Nevins counts Buchanan among the true believers and suggests that Buchanan's south of the border policies were almost certainly animated by Southern annexationist sympathy.

4   "The Latest News," *New York Herald*, 17 January 1859, p.4; "The Purchase of Cuba," *New York Herald*, 25 January 1859, 9.1.

5   Some Southerners were for Buchanan's Cuba legislation not just because of its connection to slavery, but because they felt that allowing a belligerent Spain such a prominent foothold in the Western Hemisphere was a threat to America's security. As early as the mid-1840s, Jefferson Davis had lobbied in favor of the U.S. acquiring Cuba, although he was uncomfortable with the idea of seizing the island militarily. In 1856, after reading a draft of a manuscript written by Quartermaster General Thomas Jesup that talked of the necessity of taking over Cuba, Davis wrote: "Had your views been appreciated and acted on at an early period we should have avoided the serious difficulties which must now be encountered when the necessity for the acquisition of that Island shall be made apparent to the most purblind and distorted vision." "The Acquisition of Cuba," *New York Herald*, 15 March 1859, p.1; *Jefferson Davis—The Man and His Hour* (New York: HarperPerennial, 1992), 175-76; Lynda Lasswell Crist, *The Papers of Jefferson Davis, Volume 6, 1856-1860* (Baton Rouge: Louisiana State University Press, 1998), 18-19.

6   *Congressional Globe, 2nd Session, 35th Congress* (Washington: John C. Rives, 1859), 430, 455.

7   "Difficulties in the Way of the Immediate Acquisition of Cuba," *Richmond Enquirer*, 28 January 1859, p. 2; "The Salvation of Cuba," *New York Times*, 26 January 1859, p. 1.

8   Impressed with his legal and negotiating skills, Buchanan had initially wanted Louisiana Senator Judah Benjamin to serve as his Minister to Spain, somewhat oblivious to the strain of anti-Semitism running throughout Spanish government and society. Benjamin declined the offer, as did Vice-President Breckinridge, who most likely regarded the assignment as a way for Buchanan, who resented him [see chapter eight], to remove an imagined opponent from the national scene. Buchanan finally settled on Breckinridge's cousin, William Preston, a former one-term member of Congress from Kentucky. Meanwhile,

Christopher Fallon, an American investor and financial agent for the Spanish Queen, was the man picked by Buchanan to distribute the bribe funds in Spain. Frederick Moore Binder, *James Buchanan and the American Empire* (Sclinsgorve: Susquehanna University Press, 1994), 253-54.

[9] *Congressional Globe*, p. 1079-80; William C. Harris, *Public Life of Zachariah Chandler, 1851-1875* (Lansing: Michigan Historical Commission, 1917), 46-47.

[10] "The Virginia Democracy Against the Acquisition of Cuba," *New Orleans Bee*, 8 February 1859, p.1.

[11] *Congressional Globe*, 1061.

[12] Buchanan's Cuban proposals were hardly faring better in Spain. Frederick Moore Binder notes that when William Preston was initially introduced to Spanish Foreign Minister Calderon Collantes upon his arrival in that country, "Collantes, with great emotion, brought up Buchanan's request for funds to purchase Cuba. He said it had caused great excitement throughout Spain and in the Cortes. The new American minister must know any proposal to purchase the island would result in immediate cessation of all communications between Spain and the United Sates. The warning was clear: Spain would break diplomatic relations over the mere mention of a Cuban purchase." *Congressional Globe*, 904; Binder, *James Buchanan and the American Empire*, 257.

[13] Thomas Keneally, *American Scoundrel—The Life of the Notorious Civil War General Dan Sickles* (New York: Doubleday, 2002), 130; "The Tragedy Yesterday," *Washington Evening Star*, 28 February 1859, p.3; "Dreadful Tragedy," *New York Times*, 28 February 1859, p.1.

[14] Did Buchanan fall for Teresa because she was, by all accounts, so alluring, or because Buchanan, who may have had marginal bisexual tendencies, thought Teresa was somewhat masculine in her mannerisms? Writes author Edgcumb Pinchon in a somewhat sensational description of Teresa: "There was, in fact, something boyish and forthright in her nature, a certain unguessed realism and firmness of mind...Beneath her deceptive air of slim fragility, lurked a lithe body and healthy spirit then called 'hoydenish." Edgcumb Pinchon, *Dan Sickles— Hero of Gettysburg and the "Yankee King of Spain"* (New York: Doubleday, Doran & Company, 1945), 51.52; Keneally, *American Scoundrel*, 40; W.A. Swanberg, *Sickles The Incredible* (Gettysburg: Stan Clark Military Books, 1991), 94.

[15] Speculated diarist George Templeton Strong, admittedly a Sickles critic: "Some people talk of relations between the lady [Teresa] and Old Buck, of which Dan had full notice and in which he acquiesced, and which put that vulnerable sinner in Dan's power." Allan Nevins, *The Diary of George Templeton Strong—The Turbulent Fifties, 1850-1859* (New York: Octagon Books, 1974), 441.

[16] Philip Barton Key to James Knox Polk, 26 June 1845, James K. Polk Papers, Reel 36.

17 Felix G. Fontaine, *Trial of The Hon. Daniel E. Sickles for Shooting Philip Barton Key, Esq., U.S. District Attorney, of Washington, D.C., February 27th, 1859* (New York: R.M. De Witt, 1859), 66; Nat Brandt, *The Congressman Who Got Away With Murder* (Syracuse: Syracuse University Press, 1991), 85-87.

18 According to the rules of precedence, which were closely adhered to in the Buchanan White House, Key, as an officer of the Criminal Court, was officially admitted to White House social functions only after the scheduled admittance, in fifteen-minute intervals, of Vice-President Breckenridge and members of the Cabinet and Supreme Court, but before the officers of the Army and Navy. "The Sickles Tragedy," *New York Herald*, 17 March 1859, p.8; "Political," *New York Tribune*, 3 March 1859, p. 3; "The Sickles Tragedy," *New York Tribune*, 2 March 1859, p. 6; William Seale, *The President's House—A History, Volume One* (Washington: White House Historical Association, 1986), 349.

19 Buchanan largely escaped criticism in the aftermath of the shooting and subsequent trial. The *Pittsburgh Gazette* was one of the few papers to broach the topic of his role in the scandal, noting: "The President himself does not seem conscious of the unpleasant part he has taken in this affair, but with characteristic recklessness, goes on mixing himself with it to an unlimited extent. He has even forgotten his position as a citizen and a high public official as to write a letter of condolence to Sickles since his imprisonment. His folly could not demand from him a greater sacrifice." The article was re-published in the anti-Buchanan *Chicago Tribune*. "Old Buck as a Ladies' Man," *Chicago Tribune*, 18 March 1859, p. 2.

20 Fontaine, 77; Brandt, 131; "Local News," *Washington Evening Star*, 28 February 1859, p.3; "The Sickles Tragedy," *New York Tribune*, 2 March 1859, p.6.

21 Writes W. A. Swanberg of the contrasts between Sickles' defense team and the outgunned Ould: "This contest was obviously so one-sided that friends of Key pleaded with the President to appoint some outstanding lawyer to assist Ould, but he refused." Swanberg adds: "One wonders how Prosecutor Ould, who held his office at the pleasure of the President and may have suspected that any really energetic conduct of the prosecution might turn the President's pleasure to anger, must have felt." Swanberg, *Sickles the Incredible*, 63-64, 66; Nat Brandt, *The Congressman Who Got Away With Murder*, 156.

22 "Interesting from Washington," *New York Herald*, 4 April 1859, p.4.

23 Crist, *The Papers of Jefferson Davis, Volume 6, 1856-1860*, 243-44.

24 Whatever fears Buchanan may have had concerning how he would be portrayed during the coverage of the Sickles scandal, the shooting and subsequent trial proved to be one of the greatest stories of the day, with reporters relegating Buchanan to a supporting role in the tragedy. The day after the shooting, the *Washington Evening Star* apologized to its readers, noting that it had run out of copies of previous day's edition: "Our sales of papers yesterday ran up to an

aggregate of full three thousand copies above the Star's usual edition," the paper announced. The national picture weekly, *Frank Leslie's Illustrated News*, with a normal press run of 100,000, printed over 200,000 copies with its first edition coverage of the shooting. Every major paper in the country gave the murder and trial extensive and usually front-page coverage. "An Apology." *Washington Evening Star*, 1 March 1859, p.3; "The Sickles Tragedy," *Baltimore Sun*, 15 March 1859, p.2; Keneally, *American Scoundrel*, 154. For an example of the initial reporting, see "The Lafayette Square Tragedy," *Washington Daily Union*, 1 March 1859, p.3; "The Tragedy in Washington," *Philadelphia Public Ledger*, 1 March 1859, p.1; "The Sickles Tragedy at Washington," *Harper's Weekly*, 12 March 1859, p. 168-70; "The Washington Tragedy," *Chicago Tribune*, 5 March 1859, p.2; "Important from Washington," *New York Tribune*, 4 March 1859, p.3; "Deplorable Occurrence," *Daily National Intelligencer*, 28 February 1859, p.2; "The Washington Tragedy," *New York Herald*, 2 March 1859, p.2; "Correspondence of the Courier," *Charleston Courier*, 3 March 1859, p.4. For the verdict: "The Washington Tragedy," *New York Herald*, 27 April 1859, p.2; "The Sickles Tragedy," *New York Times*, 27 April 1859, p.1; "The Sickles Tragedy," *Baltimore Sun*, 27 April 1859, p.1; "Moral of the Sickles Trial," *Daily Picayune*, 28 April 1859, p.1; "The Sickles Verdict," *Harper's Weekly*, 7 May 1859, p.290.

[25] "The President's Visit to North Carolina," *Philadelphia Public Ledger*, 3 June 1859, p.1; "President Buchanan in North Carolina," *Richmond Enquirer*, 7 June 1859, p.3.

[26] Buchanan got off a rare joke when his caravan stopped in Raleigh. "You are a sovereign people and here I am a creature appointed by them, not to rule over them, but to administer the government according to their wish and to be responsible to them for the manner in which I do so," he told a crowd of locals. "The worst of it is that I am held responsible for the many things I do not do." "The President in North Carolina," *New York Herald*, 4 June 1859, p.2; "Reception of President Buchanan at Raleigh," *New York Times*, 6 June 1859, p.4; Philip G. Auchampaugh, "James Buchanan, the Squire from Lancaster: The Squire at Home," *Pennsylvania Magazine of History and Biography*, Volume 56, Number 1 (1932), 25.

[27] A reporter for the *New York Herald* took note of the 68 year-old Buchanan's resilience as he arrived in Chapel Hill after an uncomfortable trip from Raleigh: "I venture to say that the President endured more hardship in his passage from the railroad here than along the whole route from Washington. He was literally white with dust when he reached here, and to add to the inconvenience, the heat was more intense than it had been since he entered upon his tour. I am surprised that he has withstood the fatigue of the journey so well. Between the travel, the dust, heat and laborious ordeal of hand shaking, which he has to go through at intervals of every ten or twenty minutes during the day, I have no doubt he

finds his physical capacity put vigorously to the test." "The President's Trip to North Carolina," *New York Herald*, 6 June 1859, p.8; Harry McKown, "James Buchanan Visits the University of North Carolina," lib.edu/ncc/ref/nchistory. June2009/index/html. Accessed on June 8, 2012.

28 "The President's Trip to North Carolina," *New York Herald*, 6 June 1859, p.8.

29 "The President's Visit to North Carolina," *New York Herald*, 7 June 1859, p.8; "President Buchanan in North Carolina," *Richmond Enquirer*, 7 June 1859, p.2.

30 Manly Wade Wellman, *The County of Warren, North Carolina, 1586-1917* (Chapel Hill: University of North Carolina Press, 1959) 131; *North Carolina Biographical Dictionary, Second Edition* (New York: Somerset Publishers, 1999), 198-200; "North Carolina's Futile Rebellion Against the United States," oldnorthstateskeptic.com, accessed on 18 June 2014.

31 "President Buchanan Fairly in Field for Re-nomination," *Richmond Enquirer*, 29 July 1859, p.2; "Letter from President Buchanan Declining a Re-Nomination," *Richmond Dispatch*, 1 August 1859, p. 3; Moore, *Works of James Buchanan, Volume X, 1856-1860*, 327-28.

32 James Buchanan to Robert Tyler, 15 October 1859, John Tyler Papers, Reel 2, Series 1.

CHAPTER SIX NOTES

1 "The Abolition Invasion," *Richmond Dispatch*, 22 October 1859, p.1.

2 Tony Horwitz, *Midnight Rising—John Brown and the Raid that Sparked the Civil War* (New York: Henry Holt and Company, 2011), 140-41. For an interesting study on the role played by John Brown's wife, daughter, and daughters in-law leading up to the Harper Ferry attack, see Bonnie Laughlin-Schultz, *The Tie that Bound Us: The Women of John Brown's Family and the Legacy of Radical Abolitionism* (Ithaca: Cornell University Press, 2013).

3 Ibid., 140-41, 174.

4 "It's a moment full of peril," Garrett remarked in his second dispatch to Buchanan. The B&O head may have been, despite the emergency, reluctant to speak so bluntly to a sitting President. He was just 38 years old and had only taken over the leadership of the B&O the year before. Garrett would go on to prove himself essential to the Union cause during the Civil War (while earning huge wartime profits for his company) by continually up-grading and expanding the B&O's rail lines, which in turn guaranteed an ongoing movement of troops, animals and supplies. "The Insurrection," *Richmond Dispatch*, 19 October 1859, p.1; "Harper's Ferry Insurrection," *Daily Picayune*, 19 October 1859, p.1; "Insurrection at Harper's Ferry," *Daily National Intelligencer*, 19 October 1859, p.2.; Allan Keller, *Thunder at Harper's Ferry* (Englewood Cliffs: Prentice-Hall, Inc., 1958), 68.

5   "Insurrectionary Outbreak at Harper's Ferry," *Richmond Dispatch*, 18 October 1859, p.3; "Servile Insurrection," *New York Times*, 18 October 1859, p.1.

6   In his biography of Lee, author Clifford Dowdey writes that the Colonel was working in his study when Stuart arrived. Upon hearing the reason for Stuart's visit, Lee left at once, still in his civilian clothing. Later arriving at Harper's Ferry, Lee, according to Dowdey, "soon appraised the violence as being contained. He found nothing of the slave uprising they had feared from the wild messages. The mountains around Harper's Ferry supported no plantations, and there were few slaves in the region." Keller, *Thunder at Harper's Ferry*, 68; Clifford Dowdey, *Lee* (Boston: Little, Brown & Company, 1965), 116-18.

7   Supposedly after Missouri Governor Robert Stewart put a $3,000 price on Brown's head for the Kansas attack, Buchanan ponied up an additional $250. If true, Buchanan did this as a private citizen, as the attack took place in 1856. David S. Reynolds, *John Brown, Abolitionist—The Man Who Killed Slavery, Sparked the Civil War, and Seeded Civil Rights* (New York: Alfred A. Knopf, 2005), 279.

8   "Our Washington Correspondent," *New York Herald*, 20 October 1859, p.3; "Harper's Ferry Insurrection," *Daily Picayune*, 22 October 1859, p.1; "Local Matters," *Daily National Intelligencer*, 22 October 1859, p.3.

9   "A Night of Alarm," *Washington Evening Star*, 18 October 1859, p.3; "A Night of Alarm in Washington," *New York Herald*, 20 October 1859, p.3; "Card from Mr. Lewis Clephane of the Washington Era," *New York Herald*, 23 October 1859, p.3.

10   "The Republican Association of this City," *Daily National Intelligencer*, 26 October 1859, p.3.

11   Not until his important Cooper Institute address of February 27, 1860 did Lincoln fully address the Democratic claim that Republicans had helped organize and fund Brown's raid: "You charge that we stir up insurrections among your slaves. We deny it; and what is your proof? Harper's Ferry! John Brown! John Brown was no Republican; and you have failed to implicate a single Republican in his Harper's Ferry enterprise. If any member of our party is guilty in that matter, you know it or you do not know it. If you know it, you are inexcusable for not designating the man and proving the fact. If you do not know it, you are inexcusable for asserting it, and especially for persisting in the assertion after you have tried and failed to make the proof. You need not be told that persisting in a charge which one does not know to be true is simply malicious slander." "Correspondence of the Mercury," *Charleston Mercury*, 26 October 1859, p.1; Roy P. Basler, *The Collected Works of Abraham Lincoln, Volume III* (New Brunswick: Rutgers University Press, 1953), 522-50.

12   "Speech of Senator Wilson of Massachusetts," *New York Herald*, 20 October 1859, p.8.

13   "Apart from dispatching federal troops to the scene, President Buchanan did little and said less about Harper's Ferry," writes Brown biographer Tony Horwitz. "Known as a 'Northern man with Southern principles,' he was content to let Virginians take the lead. As he later wrote the prosecutor who took charge of trying the insurgents, the question of jurisdiction in Harper's Ferry was a 'matter quite indifferent to me.'" "The Political Campaign," *New York Herald*, 3 November 1859, p.10; Horwitz, *Midnight Rising*, 195.

14   "The Political Campaign," *New York Herald*, 3 November 1859, p.10.

15   Franklin Pierce to Faneuil Hall Union Meeting, 2 December 1859, Franklin Pierce Papers, Series 3, Reel 2.

16   Ibid.

17   Allan Nevins, *The Emergence of Lincoln—Volume II, Prologue to the Civil War, 1859-1861* (New York: Charles Scribner's Sons, 1950), 105-06.

18   "Administration View," *New York Times*, 21 October 1859, p.1.

19   William C. Davis, *Jefferson Davis—The Man and His Hour, A Biography* (New York: Harper Perennial, 1992), 276.

20   "The Harper Ferry Outbreak," *Daily Picayune*, 22 October 1859, p.1.

21   Among the witnesses was the actor John Wilkes Booth, who, although disagreeing with everything Brown stood for, was nonetheless impressed with Brown's calm demeanor when Brown was forced to sit on his own coffin while being driven to the execution site. When he saw Brown gazing towards the horizon as the hangman's rope was slipped over his head, Booth thought he was most likely looking to see if anyone was going to rescue him. "He was a brave old man," Booth later said. "His heart must have been broken when he felt himself deserted." Nora Titone, *My Thoughts Be Bloody—The Bitter Rivalry Between Edwin and John Wilkes Booth That Led To An American Tragedy* (New York: Free Press, 2010), 212.

22   Once again, Buchanan, living in another time and era, hoped the ongoing slavery debate, which was animated by the John Brown invasion, would just end. After his initial reference to Harper's Ferry, Buchanan quoted philosopher Edmund Burke: "We ought to reflect that in this age, and especially in this country, there is an incessant flux and reflux of public opinion. Questions which in their day assumed a most threatening aspect have now nearly gone from the memory of men. They are 'volcanoes burnt out, and on the lava and ashes and squalid scoria of old eruptions grow the peaceful olive, the cheering vine, and the sustaining corn.' Such, in my opinion, will prove to be the fate of the present sectional excitement should those who wisely seek to apply the remedy continue always to confine their efforts within the pale of the Constitution. If this course be pursued, the existing agitation on the subject of domestic slavery, like everything human, will have its day, and give place to other and less threatening controversies." John Bassett Moore, *Works of James*

Buchanan, Volume X, 1856-1860 (Philadelphia: J.B. Lippincott, 1910), 339-40; *Message from the President of the United States to the Two Houses of Congress at the Commencement of the First Session of the Thirty-Sixth Congress* (Washington: George W. Bowman, 1860), 3-26.

CHAPTER SEVEN NOTES

[1] A North Carolinian, Helper came to the anti-slavery movement almost by accident. He had written a book taking a whimsical view of the California gold rush called *The Land of the Gold.* In it, he lightly criticized slavery. His pro-slavery Virginia publisher subsequently demanded that he remove those passages. Helper agreed, but the episode left him with the idea that if pro-slavery advocates were for censorship, they might be wrong about other things, too. Making it his mission to explore slavery from both an economic and social perspective, Helper by 1857 had come to the conclusion that the system was unworkable and damaging to everyone in the South, including slaves and slaveholders. That Helper was a Southerner obviously helped spur sales of his book in the North. But his place of origin was also the cause of great resentment against him among fellow Southerners—certainly Southern members of the House—who quickly came to regard him as a traitor. Hinton Rowan Helper, *The Impending Crisis of the South: How to Meet It* (New York: Burdick Brothers, 1857), 363; Ollinger Crenshaw, "The Speakership Contest of 1859-1860—John Sherman's Election A Cause of Disruption?" *Mississippi Valley Historical Review,* Volume XXIX, Number 2, September 1942, 323-24; David Brown, "Attacking Slavery From Within: The Making of the Impending Crisis of the South," *Journal of Southern History,* August 2004, Volume LXX, Number 3, 541-76; *Journal of the House of Representatives of the United States, First Session, Thirty-Sixth Congress* (Washington: Thomas H. For, 1859), 195-219.

[2] Some Republicans thought the move to ban Helper's book might actually help the anti-slavery cause within the South on the chance that a minority of Southerners, like Helper, would be offended by such censorship. "Many of them have been reading Helper's Crisis and think there must be a 'conflict,' of some sort, if the right to free speech is attempted to be supplanted," thought Ohio Republican Albert Tyler in a letter to William Seward. "The play of eight weeks [the Speakership battle] has produced effects of great importance upon the country. It has alarmed no one at the North, except those who fear that this trade may be affected, while it has awakened a conservative spirit at the South that chafes under the initiation of such tyranny." Rachel Sherman Thorndike, *The Sherman Letters—Correspondence Between General and Senator Sherman from 1837 to 1891* (New York: Charles Scribner's Sons, 1894), 78-79; Albert Tyler to William Seward, 6 February 1860, Papers of William Seward, Reel 59.

3   *Congressional Globe, 1ˢᵗ Session, 36ᵗʰ Congress* (Washington: John C. Rives, 1860), 18.

4   Ibid., 386-93.

5   Ibid., 21.

6   In his generally candid memoirs, Sherman writes of his withdrawal: "I was entirely satisfied with the result. I had received every Republican vote and the votes of a large number of anti-Nebraska Democrats and Americans [members of the American Party]. No cloud rested upon me, no allegation of misconduct or unfitness was made against me. I would have been easily and quickly elected but for the abnormal excitement created by Brown's invasion and the bitterness of political antagonism exiting at that time." The 63 year-old Pennington would be described by Charles Francis Adams, Sr., as a "big man," whose "legs sprawl out over the room and his boots are very prominent and he keeps his knife in his hands, opening it and shutting it while he talks." Pennington almost immediately found himself out of his depth, confused about House rules and procedures and lacking the confidence needed to take control of the often unruly chamber. A reporter for the *New York Times*, observing Pennington at work, said that he "appears lost in a maidenly muddle." The Washington correspondent for the *Charleston Courier* said Pennington was "slow, confused, and seems to be a good natured man with thick notions and a nervous perspiration constantly upon him." Perhaps it was no surprise that within a week of his Speakership, Pennington would remark that had he known what awaited him, he would not have taken the job. John Sherman, *John Sherman's Recollections of Forty Years in the House, Senate and Cabinet: An Autobiography, Volume I* (Chicago: The Werner Company, 1895), 179; Charles Francis Adams, Sr., to Charles Francis Adams, Jr., 29 December 1860, The Adams Papers, Reel 550; "From Washington," *Springfield Daily Republican*, 30 January 1860, p.4; "Important from Washington," *New York Herald*, 31 January 1860, p.1; "The Floor from the Galleries," *New York Times*, 2 February 1860, p. 4; "Correspondence of the Mercury," *Charleston Mercury*, 7 February 1860, p. 1; "Correspondence of the Courier," *Charleston Courier*, 11 February 1860, p. 4.

7   The fact that there were actually more Republicans than Democrats at Buchanan's party prompted the *New York Herald* correspondent to wonder: "Perhaps, as Mr. Buchanan has protested over and over again that he is not a candidate, and as it is known that he has not singled out any particular candidate for the succession, the Democrats of Congress are playing hide and seek in order to bring him out. No matter. As the Charleston [Democratic Presidential] Convention draws near, we shall find them increasing at these receptions; for all factions of the Democracy have learned enough to know that they cannot go down to Charleston without the administration, nor come away

from Charleston without recognizing it as the living head and front of the party." "Our Washington Correspondent," *New York Herald*, 14 February 1860, p.10.

8   The letter reveals a comfortable informality on Buchanan's part rarely seen in public: "Old Man!" Buchanan begins, "You know I like to talk to you & you know that I like to write to you, but with these devilish ups and downs of living here a person hasn't much chance. I want you to talk to me like a father & give some useful instruction to your dutiful son, if you don't intend coming over her soon, where we could converse with less trouble. I want some instruction from you in politics, so as to help me understand some of the things that are going on." James Buchanan to Robert Tyler, 21 February 1860, John Tyler Papers, Reel 2, Series 1.

9   Arthur Schlesinger, *Congress Investigates—A Documented History, 1792-1974* (New York: Chelsea House, 1983), 225; "News from Washington," *New York Herald*, 9 March 1860, p.4.

10   Ibid., 229.

11   Explaining how money was used in both the 1856 and 1858 campaigns in Pennsylvania, Wendell provided an answer that must have left the Covode Committee members wondering what they had gotten into: "I would draw a check for a given amount of money and take it with me when I went to Philadelphia, or I would draw my check in Philadelphia and swap checks with some friend in Philadelphia who would give me the money for my draft on my banker here; and I would divide the money up and give it out to different parties; I would, perhaps, make a bet [contribution] of $500, and give $500 to $1,000 in different districts. But this was all mixed up so that I really could not tell exactly how it was all done, as I did not keep a minute of the details, although my books will show the entire amount I spent for party purposes. For instance, there would be an entry of a check for '$5,000 political,' but I would not remember who got all that money, although I might remember $1,000 or $2,000 of it." *Covode Investigation* (Washington: Government Printing Office, 1860), 459-64, 471; Schlesinger, *Congress Investigates*, 238-39.

12   Ibid., 471078.

13   Buchanan additionally made the argument, one subsequently advanced by modern day Presidents, that he was going to battle the committee not for himself, but for the sanctity and power of the office of the President. The Covode proceedings, he contended, "are calculated to foster a band of interested parasites and informers, ever ready, for their own advantage, to swear ex parte committees to pretended private conversations between the President and themselves, incapable, from their nature, of being disproved; thus furnishing material for harassing him, degrading him in the eyes of the country, and eventually, should he be a weak or timid man, rendering him subservient to improper influences, in order to avoid such persecutions and annoyances; because they tend to destroy

that harmonious action for the common good, which ought to be maintained, and which I scarcely desire to cherish, between coordinate branches of the Government; and finally, because if unresisted, they would establish a precedent dangerous and embarrassing to all my successors, to whatever party they might be attached." *Congress Investigates*, 243-47; James Bassett Moore, *The Works of James Buchanan, Volume X, 1856-1860* (New York: Antiquarian Press, 1960), 399-405; "President Buchanan on Party and Prerogative," *New York Tribune*, 31 March 1860, p.6.

[14]   That Sherman served as the point man defending the existence of the Covode investigation was no accident. Although he had lost the Speakership fight, Sherman was generally regarded as the power behind the throne in the 36th Congress, a fact seen by the fact that a willing Pennington signed off on all of the members Sherman had named to head up the major House committees. Sherman later explained that during the Speakership fight he had the "full opportunity to estimate the capacity and qualifications of different members for committee positions, and had the committees substantially formed when Pennington was elected. I handed the list to him, for which he thanked me kindly, saying that he had but little knowledge of the personal qualifications of the Members. With some modifications, made necessary by my defeat and his election as speaker, he adopted the list as his own." Sherman, *John Sherman's Recollections of Forty Years in the House, Senate and Cabinet*, 179, 248-49.

[15]   Because Buchanan in his formal protest sought to present a definition of presidential rights, a portion of the Judiciary Committee report addressed the question of executive branch responsibility. The committee, the report proclaimed, "cannot restrain an expression of their deep regret that an officer who prides himself upon the fact that 'the people have thought proper to invest him with the most honorable, responsible, and dignified office in the world,' and who declares he feels 'proudly conscious that there is no public act of his (my) life which will not bear the strictest scrutiny,' and that he defies 'all investigation,' should forget, amid the surroundings of place and power and flattery, that he is but the servant of that same people, and that he should shrink back in anger or terror from a simple inquiry into his stewardship. This is the first time under a republic a Chief Executive has left a recorded admission that he has been made oblivious of the origin and ephemeral character of his position by the revelries of its enjoyment." *Congress Investigates*, 256-64.

[16]   The *Washington Union* was renamed the *Washington Constitution* in 1859. John Tebbel and Sarah Miles Watt, *The Press and the Presidency—From George Washington to Ronald Reagan* (New York: Oxford University Press, 1985), 161; Moore, *The Works of James Buchanan, Volume X, 1856-1860*, 104; "What's In a Name?" *New York Times*, 13 April 1859, p.3.

[17]   Ibid.

18 Forney began his anti-Buchanan speech on a high note, saying that his fondest goal in 1856 was the election of Buchanan as president. "I had no higher hope in life beyond that—no aim or object. Then all was concentrated in the one absorbing feeling to see that man's aspirations carried out to successful issue. I assisted in his triumph. I came back to the State where I was born, and there, with whatever selfishness was in me—if any—I gave all to that man and his cause." *Congress Investigates*, 301-04; "From Washington," *New York Times*, 4 February 1860, p.1; "The Clerk and the President," *New York Times*, 10 February 1860, p.1.

19 Ibid., 291-301.

20 "From Washington," *New York Times*, 14 June 1860, p. 1.

21 *Press and the Presidency*, 165.

22 Buchanan added that far from rewarding friends with political office and favors, he was averse to such practices: "In performing my duty, I have endeavored to be not only pure but unsuspected. I have never had any concern in awarding contracts, but have left them to be given by heads of the appropriate departments. I have ever detested that all jobs, and no man, at any period of my life, has ever approached me on such a subject." Ibid.

23 "Position of Mr. Buchanan," *New York Herald*, 26 June 1860, p.6.

24 There was no small amount of crowing in this final Buchanan communication to the House. "I have passed triumphantly through this ordeal. My vindication is complete. The committee have [sic] reported no resolution looking to an impeachment against me; no resolution of censure; not even a resolution pointing out any abuses in any of the Executive Departments to be corrected by legislation." *Congress Investigates*, 314-20; *Journal of the House of Representatives of the United States, First Session, Thirty-Sixth Congress, Volume Two* (Washington: Thomas H. Ford, 1860), 1218-1225; Moore, *The Works of James Buchanan, Volume X, 1856-1860*, 435-43.

25 *Congress Investigates*, 223.

26 Ibid.

CHAPTER EIGHT NOTES

1 Leon G. Tyler, *The Letters and Times of the Tylers—Volume II* (New York: DaCapa Press, 1970), 558; James Buchanan to Robert Tyler, 2 February 1860, John Tyler Papers, Reel 2, Series 1.

2 Douglas biographer Damon Wells contends that what mattered most to Buchanan in the spring of 1860 was stopping Douglas. "Buchanan probably wished in his heart to seek a second term, but he must have recognized that his chances for re-nomination were slim and those for re-election practically nonexistent," writes Wells. "But if James Buchanan in 1860 could not himself

gain a second term, he could at least prevent Stephen Douglas from getting the Democratic nomination. He sent his political henchmen South in hordes for the one purpose of cutting down the Little Giant." In the wake of the Charleston meeting, which saw both Douglas and Buchanan on the losing side, Republicans supporters declared they were delighted by the divisions within the Democratic Party. "They are irretrievably split to pieces," declared William Robinson, a columnist for the *Springfield Daily Republican*. "They have no principles in common. And they hate each other, as men, with invincible hatred." "What's to Be Done at Charleston?" *New York Herald*, 30 January 1860, p. 6; Damon Wells, *Stephen Douglas—The Last Years, 1857-1861* (Austin: University of Texas Press, 1971), 211; "From Boston," *Springfield Daily Republican*, 4 May 1860, p.2.

3   John Bassett Moore, *Works of James Buchanan, Volume X—1856-1860* (Philadelphia: J.B. Lippincott Company, 1910), 416-17.

4   Breckinridge as vice-president often displayed his independence from Buchanan: even though it was obvious, for example, that in 1858 Buchanan wanted to see Douglas defeated in his bid-for re-election, Breckinridge made a point of endorsing the Illinois Senator. William C. Davis, *Breckinridge—Statesman, Soldier and Symbol* (Baton Rouge: Louisiana State University Press, 1974), 139-46; Robert W. Johannsen, *Stephen A. Douglas* (New York: Oxford University Press, 1973), 652.

5   Leslie H. Southwick characterizes Breckinridge as a man with "immense talents." "His speeches were exceptional, being noted for their dramatic style and clarity. His appearance was inspiring, as he was a tall, handsome, and graceful figure. His manners were old South—gracious, open and friendly. He had considerable personal courage, as demonstrated both in politics and war. He had magnetism, even charisma. For all of the bitter hatreds that the divisive issues preceding the Civil War engendered, Breckinridge was singular in his friendships with even the most diametrically opposed politicians. He fought them verbally but then dined graciously. Respect for Breckinridge was not limited to his political friends." Leslie H. Southwick, *Presidential Also-Rans and Running Mates, 1788-1980* (Jefferson, North Carolina: McFarland & Company, 1984), 262-70; Davis, *Breckinridge*, 207-08; Elbert B. Smith, *The Presidency of James Buchanan* (Lawrence: University Press of Kansas, 1975), 124-25.

6   "The Baltimore Convention," *New York Times*, 20 June 1860, p.1; "Presidential," *New York Times*, 21 June 1860, p.1.

7   Davis, *Breckinridge*, 224-27.

8   The Lincoln delegate effort has often been praised. But nearly as important was the amateurish convention work of two of Lincoln's most important competitors, Salmon P. Chase and William Seward. Chase biographer John Niven writes of the Chase's Chicago activities, which would see him eventually lose the support of even his own Ohio: "The fact that he had not designated any one

of a number of capable politicians who were loyal to him and were attending the convention…meant either that he had resigned himself to defeat or, more likely, that he expected Ohio to act as a unit behind his candidacy." Niven goes on to assert that Chase may have thought his service as the first Republican governor of Ohio would be enough to attract delegates to his banner and for that reason didn't need to mount an active convention campaign. Seward biographer Glyndon G. Van Deusen, meanwhile, speculates that the New Yorker had no game plan at all in Chicago, especially when it came to responding to concerns that he was too radical on the slavery issue. "Plainly, the delegates, opposed though they were to its [slavery's] extension, committed though they were to its eventual extinction, were anxious to enhance the party's chances in the border slave states, and to ensure victory in Illinois and Indiana where there was strong pro-slavery sentiment. How could this be done with Seward as a candidate?" A more recent Seward biographer, Walter Stahr, also notes that the Lincoln forces in Chicago, by printing extra tickets for the day of the nomination and distributing them to supporters, packed the hall for their man, roaring at every mention of his name, and thus making it seem to undecided delegates that Lincoln was more popular across the party than he really was. Seward additionally may have been lulled into complacency by overly-confident New York supporters. As late as the night before the balloting, New York Republican leader Edwin Morgan, in Chicago, was certain that the delegates would simply turn to Seward en masse, wiring Seward: "You have no doubt of a favorable result tomorrow." Compare this with the more nuanced approach of the Lincoln team, which emphasized gradually building delegate support, as seen in a message to Lincoln from one of his delegate-hunters, Nathan Knapp: "We are laboring to make you the second choice of all the delegations where we cannot make you the first choice." John Niven, *Salmon P. Chase—A Biography* (New York: Oxford University Press, 1995), 217; Glyndon G. Van Deusen, *William Henry Seward* (New York: Oxford University Press, 1967), 225-27; Walter Stahr, *Seward—Lincoln's Indispensable Man* (New York: Simon & Schuster, 2012), 185-89, 194-95; Edwin Morgan to William Seward, 17 May 1860, Papers of William H. Seward, Reel 159; Nathan Knapp to Abraham Lincoln, 16 May 1860, Abraham Lincoln Papers, Reel 6.

[9] "From Washington," *New York Times*, 26 June 1860, p.1; "The Southern Democracy," *New York Times*, 28 June 1860, p.1.; Davis, *Breckinridge*, 224-27.

[10] "Interesting Interview Between Wood and the President," *New York Times*, 30 June 1860, p.1; Jerome Mushkat, *Fernando Wood—A Political Biography* (Kent: Kent State University Press, 1994), 106.

[11] "President Buchanan's Speech," *New York Tribune*, 12 July 1860, p.5; "Washington Correspondence," *Baltimore American*, 12 July 1860, p.1; Moore, *The Works of James Buchanan, Volume X, 1856-1860*, 457-64.

12   "The President on the Rival Tickets," *Springfield Daily Republican*, 16 July 1860, p.2.

13   "National Democratic Mass Meeting," *New York Herald*, 19 July 1860, p.1; Moore, *Works of James Buchanan, Volume X, 1856-1860*, 465.

14   "Movements of Mr. Douglas," *New York Herald*, 1 August 1860, p.5.

15   Notes Breckinridge biographer William C. Davis: "Buchanan, who was concentrating chiefly on winning Pennsylvania for him [Breckinridge], began removing office holders who favored Douglas. In public he denied it, of course, but men in Tennessee, Massachusetts, Vermont, Indiana, Ohio and New York lost their jobs and were replaced by Breckinridge men." "The President and Mr. Douglas," *Richmond Enquirer*, 11 September 1860, p.4; Davis, *Breckinridge*, 235.

16   Bell was nearly invisible during the fall campaign. Breckinridge limited his appearances to a few border states, while the Lincoln campaign delegated such prominent Republicans as Seward, Michigan Senator Zachariah Chandler, and Indiana Congressman Schuyler Colfax to speak for him. Only Douglas on a daily basis brought his case to the people. Writes Douglas biographer Wells: "For the first time, a candidate for the presidency took to the national stump. Douglas visited almost every section of the country, at least once. He spoke two or three times a day, usually in the open air under the burning sun of a Midwestern summer or the raw autumn chill of New England, and he overtaxed a constitution that was at best frail and for too long been called upon for almost superhuman feats of endurance." "Movements of Mr. Douglas," *New York Tribune*, 8 September 1860, p.7; Wells, *Stephen Douglas*, 241.

17   "The Presidential Canvass," *New York Herald*, 9 September 1860, p.1.

18   Davis, an Illinois circuit court judge, was more than just a part of the Lincoln campaign team. According to Doris Kearns Goodwin, he was one of Lincoln's closest friends in Springfield: "The two men took lazy strolls along the river, shared accommodations in various villages, read books in common, and enjoyed long conversations on the rides from one county to the next." David Davis to Abraham Lincoln, 12 August 1860, Reel 8; Doris Kearns Goodwin, *Team of Rivals—The Political Genius of Abraham Lincoln* (New York: Simon & Schuster, 2005), 150.

19   Often forgotten in the 1860 election is the vituperation and outright demagoguery that characterized the efforts of the major candidate supporters. *Charleston Mercury* publisher Robert Barnwell Rhett, a Breckinridge man, declared that because Lincoln's running mate, Hannibal Hamlin, had dark features, he was "what we call a mulatto." Rhett added that he was outraged that Republicans would dare to "place over the South a man who has Negro blood in his veins." The *Cleveland Plain Dealer* charged that should Lincoln win "We shall have the nigger at the polls, the nigger on our juries, niggers in the Legislature, in our public offices," all of which will contribute to a "common

mulattodom." Republicans, meanwhile, made much of the fact that Douglas had married a Catholic and had once visited the Pope in Rome. Notes Lincoln biographer Richard Carwardine: "Republicans' anti-Catholicism played upon a number of related but distinct fears, the theological-ecclesiastical anxieties of staunch Protestants who regarded Rome as the Antichrist and the murderer of religious liberties." "Pennsylvania Politics," *New York Times*, 20 October 1860, p.1; "A Remarkable Discovery," *Baltimore American*, 19 July 1860, p.1; Charles Eugene Hamlin, *The Life and Times of Hannibal Hamlin* (Cambridge: Riverdale Press, 1899), 355; Michael Burlingame, *Abraham Lincoln—A Life* (Baltimore: Johns Hopkins University, 2008), 632; Richard Carwardine, *Lincoln—A Life of Purpose and Power* (New York: Alfred A. Knopf, 2006), 124-25.

[20] One of the few important leaders in the South to support Douglas, Stephens was wary of the secession movement, but also thought it wasn't being taken seriously enough in the North. "The Northern people do not know what dangers threaten their country," he told the *New York Herald* reporter. "They appear to think lightly of what is said at the South, and to treat with contempt the protests the Southerners make against the continual warfare the abolitionists are making upon their social institutions." "The Coming Struggle," *New York Herald*, 29 September 1860, p.2

[21] Lynda Lasswell Crist, *The Papers of Jefferson Davis, Volume 6, 1856-1860* (Baton Rouge: Louisiana State University Press, 1989), 366-67; "Political," *Baltimore American*, 29 October 1860, p.1.

[22] Roy P. Basler, *The Collected Works of Abraham Lincoln, Volume IV* (New Brunswick: Rutgers University Press, 1953), 126-27.

[23] Notes Wells of the fusion movement: "At the very least, this strategy hoped to throw the presidential election into the House of Representatives by preventing Lincoln from obtaining a majority in the electoral college almost by default, for if no slate of electors pledged to a single opposition candidate could command a plurality in that state, that state's entire electoral vote might pass to Lincoln." Robert W. Johannsen contends that Douglas' opposition to fusion was rooted in his belief that "only he, of all the candidates, could beat Lincoln. Additionally, fusion with the Breckinridge party would in effect recognize the legitimacy of the Vice-President's nomination and would seriously cloud Douglas' campaign for leadership of the Democratic party." Franklin Pierce to James Campbell, 17 October 1860, Franklin Pierce Papers, Reel 2, Series 1; Wells, *Stephen Douglas*, 244; Johannsen, *Stephen A. Douglas*, 793.

[24] Simon Cameron to Abraham Lincoln, 6 November 1860, Abraham Lincoln Papers, Reel 10.

[25] James Buchanan, *Mr. Buchanan's Administration on the Eve of the Rebellion* (Freeport: Books for Libraries Press, 1866), 108-09.

[26] Ibid.

CHAPTER NINE NOTES

1 James Buchanan, *Mr. Buchanan's Administration on the Eve of the Rebellion* (Freeport, New York: 1866), 99-107.

2 Bruce Catton describes the status of the late 1860 federal Army: "The entire United States Army at that moment numbered hardly more than 16,000 officers and men, and these were scattered all over the continental United States, guarding the frontiers, protecting emigrant trains, overawing contumacious Indiana, and in general trying to do a very large job with inadequate means." Buchanan, *Mr. Buchanan's Administration on the Eve of the Rebellion*, 99-107; Bruce Catton, *The Coming Fury* (New York: Doubleday, 1861), 120.

3 William Seale, *The President's House—A History, Volume One* (Washington: White House Historical Association, 1986), 357.

4 "The Crisis in the South," *New York Herald*, 9 November 1860, p.1; "The Latest News," *New York Tribune*, 8 November 1860, p.4.

5 Ernest B. Ferguson, *Freedom Rising—Washington in the Civil War* (New York: Vintage Books, 2004), 6-10; "Washington City on the Night of the Election," *Washington Evening Star*, 7 November 1860, p. 3; "Local Matters," *Daily National Intelligencer*, 8 November 1860, p.1; "From Our Washington Correspondent," *The Independent,* 15 November 1860, p. 1.

6 "Feeling in South Carolina," *New York Times*, 13 November 1860, p.1; "Compliment to the Hon. L.M. Keitt," *Charleston Mercury*, 13 November 1860, p.3.

7 "Important from the Federal Capital," *Charleston Mercury*, 24 November 1860, p.2.

8 "The accusation of timidity and indecision is the most preposterous," Black would later say of Buchanan. "His faults were of another kind: his resolutions once formed were generally immovable to a degree that bordered on obstinacy." George Ticknor Curtis, *Life of James Buchanan, Volume II* (New York: Harper & Brothers, 1883), 319; Chauncey F. Black, *Essays and Speeches of Jeremiah S. Black* (New York: Appleton and Company), 1885), 251.

9 Black left one opening for Buchanan: "Whether Congress has the constitutional right to make war against any of more States, and require the Executive of the Federal Government to carry it on by means of force to be drawn from the other States is a question for Congress to consider." Daniel Farber, *Lincoln's Constitution* (Chicago: University of Chicago Press, 2003), 75-76; Francis Newton Thorpe, "Jeremiah S. Black," *Pennsylvania Magazine of History and Biography*, Volume L, Number 198, April 1926, 117-129.

10 "Important from the South," *New York Herald*, 23 November 1860, p.1.

11 Ibid.

[12] W. A. Swanberg, *First Blood—The Story of Fort Sumter* (New York: Penguin Books, 1992), 56.

[13] Ibid. 58

[14] "From Washington," *New York Tribune*, 24 November 1860, p.9.

[15] Buchanan, *Mr. Buchanan's Administration on the Eve of the Rebellion*, 113.

[16] *Congressional Globe—2nd Session of the 36th Congress* (Washington: John C. Rives, 1860), 12.

[17] Historical interpretations of Buchanan's message have been uniformly critical, with each succeeding generation of scholars repeating the interpretations of their predecessors. In 1901 John W. Burgess, a Columbia University law professor, lauded Buchanan as a man of judgment and patriotism, but added "How he could have written such a message is to men of the present almost past comprehension. It was the greatest encouragement to secession which could have possibly been given. It meant, whether the President so intended it or not—and he certainly did not intend it—that the secessionists should have until the 4th of the following March to withdraw their 'States' from the union, and organize a new government of their own without any serious impediment from the Administration at Washington." In 1950 the most famous Civil War political historian, Allan Nevins, described Buchanan's message as symptomatic of a "complete paralysis" as well as a "national helplessness." More than two decades later, James McPherson labelled the message a "confession of impotence," while Don Fehrenbacher, repeating the impotence argument, claimed the message "offered no resistance to the South's departure from the old Union." Nevins, McPherson and Fehrenbacher blame Buchanan for not seizing a Constitutional power that did not exist: the right to force a seceding state back into the Union. Even more, they are all silent when it came to what Buchanan actually could do. Buchanan presidency scholar Elbert B. Smith provides an entirely different take on the message, saying that while it was anything but inspiring, it indicated that Buchanan showed a "greater awareness of the bloodshed and mass suffering a civil war would bring than did either Abraham Lincoln or Jefferson Davis. Through his Southern associations and sympathies he understood the depth of Southern anger, pride, fears, determination and courage. As a Northerner and Union lover he also knew the blood, treasure and power the North could and would expand for the Union if a military confrontation occurred. When Lincoln and Davis ultimately put their faith in war, each apparently expected only a quick, easy victory, but James Buchanan had no such illusions." One of the most enlightened takes on Buchanan's message was offered by Kenneth Stampp during a 1991 roundtable of Buchanan scholars at Marshall College. Acknowledging that the message was "much maligned in the press," Stampp argues that what Buchanan did in that message was to "say exactly what Lincoln said. There is a difference between enforcing the law and protecting American

property and coercing a state, and Buchanan denied the right of the federal government to coerce a state, and so did Lincoln. But he also said that the government had the right to protect its property. He said further that the powers of the president, as defined by federal law, were not adequate, and he threw it up to Congress to provide additional powers and the Congress never did, even after the South left the Union and resigned from Congress and the Republicans had a majority." James W. Burgess, *The Civil War and the Constitution, 1859-1865, Volume I* (Port Washington, New York: Kennikat Press, 1972), 85; Allan Nevins, *The Emergence of Lincoln, Volume II* (New York: Charles Scribner's Sons, 1950), 352; James McPherson, *Battle Cry of Freedom—The Civil War Era* (New York: Ballantine Books, 1989), 248; Don Fehrenbacher, *The Slaveholding Republic— An Account of the United States Government's Relations to Slavery* (New York: Oxford University Press, 2001), 304; Elbert B. Smith, *The Presidency of James Buchanan* (Lawrence: University Press of Kansas, 1975), 152; "James Buchanan and the Political Crisis of the 1850s: A Panel Discussion," *Pennsylvania History*, Volume 60, Number Three, July 1993, 261-87.

18   John Bassett Moore, *Works of James Buchanan, Volume XI, 1860-1868* (New York: Antiquarian Press, 1960), 7-43; John W. Quist and Michael J. Birkner, *James Buchanan and the Coming of the Civil War* (Gainesville: University Press of Florida, 2013), 170.

19   The right of secession is not recognized in the Constitution, nor is it denied. Article VII of that document declares that "the ratification of the conventions of nine states shall be sufficient for the establishment of this Constitution between the states so ratifying the same." Secessionists argued that this article, by not saying anything directly about dissolution, especially expressly forbidding it, in fact made it legal. Other scholars think that is taking a lot for granted. Writes Conrad Black: "It is very difficult to find any legal rationale for the American states simply purporting to secede as if they had an untrammeled right at all times to promote themselves from subordinate jurisdictions in a federal state to sovereignty, merely by vote of a convention struck by act of the state legislature." But Sanford Levinson, University of Texas law professor, argues that the Constitution does not speak "clearly with regard to the legitimacy of secession, so that we can easily decide who the winners and losers are in any debate about the issue. Instead, the opposite is true: the Constitution speaks with a notable lack of clarity. This means, at the very least, that men and women of good faith can most certainly disagree about its meaning." *The Declaration of Independence and the Constitution of the United States* (Williamsburg: Colonial Williamsburg Foundation, 2011), 30; Conrad Black, *Flight of the Eagle—The Grand Strategies that Brought America from Colonial Dependence to World Leadership* (New York: Encounter Books, 2013), 222; Sanford Levinson, "Perpetual Union, 'Free Love,'

and Secession" On the Limits to the 'Consent of the Governed,'" *Tulsa Law Review*, Volume 39, Number 3, Spring 2004, 457-483.

[20] Harriet Beecher Stowe, "The President's Message," *The Independent*, 20 December 1860, p.1; Sherman's remarks were made in a letter he had sent to a Republican leadership conference in Pennsylvania. John Sherman to William Read, 22 December 1860, Papers of William T. Sherman, Reel 5; Charles Francis Adams, Sr. to Charles Francis Adams, Sr., 15 December 1860, The Adams Papers, Reel 550.

[21] *Congressional Globe*, 9.

[22] Despite his public opposition to Buchanan, Seward at this time was privately doing what he could to manipulate administration policy. He was secretly in talks with the man who would become Buchanan's new Attorney General, Edwin Stanton, a staunch Unionist, and would drum up support for Buchanan's nomination of New Yorker and Unionist John Dix as the new Secretary of the Treasury. Seward's activities were obviously not designed to help Buchanan succeed politically, but rather to keep and maintain a pro-Union White House line until Lincoln could take office. "News and Gossip from Washington," *Springfield Daily Republican*, 8 December 1860, p.4; Glyndon G. Van Deusen, *William Henry Seward* (New York: Oxford University, 1967), 244; Walter Stahr, *Seward—Lincoln's Indispensable Man* (New York: Simon & Schuster, 2012), 211-12.

[23] Buchanan's message also bombed with Union loyalists in the border states. Daniel Miller, a Maryland physician, in a letter to Tennessee Senator Andrew Johnson, chartacterized Buchanan as "the old thing," and his message as a "silly paper," adding: "Why did he not man the Forts, we think he stands a perjured villain before the whole World in not enforcing the Laws and in not supporting the Constitution. Benedict Arnold could have done no worse." *Congressional Globe*, 14, 29; Douglas R. Egerton, *Year of the Meteors—Stephen Douglas, Abraham Lincoln, and the Election That Brought on the Civil War* (New York: Bloomsbury Press, 2010), 226; William C. Davis, *Jefferson Davis—The Man and His Hour, a Biography* (New York: Harper Perennial, 1992), 288; Leroy P. Graf, *The Papers of Andrew Johnson, Volume 4, 1860-1861* (Knoxville: University of Tennessee Press, 1976), 93-95.

[24] Egerton, *Year of the Meteors*, 226-27; Philip S. Klein, *President James Buchanan—A Biography* (Newton, Connecticut: American Political Biography Press, 2010), 15.

CHAPTER TEN NOTES

[1] Cooper spared Buchanan the embarrassment of announcing that he was joining the Confederate cause until Buchanan was out of office, becoming, on the appointment of Jefferson Davis, adjutant and inspector general for the

Confederacy. *War of the Rebellion, Official Records of the Union and Confederate Armies—Series I, Volume 1* (Washington: Government Printing Office, 1880), 99; William C. Davis, *"A Government of our Own"—The Making of the Confederacy* (New York: The Free Press, 1994), 211; David S. Heidler and Jeanne T. Heidler, *Encyclopedia of the American Civil War—A Political, Social and Military History* (New York: W.W. Norton & Company, 2000), 497.

[2]   The second correspondence from Anderson, dated December 22, 1860, revealed the Major's frustration with the impotency of his position as defined by Floyd and, by inference, Buchanan. "I must confess that I think where an officer is placed in as delicate position as the one I occupy that he should have the entire control over all persons connected in any way with the work intrusted to him," Anderson wrote to Cooper. "Responsibility and power to control ought to go together." *War of the Rebellion, Series I Volume 1*, 99, 105.

[3]   Writes Bruce Catton: "Anderson was a lean, graying veteran, clean-shaven, noted both for an excellent combat record (he had won brevets for gallantry in the Black Hawk and Mexican wars and had been wounded at Molino Del Ray) and for a mildly bookish quality, which was somewhat rare among army officers at that time. He had translated French texts on artillery and these were used as manuals of instruction, he had served with credit on various War Department boards, and he was known to be an industrious and energetic officer. It seemed important, too, that he was a Southerner. His principles were considered pro-slavery, and some of the officers at Fort Sumter told each other that this was why Secretary Floyd had chosen him." Bruce Catton, *The Coming Fury* (Garden City: Doubleday & Company, 1961), 143.

[4]   After ordering Anderson to defend the forts in the harbor to the "last extremity," Floyd wrote: "Under these instructions, you might infer that you are required to make a vain and useless sacrifice of your own life and the lives of the men under your command, upon a mere point of honor. This is far from the President's intentions. You are to exercise a sound military discretion on this subject." Written by Floyd on December 21, this communication was received by Anderson on December 23, 1860. *War of the Rebellion, Series I, Volume 1*, 103.

[5]   Floyd and Assistant Adjutant General Don Carlos Buell, on December 11, 1860, defined the limits of Anderson's mission after the Major requested the use of additional troops: "You are carefully to avoid every act which would needlessly tend to provoke aggression; and for that reason you are not, without evident and imminent necessity, to take up any position which could be construed into the assumption of a hostile attitude. But you are to hold possession of the forts in this harbor, and if attacked you are to defend yourself to the last extremity. The smallness of your force will not permit you, perhaps, to occupy more than one of the three forts, but an attack on or attempt to take possession of either of them will be regarded as an act of hostility, and you may then put your command

into either of them which you may deem most proper to increase its power of resistance." *War of the Rebellion, Series I, Volume 1,*117; "The Latest News," *New York Tribune,* 1 January 1861, p. 5.

6   Because it was obviously not a pro-North abolitionist publication, but also because it was wary of the secessionist movement, the *Daily Picayune* reported with some skepticism on all aspects of the emerging crises. "The Latest News," *Daily Picayune,* 30 December 1860, p. 6.

7   "Gossip from the Federal Capital," *Charleston Mercury,* 29 December 1860, p. 6.

8   Write John Tebbel and Sarah Miles Watts: "The pro-Southern editorials of William Browne that appeared in the *Washington Constitution,* regarded as the semiofficial administration paper, were presumed to reflect the views of the President. Buchanan, however, was not responsible for what Browne wrote and, in fact, was not in accord with most of what he said." Varina Davis, for one, admired Browne, telling Jefferson Davis "No one rings like the true metal so much as Constitution Browne, who is enthusiastic, and thoroughgoing, repudiates Mr. Buchanan's views openly, assuming Secession responsibility." John Basset Moore, *The Works of James Buchanan—Volume XI, 1860-1868* (New York: Antiquarian Press, 1960), 75; John Tebbel and Sarah Miles Watts, *The Press and the Presidency—From George Washington to Ronald Reagan* (New York: Oxford University Press, 1985), 164; Lynda Laswell Crist, *Papers of Jefferson Davis, Volume 6, 1856-1860* (Baton Rouge, Louisiana State University Press, 1989), 371-74.

9   *War of the Rebellion, Series I, Volume 1,* 3.

10 The *Boston Evening Transcript* spoke for many in the North when it wrote: "Major Anderson is now unquestionably the most popular man in the country. The combination of his character of modesty, and the entire absence of anything like bravado in his intrepidity, have attracted to him universal respect and admiration." "Major Anderson's Coup d'Etat," *Springfield Daily Republican,* 31 December 1860, p. 2; "Major Anderson," *Boston Evening Transcript,* 7 January 1861, p. 3.

11 Allan Nevins, *The Emergence of Lincoln, Volume II* (New York: Charles Scribner's Sons, 1950), 368.

12 *War of the Rebellion, Series I, Volume 1,* 3.

13 Ibid., 3-4.

14 Ibid.

15 "Is the President Wrong or Right?" *Philadelphia Public Ledger,* 1 January 1861, p. 1.

16 Holt would remain loyal to Buchanan, as well as to Lincoln, whom he served as judge advocate general. The most controversial aspect of his career came after the Civil War when he presided over the trial of the Lincoln assassination conspirators, aggressively pushing for a quick result and failing to inform

President Johnson of a call for leniency on the part of the trial commissioners for Mary Surratt, who was executed on July 7, 1865. The troubling story of Surratt's execution is explored in film maker Robert Redford's 2011 *The Conspirator*. Moore, *The Works of James Buchanan, Volume XI, 1860-1868*, 84-91; Michael W. Kaufman, *American Brutus—John Wilkes Booth and the Lincoln Conspiracies* (New York: Random House, 2004), 375-382-83, 388-89; A. O. Allen, "History's Loose Ends and a Tightening Noose," *New York Times*, 14 April 2011, p. 8.

[17]   *War of the Rebellion, Series III, Volume 1* (Washington: Government Printing Office, 1899), 1-22.

[18]   In the earlier part of his address, Floyd referenced Buchanan's 1856 election, obviously a triumph for the South, as something less than that: "Four years ago at the electoral dinner in this house we congratulated ourselves upon the result of the great battle through which we had passed. If there was a lurking sentiment in the bosom of some that all was not all quite as it should be—if the demon came up in spite of us and intimated that the triumph we achieved was not quite the triumph of the majority—that it solved no great principle—that it was alone a quieting of the confederacy for the moment, still there was a general feeling of triumph and an abiding hope in the minds of the people that in the future all would be well." "The Floyd Banquet," *New York Herald*, 17 January 1861, p. 2.

[19]   Ironically, during the Civil War, it would be Theodorus Myer's uncle, Theodorus Bailey, serving as a rear admiral in the Eastern Gulf Squadron, who would be assigned to report on the early 1863 Confederate destruction of the *Harriet Lane*, the 750-ton steamed named in honor of Buchanan's niece.

[20]   The commissioners, Robert W. Barnwell, James H. Adams and James L. Orr, conclude: "We urge upon you the immediate withdrawal of the troops from the harbor of Charleston. Under present circumstances they are a standing menace which renders negotiations impossible, and, as our recent experience shows, threatens speedily to bring to a bloody issue questions which ought to be settled with temperance and judgment." *War of the Rebellion, Series I, Volume 1*, 109-10.

[21]   D. F. Jamison, president of South Carolina's secession convention, told the commissioners that their assignment was nothing less than preserving the "peace and amity between this Commonwealth and the Government of Washington." At the same time the commissioners were delegated to secure possession from the U.S. government all "forts, magazines, light-houses and other real estate, with their appurtenances, within the limits of South Carolina." Ibid, 111-12.

[22]   Benjamin Thomas and Harold Hyman, *Stanton—The Life and Times of Lincoln's Secretary of War* (New York: Alfred A. Knopf, 1962), 98.

[23]   Buchanan reveals how out of touch he was with South Carolina's intentions when he notes of the demand that the federal government entirely withdraw from the Charleston harbor: "Such an idea was never thought of by me in any possible contingency. No allusion has ever been made to it in any communications

between myself and any human being." *War of the Rebellion, Series I, Volume 1*, 115-18.

24 Ibid., 4-8.

25 Four days later the *Tribune* was back to its usual form. With no perceptible change in the new pro-North administration policy over the course of those four days, the Washington correspondent for the paper nevertheless opened his dispatch with the following: "The doubts of the President being able to stand up against the revolutionists still linger. He has been so long under their inspirations and manipulations, that he is almost incapable of taking a correct view of things." That judgment was fair enough, but it was followed by a sentence taking a swipe at both Buchanan's supposed femininity as well as his age: "It is dreadful to have such a loose-jointed and decaying piece of mortality at the helm of the state in such a time as this." "Important from Washington," *New York Tribune*, 1 January 1861, p. 5; "From Washington," *New York Tribune*, 5 January 1861, p. 6.

CHAPTER ELEVEN NOTES

1 Benjamin P. Thomas and Harold M. Hyman, *Stanton—The Life and Times of Lincoln's Secretary of War* (New York: Alfred A. Knopf, 1962), 95-96; Roy Franklin Nichols, *The Disruption of American Democracy* (New York: Collier Books, 1962), 424-26.

2 Thomas and Hyman, *Stanton—The Life and Times of Lincoln's Secretary of War*, 98.

3 Elbert Smith, *The Presidency of James Buchanan* (Lawrence: University Press of Kansas, 1975), 181.

4 Ibid.

5 Ibid; Nichols, *The Disruption of American Democracy*, 426.

6 Ibid.; Philip S. Klein, *President James Buchanan—A Biography* (Newton: American Political Biography Press, 2010), 380-81; Elizabeth D. Leonard, *Lincoln's Forgotten Ally—Judge Advocate General Joseph Holt of Kentucky* (Chapel Hill: University of North Carolina Press, 2011), 111.

7 Cleverly framing the failure of the *Star of the West* mission like the lawyer that he was, Thaddeus Stevens on January 29 would say that he had heard that Buchanan had purposely left the federal forts along the Charleston Harbor defenseless, but added "I cannot bring myself to believe it; I will not believe it; for it would make Mr. Buchanan a more odious traitor than Benedict Arnold. Every drop of blood that shall be shed in the conflict would sit heavy on his soul forever." But just as quickly as Stevens claimed to discard that indictment, he rhetorically sustained it, noting that "the charge seems to receive some countenance from the fact that but a handful of men are in the remaining fort,

without any effectual attempt to reinforce them; while the rebels are inclosing them with formidable works, and openly declare the intention to take it." Stevens then acknowledged that Buchanan did, in fact, send the *Star of the West* to supply the men at Fort Sumter, "but our flag was insulted, and the unarmed vessel driven off; and no effort has been made to avenge the insult." He concluded by predicting that if Fort Sumter would finally be attacked, and the men inside it were to die as a result, "how wretched must be the miserble man [Buchanan] who permits it. The fires of remorse will forever burn in his bosom as fiercely as the infernal fires of Phlegethon." John Bassett Moore, *Works of James Buchanan, Volume XI, 1860-1868* (New York: Antiquarian Press, 1960), 7-43, Nichols, *The Disruption of American Democracy*, 431; Beverly Wilson Palmer, *The Selected Papers of Thaddeus Stevens, Volume 1: January 1814-March 1865* (Pittsburgh: University of Pittsburgh Press, 1997), 193.

[8] James Buchanan, *Mr. Buchanan's Administration on the Eve of the Rebellion* (New York: Books for Libraries Press, 1960), 134.

[9] Crittenden numbered himself among those who were bewildered by Buchanan's December 3 message to Congress. "I do not agree that there is no power in the President to preserve the Union," he said in response. "If we have a Union at all, and if, as the President thinks, there is no right to secede on the part of any State (and I agree with him on that), I think there is a right to employ our power to preserve the Union. I do not say how we should apply it—I leave that open." *Congressional Globe—2nd Session of the 36th Congress* (Washington: John C. Rives, 1861), 5; Ann Mary Coleman, *The Life of John C. Crittenden* (Philadelphia: J.B. Lippincott, 1871), 221.

[10] William C. Davis, *Jefferson Davis—The Man and His Hour* (New York: Harper Perennial, 1992), 290-91; *Congressional Globe*, 28.

[11] The 69 year-old Green had served as the influential editor of the *United States Telegraph* during the presidency of John Quincy Adams, and supported Andrew Jackson and Martin Van Buren, before securing a post from President William Henry Harrison in 1841 as the Governor of the Florida Territory. Lincoln was serving out his one term in Congress in the late 1840s when he and Green, living in the same boarding house, became friends. David Woodard, "Abraham Lincoln, Duff Green, and the Mysterious Trumbull Letter," *Civil War History*, Volume Forty-Two, Number Three, September 1996, 215; H.W. Brands, *Andrew Jackson—His Life and Times* (New York: Doubleday & Company, 2005), 416; Roy P. Basler, *The Collected Works of Abraham Lincoln, Volume 1* (New Brunswick: Rutgers University Press, 1953), 419; Basler, *The Collected Works of Abraham Lincoln, Volume 2* (New Brunswick: Rutgers University Press, 1953), 49-52; Klein, *President James Buchanan*, 385-86.

[12] Woodard, "Abraham Lincoln, Duff Green and the Mysterious Trumbull Letter," 216.

13   George Ticknor Curtis, *Life of James Buchanan, Volume II* (New York: Harper & Brothers, 1883), 426.

14   "To the Associated Press," *New York Tribune*, 3 January 1861, p.4; Lyon G. Tyler, *The Letters and Times of the Tylers—Volume II* (New York: Da Capo Press, 1970), 578.

15   "Letter from President Tyler," *Richmond Enquirer*, 18 January 1861, p.1.

16   Tyler, *The Letters and Times of the Tylers—Volume II*, 590.

17   "What Mr. Buchanan Proposes to do After the Fourth of March," *Richmond Dispatch*, 4 March 1861, p.1.

18   Worried that Buchanan might still throw in with or capitulate to the secessionists, Stanton at this time was secretly talking to various Republican leaders, seeking their support in the unlikely event of a Southern coup in Washington. Note Stanton biographers Benjamin P. Thomas and Harold M. Hyman: "Stanton was playing both sides, for he had to retain Buchanan's confidence or else lose all influence with the uncertain President. Stanton's liason role with the Republicans was the secret one, although his Unionist position in cabinet proceedings was frank enough." Edward Stanton to Salmon P. Chase, 23 January 1861, Salmon P. Chase Papers, Reel 14; Thomas and Hyman, *Stanton—The Life and Times of Lincoln's Secretary of War*, 111-12.

19   "Affairs at the Capital," *Boston Evening Transcript*, 13 February 1861, p.2.

20   Tyler, *The Letters and Times of the Tylers*, 612.

21   James Buchanan to John Tyler, 21 February 1861, John Tyler Papers, Reel 2, Series 1.

22   "Washington's Birthday at the Federal Capital," *New York Tribune*, 25 February 1861, p.6; W.A. Swanberg, *Sickles the Incredible* (New York: Charles Scribner's Sons, 1956), 112.

23   William Seale, *The President's House—A History, Volume I* (Washington: White House Historical Association, 1986), 360.

24   Curtis, *Life of James Buchanan, Volume II*, 636; Seale, *The President's House—A History, Volume I*, 363.

25   "Interesting Scenes at the White House and Willard's Hotel," *New York Herald*, 26 February 1861, p.1.

26   Moore, *Works of James Buchanan, Volume XI, 1860-1868*, 152-54.

27   Michael P. Riccards, *The Ferocious Engine of Democracy—A History of the American Presidency, Volume One* (Lanham: Madison Books, 1995), 210.

28   Michael Burlingame, *At Lincoln's Side—John Hay's Civil War Correspondence and Selected Writings* (Carbondale: Southern Illinois University, 2006), 118-19.

29   Working as a journalist in 1860, the young Adams would soon join the 1st Massachusetts Cavalry. Three weeks after the inaugural, Lincoln named Adams' father, Charles Francis Adams, Sr., to Buchanan's old post as minister to Great Britain. Charles Francis Adams, *Charles Francis Adams 1835-1915—An*

Autobiography (New York: Russell and Russell, 1916), 96-97; David S. Heidler and Jeanne T. Heidler, *Encyclopedia of the American Civil War* (New York: W.W. Norton & Company, 2000), 8-11.

30   Abraham Lincoln 1861 Inaugural Speech, 4 March 1861, Abraham Lincoln Papers, Reel 18.

31   "The Presidential Inaugural," *Springfield Daily Republican*, 6 March 1861, p.2.

CHAPTER TWELVE NOTES

1   Philip Shriver Klein, *President Buchanan—A Biography* (Falls Creek: Pennsylvania State University Press, 1962), 403-04; "Mr. Buchanan's Reception at Lancaster," *Philadelphia Public Ledger,* 12 March 1861, p.1.

2   Buchanan initially thought his former Secretary of State and Attorney General Jeremiah Black would write his biography. But after Buchanan endorsed Lincoln's war aims, Black dropped out of the project arguing that he could not reconcile Buchanan's conflicting secession stand as president with his new pro-war stand as ex-president. Stephen Patrick O'Hara, "'The Verdict of History'—Defining and Defending James Buchanan Through Public Memorialization," Master's thesis, 30 April 2012, Virginia Polytechnic Institute and State University, 49.

3   Although Buchanan retained Bennett's support to the very end of his presidency, the two men parted ways in 1862 after the *New York Herald* claimed that Buchanan had stolen a picture of Queen Victoria and other members of the Royal Family given to him during an 1860 visit to the U.S. by the Prince of Wales. Buchanan vigorously denied the charge. When the paper subsequently also criticized Buchanan's record as president, suggesting that his actions encouraged secession, Buchanan unintentionally revealed more than he intended when he complained to his nephew James Buchanan Henry: "From a spirit of malignity & supposing that the world may have forgotten the circumstances, [the *Herald*] takes every occasion to blame me for my supine-ness." George Ticknor Curtis, *Life of James Buchanan, Volume II* (New York: Harper & Brothers, 1883), 530-31; John Tebbel, Sarah Miles Watts, *The Press and the Presidency—From George Washington to Ronald Reagan* (New York: Oxford University Press, 1985), 165.

4   After the Confederate assault on Fort Sumter Buchanan privately proclaimed that his policies regarding the installation had been correct all along, although he admitted to being worried that Congressional Republicans, obviously in an attempt to further damage his reputation, might want to launch an investigation into his administration's policies on the matter. "I had supposed there would be some investigation in regard to Fort Sumter, but I find I have been mistaken," Buchanan said in correspondence dated April 30, 1861. This letter is reproduced in the Library of Congress' microfilmed Theodore Roosevelt letters collection. There is no indication of the letter's recipient, but most likely it was sent

to Judge James Roosevelt, the granduncle of Theodore Roosevelt who had been appointed U.S. District Attorney for southern New York by Buchanan. Theodore Roosevelt himself, who greatly admired Lincoln, later maintained that popular support for Lincoln only naturally meant opposing Buchanan: "No man could effectively stand by President Lincoln unless he stood against President Buchanan," Roosevelt remarked in a 1915 speech. James Buchanan, 20 April 1861, Theodore Roosevelt Papers, Reel One. David Pietrusza, *1920—The Year of the Six Presidents* (New York: Carroll & Graff Publishers, 2007), 170.

5   In a letter to John Dix just a week after the Confederate attack on Fort Sumter, Buchanan remarked "When the major [Robert Anderson] in a firm and patriotic manner, refused to surrender the fort to [General P.T.] Beauregard, it seems he informed him that his provisions would last but a few days. What an outrage this was, after this information, to fire on the fort." Curtis, *Life of James Buchanan, Volume II*, 541, 544.

6   Several days before this letter, Buchanan publicly vowed his support for the war, in the process denouncing a bid by Northern Peace Democrats calling for a negotiated settlement with the South. "This is the moment for action—prompt, energetic and united action—and not for the discussion of peace propositions," he said in a letter that was read aloud to a pro-Union gathering in Haynesville, Pennsylvania. "These would be rejected by the states that seceded, unless we should offer to recognize their independence, which is entirely out of the question." Curtis, *Life of James Buchanan, Volume II*, 566-67; ""Ex-President Buchanan on the War," *New Hampshire Sentinel*, 10 October 1861, p.2.

7   Buchanan resented the fact that his former Attorney General, Edwin Stanton, had accepted a new job in January 1862 as Secretary of War in the Lincoln administration. "He is a sound, clear-headed, persevering and practical lawyer, and is quite eminent, especially in patent cases," Buchanan told Harriet on January 16, before acidly adding, incorrectly, "He never took much part in cabinet councils, because his office did not require it. He was always on my side and flattered me ad nauseum," Curtis, *Life of James Buchanan, Volume II*, 572, 533.

8   Steven Woodworth argues that Davis appointed Floyd brigadier general primarily to assuage Floyd supporters in Virginia. Allen Nevins says that as a brigadier general Floyd proved himself to be the "same muddle-headed incompetent who had been Secretary of War under Buchanan." During the February 1862 battle of Fort Donnelson, Floyd, in command of the fort, mismanaged Confederate defenses to the point where some 15,000 of his soldiers were forced to surrender to Ulysses S. Grant. Floyd escaped to Nashville. "Though it was Floyd's duty to remain with his troops," writes Nevins, "he knew that capture would mean trial in Washington for the theft of public funds when he was Secretary of War, if not for treason." Steven Woodworth, *Jefferson Davis and His Generals—The*

Failure of Confederate Command in the West (Lawrence: University Press of Kansas, 1990), 80; Allen Nevins, *The War for the Union, Volume II: War Becomes Revolution, 1862-1863* (New York: Charles Scribner's Sons, 1960), 23-26.

9   Chris DeRose, *The President's War—Six American Presidents and the Civil War That Divided Them* (Guilford, Connecticut, Lyons Press, 2014), 247; "Lieutenant General Scott's Opinion," *Daily National Intelligencer*, 21 October 1862, p.3; "Letter from President Buchanan," *Daily National Intelligencer*, 1 November 1862, p.2; "Old Mother Buchanan at Wheatland," *Harper's Weekly*, 29 November 1862, p.768; Klein, *President James Buchanan*, 410; David Herbert Donald, *Lincoln* (New York: Touchstone, 1995), 373.

10 James Buchanan to Harriett Lane, 3 August 1862, Papers of James Buchanan and Harriet L. Johnston, Reel 2.

11 Buchannan's pessimism regarding Democrat Party fortunes in 1864 came despite a mid-term 1862 election that delighted him, seeing Democratic gains across the country, particularly in Pennsylvania where the party more than doubled its Congressional representation. Curtis, *Life of James Buchanan, Volume II*, 616; "The Election in Pennsylvania," *New York Tribune*, 15 October 1862, p.1; "The State Elections," *Springfield Daily Republican*, 17 October 1862, p.2.

12 Even though Buchanan made a policy of never criticizing Lincoln in public and was even, to a degree, supportive of him in his private correspondence, he sometimes thought Lincoln went too far. When Lincoln in June 1864 spoke to a Union League meeting in Philadelphia, bluntly remarking that "We are going through with our task, as far as I am concerned, even if it takes us three years longer," and later asking young boys in the audience if they would be willing to serve, Buchanan remarked "What an extraordinary speech Mr. Lincoln has made to the Union Leaguers in Philadelphia! They have promised with a shout to march to the front at his call and shed their blood, if need be, in the cause of their country. I have no doubt he will afford them that opportunity." Curtis, *Life of James Buchanan, Volume II*, 617; "The President's Visit to Philadelphia," *New York Tribune*, 17 June 1864, p.5.

13 Curtis, *Life of James Buchanan, Volume II*, 625-626.

14 In the middle of the 1864 campaign, Buchanan was attacked from an unexpected quarter. William Henry Hurlbert, a reporter for the *New York World*, authored a book designed to refute Republican attacks on General McClellan's military record. In chronicling McClellan's activities during the years of the Buchanan presidency, Hurlbert wrote: "Mr. Buchanan was a politician grown old in the small intrigues of party. Neither by nature nor by experience was he fitted to hold the even balance of a wise authority between the angry sections. His administration completed the ruin of the Republic." Curtis, *Life of James Buchanan, Volume II*, 626; William Henry Hurlbert, *General McClellan and the Conduct of the War* (New York: Sheldon and Company, 1864), 1864),

54; see also, Stephen W. Sears, "McClellan and the Peace Plank of 1864: A Reappraisal," *Civil War History*, Volume XXXVI, Number 1, March 1990, 57-64; "The Chicago Candidate and Platform," *New York Evening Post*, 9 September 1864, p.2.

15 Curtis, *Life of James Buchanan, Volume II*, 629-30.

16 Klein, *President James Buchanan*, 421.

17 Curtis, *Life of James Buchanan, Volume II*, 633-34.

18 Robert J. Scarry, *Millard Fillmore* (Jefferson, North Carolina: McFarland & Company, 2001), 320-21, 400; James O. Lyford, *History of Concord, New Hampshire, Volume II*,(Concord: City of Concord, 1896), 1195-97; "Mob Demonstrations—Speech by General Pierce," *New Hampshire Patriot*, 19 April 1865, p.2., col.4; "An Insult to an Ex-President," *New Orleans Bee*, 2 May 1865, p.1, col. 2.

19 John Bassett Moore, *The Works of James Buchanan, Volume XI, 1860-1868* (New York: Antiquarian Press, 1960), 381.

20 Ibid.

21 The feeling was mutual. Johnson had never been much impressed with Buchanan, deriding him in 1856 as the "slowest man" among that year's probable candidates for the Democrat nomination, and offering only nominal support for the Buchanan-Breckinridge ticket in the fall. Johnson appeared to also have a problem with the fact that Buchanan was a life-long bachelor, noting during one debate that he could not trust the judgment of a man "whose bosom has never swelled with emotions for wife or children." Curtis, *Life of James Buchanan, Volume II*, 640; Hans L. Trefousse, *Andrew Johnson—A Biography* (New York: W.W. Norton & Company, 1989), 103; Leroy P. Graf, *Papers of Andrew Johnson, Volume 3, 1858-1860* (Knoxville: University of Tennessee Press, 1972), 631, 641.

22 "The Philadelphia Convention," *New York Times*, 17 July 1866, p. 5; "National Union Convention," *New York Observer*, 23 August 1866, p. 27; "The Arm-in-Arm Convention," *Civil War History*, Volume Fourteen, Number Two, June 1868, 101-19.

23 Perhaps the greatest damage to Johnson as a result of his behavior on the campaign trail was the loss of the *New York Times* and *New York Herald*, both of which had been editorially supporting the President in his ongoing struggles with the Radical Republicans. "The President's Mistake," *New York Times*, 7 September 1866, p. 9; William B. Phillips to Andrew Johnson, 16 September 1866, Andrew Johnson Papers, Series 1, Reel 24.

24 Curtis, *Life of James Buchanan*, Volume II, 651.

25 The book had been anticipated in the nation's press. The *Philadelphia Press*, in the spring of 1865, predicted that Buchanan's memoirs would "explode the whole arsenal of lies which has supplied powder for the whole Republican party for four years," while the *Chicago Tribune* condemned Buchanan for writing in

his "calm, easy and undisturbed retreat," while "others were fighting, dying, and toiling to staunch the bleeding wounds of the Republic." Writes Buchanan historian Michael J. Birkner: "A reader will need to look hard to find any instance in the book, or in Buchanan's private correspondence, when he felt he had erred." "Mr. Buchanan's Administration," *New York Times*, 18 February 1866, p.1; "Old Buchanan," *Chicago Tribune*, 29 April 1865, p.2; O'Hara, "'The Verdict of History,'" 56-57; John W. Quest and Michael J. Birkner, *James Buchanan and the Coming of the Civil War* (Gainesville: University Press of Florida, 2013), 275; "Allen Cole, "Asserting His Authority: James Buchanan's Failed Vindication," *Pennsylvania History*, Volume 70, Number 1, Winter 2003, 81-97.

26 John Abbott, *Lives of the Presidents of the United States of America* (Boston: B.B. Russell and Company, 1867), 358-59.

27 Curtis, *Life of James Buchanan, Volume II*, 652.

28 Various historians' polls through the years have consistently listed Buchanan at or near the bottom in presidential rankings. In 2007 *US News & World Report* averaged out the results of such listings, including a 1999 C-Span survey and scholars' poll conducted by the *Wall Street Journal* in 2005, and determined that Buchanan was regarded as the worst president in U.S. history. Jay Tolson, "Worst Presidents: A Survey of Majaor Polls," 17 February 2007, usnews.com.

29 Curtis, *Life of James Buchanan, Volume II*, 662.

30 Ibid., 659-60.

31 Klein, *President James Buchanan*, 427.

32 Johnson's proclamation on Buchanan's death was a masterpiece of brevity. "This event will occasion mourning in the nation for the loss of an eminent and honored public servant," he declared before ordering that business at the Executive Mansion and "several Executive Departments" be suspended for one day. Under the orders of Navy Secretary Gideon Welles, flags were lowered at Navy yards across the country and on all revenue vessels. Howard K. Beale, *Diary of Gideon Welles, Volume III, January 1, 1867-June 6, 1869* (New York: W.W. Norton & Company, 1960), 374-77; Paul H. Bergeron, *The Papers of Andrew Johnson, Volume 14, April-August 1868* (Knoxville: University of Tennessee Press, 1997), 156.

33 "Ex-President Buchanan," *Daily Picayune*, 3 June 1868, p.2; O'Hara, "The Verdict of History," 38; "Death of James Buchanan," *Chicago Tribune*, 2 June 1868, p.2.

34 *Congressional Globe—40th Congress, 2nd Session* (Washington: Government Printing Office, 1868), 2810-11, 2817.

Index

Printed in the United States
by Baker & Taylor Publisher Services